VOLUME EDITOR

NATHAN KOWALSKY is Assistant Professor of Philosophy, St. Joseph's College, University of Alberta. He has published essays in the journals *Environmental Ethics* and *Ethical Perspectives* and in the book *The Ranges of Evil: Multidisciplinary Studies in Human Wickedness*. He has also served as a consultant to Environment Canada (a ministry of the Canadian government).

SERIES EDITOR

FRITZ ALLHOFF is an Assistant Professor in the Philosophy Department at Western Michigan University, as well as a Senior Research Fellow at the Australian National University's Centre for Applied Philosophy and Public Ethics. In addition to editing the *Philosophy for Everyone* series, Allhoff is the volume editor or co-editor for several titles, including *Wine & Philosophy* (Wiley-Blackwell, 2007), *Whiskey & Philosophy* (with Marcus P. Adams, Wiley, 2009), and *Food & Philosophy* (with Dave Monroe, Wiley-Blackwell, 2007).

PHILOSOPHY FOR EVERYONE

Series editor: Fritz Allhoff

Not so much a subject matter, philosophy is a way of thinking. Thinking not just about the Big Questions, but about little ones too. This series invites everyone to ponder things they care about, big or small, significant, serious … or just curious.

Forthcoming books in the series:

Edited by Nathan Kowalsky

HUNTING

PHILOSOPHY FOR EVERYONE

In Search of the Wild Life

Foreword by David Petersen

A John Wiley & Sons, Ltd., Publication

This edition first published 2010

© 2010 Blackwell Publishing Ltd except for editorial material and organization
© 2010 Nathan Kowalsky

Blackwell Publishing was acquired by John Wiley & Sons in February 2007.
Blackwell's publishing program has been merged with Wiley's global Scientific,
Technical, and Medical business to form Wiley-Blackwell.

Registered Office
John Wiley & Sons Ltd, The Atrium, Southern Gate, Chichester, West Sussex, PO19
8SQ, United Kingdom

Editorial Offices
350 Main Street, Malden, MA 02148–5020, USA
9600 Garsington Road, Oxford, OX4 2DQ, UK
The Atrium, Southern Gate, Chichester, West Sussex, PO19 8SQ, UK

For details of our global editorial offices, for customer services, and for information
about how to apply for permission to reuse the copyright material in this book
please see our website at www.wiley.com/wiley-blackwell.

The right of Nathan Kowalsky to be identified as the author of the editorial material
in this work has been asserted in accordance with the UK Copyright, Designs and
Patents Act 1988.

All rights reserved. No part of this publication may be reproduced, stored in a
retrieval system, or transmitted, in any form or by any means, electronic, mechanical,
photocopying, recording or otherwise, except as permitted by the UK Copyright,
Designs and Patents Act 1988, without the prior permission of the publisher.

Wiley also publishes its books in a variety of electronic formats. Some content that
appears in print may not be available in electronic books.

Designations used by companies to distinguish their products are often claimed as
trademarks. All brand names and product names used in this book are trade names,
service marks, trademarks or registered trademarks of their respective owners. The
publisher is not associated with any product or vendor mentioned in this book. This
publication is designed to provide accurate and authoritative information in regard
to the subject matter covered. It is sold on the understanding that the publisher is
not engaged in rendering professional services. If professional advice or other expert
assistance is required, the services of a competent professional should be sought.

Library of Congress Cataloging-in-Publication Data

Hunting – philosophy for everyone: in search of the wild life / Nathan Kowalsky,
editor.
    p.   cm. – (Philosophy for everyone)
  Includes bibliographical references.
  ISBN 978-1-4444-3569-9 (pbk.: alk. paper)   1. Hunting – Philosophy.
I. Kowalsky, Nathan.
  SK14.H86 2010
  179′.3–dc22

2010017112

A catalogue record for this book is available from the British Library.

Set in 10/12.5pt Plantin by SPi Publisher Services, Pondicherry, India
Printed in Singapore

01   2010

To my Grandfather, E. L. "Bud" Kowalsky (1925–2009),
whose many loves included hunting with Dad and me
out there in the wide-open lands of home.

"To illustrate all this by a similar instance, I shall observe, that there cannot be two passions more nearly resembling each other than those of hunting and philosophy, whatever disproportion may at first sight appear betwixt them."

David Hume, A Treatise of Human Nature,
book II, part III, section X

CONTENTS

FOREWORD

Hunting as Philosophy Professor

The out-of-doors is our true ancestral estate. For a mere few thousand years we have grubbed in the soil and laid brick upon brick to build the cities; but for millions of years before that we lived the leisurely, free, and adventurous life of hunters and gatherers. How can we pluck that deep root of feeling from the racial consciousness? Impossible!

Edward Abbey

In my long and shaggy life, I've known no better philosophy teacher than hunting. While non-hunters may initially scoff at the concept of "hunting as philosophy professor," the thought-provoking essay collection to follow should broaden and deepen personal insights about life and death, and the interplay between the two, for all with open minds.

In my case, as one who examines life and death through the eyes of a self-styled neo-animist, many of the most useful lessons I've learned about the nature of human nature, including especially my own, have come through the practice, in both the practical and Zen meanings of the word, of hunting.

As hunters, much is revealed about us by the tools we choose to carry afield, the strategies we employ to bring game to bag, the ethics we embrace or ignore in seeking success, how we define hunting "success," and how we talk about it all.

Yet, personal ethics aside, it's entirely logical to ask, as so many non-hunters do, why *anyone* hunts today, when it's no longer necessary for human physical survival. Put this question to the average hunter and he or she predictably will trot out such pragmatic motivations as meat, challenge, adventure, trophies (physical memorabilia), and companionship afield.

Yet in fact such "reasons" as these are merely enjoyable *products* of the hunt. Let's take it another step and ask *why* we find wild meat, big antlers, personal challenge, outdoor adventure, campfire companionship, crisp autumn sunrises, and stinky elk wallows so viscerally *exciting* as to compel us to seek them fall after fall, often at considerable cost in money, time, and energy.

As Edward Abbey suggests, the tenacious human urge to hunt, which feels so much like instinct to those of us who know it, *is* instinct, arising from the deepest primitive core of our species' memory; a genetic predisposition, often sublimated yet very much still with and within our opportunistic omnivorous species.

And the flip-side of this same coin, a self-evident biological fact that hunting's harshest philosophical critics fail to grasp or at least to acknowledge, is that a complementary instinctive *need to be hunted* is built into all evolved prey species. Without the perpetual continuation of the precise sort of physical and mental exercise provided by predation and evasion, our spectacular prey species, so beautifully sculpted by the artful knife of natural selection, would soon devolve into mere thin shadows of their artful wild selves.

Predation and evasion comprise a sacred game, without which no living thing would be the same – without which no living thing would even *be*. In a world with no predation – where no living organism sucks its sustenance from other living organisms – there would be no food, no adaptive evolution, no quality control via culling of the least fit, and no you or me.

Unfortunately, many criticisms of contemporary hunting are valid. Outdoor catalogs clog the mails, all hawking flashy lethal toys, skill-crutches, and cheater technologies targeted at contemporary Wannabee hunters who don't wannabee *real* hunters badly enough to invest the time, energy, and heart required to do it right.

Finding such traditional hunting values as woodsmanship too slow and unreliable, too many of today's dilettante sportsmen are eagerly co-opted by advertising to take such ethically bankrupt shortcuts as motorized decoys, electronic game calls, map-friendly GPS units, cell and satellite telephones, night-vision optics, space-age compound arrow-launching devices and cross-guns posing as "archery equipment," automatic game "feeders" (bait stations) that spray out showers of corn at preset times each day so that our "trophies" are conditioned to appear promptly, say at 8 a.m. and 4 p.m., thus relieving Bubba from the exhausting inconvenience of actually having to *hunt*.

To true hunters and the concerned non-hunting public, this stinky garbage – as grotesquely acted out on TV's "outdoor" channels – is embarrassingly pathetic, leaving us to ask: "What's the *point*? Why even *bother* doing a thing when there's so much cheating and self-delusion involved that both goal and gain become transparent lies?"

Happily and hopefully, standing in staunch opposition to this "new generation" of "hunters in a hurry," true, traditional-values hunters remain abundant, if far less visible – quietly thoughtful natural predators playing a proper, exacting, and essential role in the scheme of things. It is, after all (circling back to this essential key to comprehending hunting), predators, human and otherwise, who sculpted the sublime defensive tactics of their prey. Predator and prey: a quintessential symbiotic relationship and the engine that throughout life's long history powered an upward-spiraling intellectual evolution among our own species, in team with a quest for survival perfection among all creatures great and small.

Consequently, if hunting were to be banned or even unwisely restricted, rather than gains in the welfare of wildlife, as animal rights zealots envision, we would see rapid increases in wildlife overpopulation and its horrific upshots – increased run-ins with automobiles, contagious disease, genetic decline, overgrazing leading to mass starvation, and general misery all around.

The essence of wildlife is wildness. And the heartbeat of wildness is predation.

To true hunters, the game, in both meanings of the term, remains sacred, to be approached with an attitude of *process* over *product*; doing more with less, a willful body/spirit immersion in a determined effort to reconnect as honestly and humbly as possible to our innate human/animal wildness, which *is* the human soul. Above all, the true hunter's thoughts and actions are tempered by respect for our prey as expressed through self-restraint even when, as Aldo Leopold famously noted, no one is out there watching us (that's the "sporting" part). For true hunters, the trip *is* the destination and "success" is measured not by quantity of game "harvested" (a simpering agricultural euphemism) but by the quality of the overall *experience*, start to finish.

No one grows stronger by always taking the easy trail. No one grows wiser by ditching school.

Apropos to the task at hand, *Hunting – Philosophy for Everyone* takes no shortcuts. Whether you approach this book with the biases of a hunter, a non-hunter, or an animal rights advocate, don't be surprised to feel yourself, as I did, being gently jolted into having to rethink what you *thought* you knew about hunting all along. The innovative, deep-time revelations of Valerius Geist ("The Carnivorous Herbivore: Hunting and Culture in Human Evolution"), to flag but one chapter among many, are themselves worth the price of admission.

Not all hunting is the same.

Not all hunters are the same.

To blanket-brand hunting and hunters as either "bad" or "good" – black or white with no room for gray – is a trophy-class philosophical oversimplification.

We are both.

We are *Homo sapiens*.

ACKNOWLEDGMENTS

Wow, editing a book is not a one-man job! I must thank, first and foremost, Richard Kover, who started off as my editorial assistant, but who I now recognize, by rights, as my assistant editor. Richard has worked with me on this project from the beginning, kicking me in the pants to get moving with a proposal, helping to draft it and propose the subtitle that eventually stuck, going through hundreds of abstracts, providing extremely helpful first impressions of contributions, and generally hauling the load whenever necessary – in addition to his own research and writing responsibilities (including a piece for this volume). I am deeply indebted to him for his assistance.

Second, I cannot but thank the contributors themselves, who have dealt with unusually tight deadlines, to say nothing of their tolerance of my editorial pestering. I'm amazed that we all got along smashingly in spite of the incredibly volatile topic, but given everyone's caliber, it's no surprise to find myself thrilled by the quality of their finished essays. We've only communicated via the disembodied electronic media, yet it's been an honor nonetheless. You feel like friends, and I can only hope that we can actually meet someday in person – and take each other up on the apple pies, muzzleloaders, cooking over a fire under the sky, bowmaking...

Third, I want to thank *all* the people who submitted abstracts in the hope of inclusion in this volume. It was truly overwhelming to have hundreds of abstracts arrive within the short space of a month in the middle of summer holidays, and I can only hope there will be other opportunities in the future for these insightful thinkers to showcase their ideas.

We could have easily put together *two* volumes on this topic! Timothy, Jorge, Chuck, Leon, Baird, Jordan, Nathan, Keith, Samantha, Alexandria, John, Marc, Mary, Thomas, Richard, Don, Carla, Niall, Alastair ... the list of awesome possibilities just keeps on going. I do hope we'll get a chance to work together somehow, someday.

Fourth, I wish to thank the various persons and organizations who were so cooperative in helping me advertise the call for abstracts, including Larry Cahoone, Lee Foote and the Canadian Circumpolar Institute, Roger Brunt, Peter Flack and Gerhard Damm of African Indaba, T. J. Schwanky, Christine Roedlach of the Federation of Associations for Hunting and Conservation of the European Union (FACE), and more. Your support has been invaluable!

Fifth, my superiors at Wiley-Blackwell have been longsuffering and generous in their dealings with me, a newbie. Fritz Allhoff, Tiffany Mok, and Jeff Dean have provided me with advice, instruction, and other invaluable assistance at almost a moment's notice. In this vein I also want to thank Margolee Horn, Tona Cota, Tracy Yurchak, and Ashley Blum at St. Joseph's College, University of Alberta, for the administrative support they provided me throughout this process. Additionally, I am deeply indebted to Rique Edgar Brotherston, who proofread the entire manuscript, *pro bono*.

Finally (and sheepishly), I thank my loving wife Stephanie, who lived as a virtually single parent while I slaved away on this project, and our two dear daughters, Anya and Nina, who thought Daddy was sick because of all the time he spent holed up in the office. I love each of you more than I know how to say, and more than I know how to show.

Nathan Kowalsky
Edmonton, Alberta

PICKING UP THE TRAIL

An Introduction to *Hunting – Philosophy for Everyone*

If I think about it, my earliest memories of hunting are with my Dad, and seeing … nothing. Well, not *nothing*, but no deer, anyway. I do remember lots of walking, lots of grass (or snow), lots of wind, and lots of Halloween candy in my pockets. But hunting as a child never involved seeing deer, let alone shooting them. However, for some odd reason, the day *after* I went hunting, I do recall Dad showing up at school with deer in the back of the van. That was a cool way to spend a lunch hour, checking out deer with your friends in the parking lot, but they were never *my* deer.

My luck changed for the better when I reached 14, which was the first time we went out hunting with a rifle and a license in *my* hands. Dad let me use his .30–30 lever action Marlin with open sights, and somehow or other we had managed to sneak into sight of a small whitetail buck browsing in some brush on the side of a hill, easily under 100 yards away. We were laying in prone position, and had all the time in the world to get a bead on that buck. It was my shot. I sat there with him in my sights, but I couldn't pull the trigger! Nope, couldn't do it. Not because I didn't want to kill him, but because I wasn't confident I'd kill him *well*. From my perspective, my gun sights were bigger than his body, so I had no idea if that bullet would hit him in the heart or in the legs. I was okay with killing the buck (so I thought), but I wasn't okay with maiming him instead. This was nothing like shooting at a target.

So Dad took the shot instead. BANG! (Actually, all I heard was a loud, high-pitched "whee" sound that wouldn't go away, my ears being in too much shock to register anything else.) The buck fell to his knees, and thrashed around in the brush for what seemed too long, and then lay still. I remember running like hell towards him, but probably only after Dad woke me up from my ... well, you can't call it a "reverie," but it was a kind of mindlessness – as if there was only one thing that existed in the world, that buck, and my entire consciousness was nothing but a giant tube through which something else beyond me was able to look through the fabric of the universe and see that buck, right there, die. *Whoosh.*

After that, running. "Dad, is he dead? Dad, is he okay? Dad, did it hurt? Dad ... ?" There was only one thing that mattered to me: that the buck was okay. And by okay, I meant that he was *well* dead. Death was always in the cards, but it had to be *good*. Weird, huh? I loved that buck, that one, right there. He deserved the *right* kind of death. And then I cried. Good God, I cried! I guess 14-year-old boys are allowed to. It's always odd to consider why one cries. We cry when we're happy, when we're sad, when we're relieved, and when we're frustrated. We cry when we see beauty, and when we see horror. And yet neither of these things truly captured what I felt. I don't know of any words that really could. But it was *good* to cry, and it was *good* that the buck died as he did (Dad was a *good* shot).

And then, it was good that I could *touch* him.

Hunting *and* philosophy? C'mon, don't be ridiculous. The combination is almost an oxymoron! Everybody knows that philosophers don't hunt, and that hunters don't think, right? Elmer Fudd's an idiot, and Socrates hung around downtown where all the interesting people are.

Well ... yeah, not so much. But you know what I'm talking about, don't you? It doesn't matter if you're a hunter, a non-hunter, or an anti-hunter, because we're all familiar with the stereotype, and not without reason. We hear news stories about how many hunters accidentally shot their hunting companions this season, or we've heard of how hunters pull into a gas station (or a school, *cough-cough*) with a bunch of dead deer hanging out of the half-ton, and we all know that most hunters kill animals that are wild and free – even though they don't *have* to. What kind of people do this? Surely not ... philosophers.

Well let me just say this: I am a philosopher *and* a hunter, and I'm not the only one. In fact, *I am an environmental philosopher because I'm a hunter*. How's that for a paradox? Here's the thing about philosophy: if there isn't a paradox to work with, there's not much philosophy to be

NATHAN KOWALSKY

done. Hunting provides that paradox, and how! Life and death, together, right there in front of your face – and on your hands. How often do humans and wildness *touch*? Must that kind of contact with raw nature involve *death*? Why is hunting so *enjoyable*? (Where else can you get organic, free-range, grass-fed, arguably cruelty-free, roughly 100-mile diet, U-Pick meat?) It's enough to make someone think, and think hard.

You might be interested in thinking hard about hunting because you're a hunter, or a foodie, or a locavore, or a vegetarian, or a conservation biologist, or a city slicker – this book has got chapters written by all those sorts, and more! There are deep thoughts here for everyone. One can be a philosopher by profession, inclination, or otherwise – the very term means "lover of wisdom," and that isn't limited to stodgy academics smoking pipes whilst wearing waistcoats. Even so (and you may already know this), a philosopher is only good for maybe one thing: thinking hard. Don't go to them for answers, because all you'll get is more questions. But what philosophers will do is some hard thinking for you (if you believe in the division of labor), and get you philosophizing too (that is, if you don't mind).

That's what this book is for: contemplating hunting – an activity that gets the mind going, if not the blood boiling – and doing the thinking *well*. It's easy to dismiss hunters as barbaric or ignorant, but there's no denying the profound nature of the issue. Hunting *is itself* a field for pursuit, and a worthy one. It isn't often given the attention it deserves. So let's get our wits about us and follow it down.

It's fitting that we get our sights set on hunting with the guidance of the venerable hunter, nature writer, and cabin dweller, David Petersen. Dave's been hunting the land where he lives almost as long as I've been alive. He knows the secret location of Edward Abbey's grave. And he's been doing some thinking. You might be a hunter or you might not be; Mr. Petersen's got some words for the lot of us. That's why he's taking the point!

Now there are better and worse ways to hunt down your quarry, depending on what it is and where you are. What we've done is set up four practice targets, with almost five chapters aiming at each. "The Good, the Bad, and the Hunter" points us in the most obvious direction: the morality of hunting. Everybody wants to know, after all, if hunting is good or bad, and why. And that's just the beginning! What better way to start thinking about right and wrong than with a guy named Jesús? Professor Ilundáin-Agurruza (if we're speaking formally) dares us to go on a hunt with him – a philosophical hunt. Philosophers are, after all (so he says), "truth hunters," even if he isn't an animal hunter himself. With a bevy of bullet-laden puns, Jesús argues that the only way to answer the question of the value of hunting is to follow the *philosophical* ethic of "fair chase." The same courtesy hunters are supposed to extend to their prey has to be shown to their *opponents*: this makes the debate fair, and anti-hunters fair philosophical game.

But what about "fair chase" for non-human animals? The feelings of animals count for something, and animals don't like being hunted. That's where Theodore Vitali comes in, a professional member of the Boone and Crockett Club, which pretty much wrote the book on the fair chase ethic. Father Ted throws us for a loop, arguing that hunters *can't* be fair to animals. What they can do, however, is cultivate a particularly *human* excellence, one which provides a non-trivial justification for hunting – the kind which gives the prey (individually and as a species) a fighting chance. Our next contributor, Lisa Kretz, won't have any of this. She systematically criticizes the idea that hunting is somehow "environmental." It doesn't matter if hunting is natural for humans; our hunting is not good for the prey (individually or as a species), and it doesn't get us closer to the truth of nature either. This is precisely the kind of critical thinking that lies at the heart of philosophy, and her case cannot be ignored.

Tovar Cerulli proceeds to march right up the middle of this debate, as only an ex-vegan can. With drama and panache, he argues that the same sort of fundamental ethical concerns lie beneath both vegetarian and hunting practice. Say that again? Well, I'll let you read it for yourself, but you may not look at either side in the same way again. Recognizing that ethics can lead us into deeper philosophical ground, Greg Clark asks the question on everybody's mind: isn't hunting the equivalent of murdering Bambi? Rather than dancing around in the wilderness equivalent of a princess palace, he leads us deep into a mystery – one that Disney doesn't quite do justice to, and yet one that isn't served by knee-jerk criticisms of Bambi either. Clark doesn't offer us a "solution" to the "problem" of hunting so much as show us a portal into another way of experiencing the cosmos.

This is where the next part of the book points us, "The Hunter's View of the World." Part of the trouble with sorting out the morality of hunting is that not everybody knows what it's like. As usual, Hollywood hasn't done us many favors in this regard. Hunting is killing for fun, right? What a perverse way to look at the world! Well, hang on, we might not even have the right target – and shooting at a straw duck is no way to connect with the real thing. So our second goal is finding out what hunting actually *is* – how it is experienced (phenomenology), and how it can shape our view of the world (metaphysics).

Brian Seitz starts us off with an existential reflection on hunting: what it is, whether hunting for sport changes what it is to hunt, even whether or not killing is the essence of hunting, let alone the point of it! He makes the challenging case that hunting connects us to a timeless reality, which is why it is out of place with civilization and the other hyperactive degradations of our day and age. Yet, at the very same time, hunting can be a rip-roaring good time, as Alison Acton makes clear in her chapter. She takes us for a ride into that pell-mell rush which is English foxhunting. She points out that you can't take yourself too seriously when hunting, least of all when you're not the hunter, but your horse is! There's a level of trust and respect that has to exist between the human and the animal if the ancient arrangement is going to come to any fruition at all.

But there's nothing quite so timeless – and yet so current – as the once universal form of human flourishing known as hunting and gathering. Through the lens of traditional Anishinabe teachings, Jacob Wawatie (Mowegan) and Stephanie Pyne show us what the world can be like in the eyes of a people for whom hunting was a way of life. Rather than divisions between humanity and "nature," interconnections are so prominent in their stories that even hunting isn't something to investigate in isolation; it is as unremarkable as breathing, and yet one of the profound gifts given to humanity by the animals of our shared home. One might think that modern sport hunting lacks much of this character, but as Garry Marvin argues, even the trophy of a hunted animal only makes sense in terms of individual, personal connections between the prey and the hunter. Trophies are meaningless except as part of the experience of a particular hunt; they breathe life into an experience that goes beyond death. As the embodiment of memory, Garry argues that trophies perpetuate both relationship and spirit.

The third segment of this book, "Eating Nature Naturally," focuses our attention even more intensely on the issue of nature. Hunting and naturalness is a particularly appropriate topic, given current concerns about the environmental crisis, and humanity's relationship with (the rest of) nature and (other) animals. We have already seen this issue come up, in relation to both the ethics of hunting and the quality of experience facilitated by hunting. To take us further into the depths of this issue, the eminent conservation biologist Valerius Geist examines the evidence for and implications of the evolution of human beings as hunters. While there's no question that our species and its ancestors made their way in the world by hunting, he points out that it's a whole lot more complicated than that. Val argues that our apelike ancestors started out as vulnerable vegetarians, but learned to fight off predators, which is how we learned to hunt. This evolutionary step, in turn, led to a great deal of the cultural capacities that we now hold dear. Professor Geist wants us to be clear as to exactly what is at stake when we consider the relationship between human nature, hunting, and the rest of nature.

These close connections between our basic constitution and hunting other animals don't mean, however, that hunting can be pursued without any qualms at all. The archaeologist Janina Duerr argues that it's *universal* across human cultures – hunting cultures, farming cultures, herding cultures – to believe that hunting is morally problematic and must be properly performed, lest one suffer the consequences. She suggests, in effect, that it's natural to believe in a Master or Mistress of Animals, who will hunt *you* down if you don't hunt with the proper respect. Yet even if hunting ethics are "natural," that doesn't mean hunting is the best way to reconnect with "nature." In his chapter, Roger King makes the point that most hunters understand their relationship with nature to be a mind-game at best. There isn't a growing movement of hunters who want to reform society so that more people do, in fact, access nature in a more authentic way. This is an important call to action: if hunting really does bring us closer to genuine nature, then hunters should be coming up with ways in which we can overcome societies that prevent such access!

Genuine access to nature? What's that supposed to mean? The last two chapters in this section flesh that out for us, even if controversially. Jonathan Parker asks whether or not "hunting" with cameras can connect us to nature in the same way that hunting with weapons can. While he doesn't have a problem with nature photography, he does argue that hunters are different from photographers in the way that participants are different from spectators: hunting places a person directly in the middle of the logic of ecosystems, whereas at best, photography can only view these realities from a distance. T. R. Kover takes this point and runs with it: the logic of ecosystems which hunters know firsthand is that biological life is intertwined with *death*! Hunting brings us face to face with the fact that all living things die and get eaten, including ourselves. Richard goes on to argue that most anti-hunters are motivated not by a "love" of animals, but rather by the *fear* of mortality characteristic of Western culture's alienation from nature. You can't love life, after all, if you won't let it be what it is.

Implicit in the question of nature is the question of culture, as we've just seen: hunting is opposed to the dominant cultures of life-denial many of us languish in, and yet it is at the root of our species' cultural hard-wiring. Our final section, "The Antler Chandelier: Hunting in Culture, Politics, and Tradition," helps us to consider the interrelationship of hunting and various social factors. Leading this pack is the eminent philosopher and foxhunter Roger Scruton. Giving us a tour of both famous and obscure novels, operas, and other forms of literature, Roger explores the ways in which even contemporary hunting expresses profoundly human attitudes towards the land, other animals, and even the divine. There is something of the holy and the sacred in the ritual pursuit of "game," and while we may not be able to fully explain it, we can by no means ignore its centrality to the human condition.

The "oldness" of hunting has already come up as a theme, and Kay Koppedrayer, an editor for *Primitive Archer* magazine, examines the phenomenon of hunting with bow and arrow. Moreover, it's not "modern" bowhunting she's interested in; rather, bowhunting and bowmaking with old-fashioned, even self-made bows and arrows draws her attention. What is it about the hands-on, do-it-yourself attitude at the heart of traditional archery? Kay suggests that the appeal here is not to go back in time, but rather to use the past as the foundation for a present which is more robust than the usual cultural trappings of carbon-fiber, surgical steel, and electronics. Similarly, this conflicted relationship between the past-informed present and a culture of the ravenous future figures prominently in Paula Lee's chapter on hunting in visual art. Drawing on both contemporary and nineteenth-century examples, she shows how hunting presents a challenge to the dominant forces of civilization. Gustave Courbet's paintings are but one instance where transformed ideals of masculinity and naturalness are mocked by the rural, lower-class values they make obsolete.

Ah, but it's not only about masculinity. Debra Merskin proceeds to draw on feminist theory, investigating how it is that female hunters participate in an activity presently dominated by men. The analysis of hunting as a veiled metaphor for sexual predation is highly controversial, and yet Merskin suggests that there isn't anything necessarily bizarre about women participating in the hunt. Not only do women hunt for reasons similar to those of men, but the image of the female hunter has a longer history of denying male dominance than one might imagine given contemporary stereotypes. While there's plenty more to be said about sexual politics and hunting, I think Deb's right in arguing that there's no sense in denying the propriety of women hunters in light of problematic gender roles. Our final author, James Carmine, takes the political aspects of hunting and heats them up over a blazing fire! Arguing from the perspective of classical American liberalism, he claims that hunting is a right of the commoner to the commonwealth that is wild nature. The aristocracy is no more entitled to the common grace of God's Green Earth than we are. In fact, he views the modern environmental movement as the equivalent of the uppity English gentry, in that it wishes to restrict access to hunting by asserting the equality of humans with all other forms of biological life. One needn't agree with Jim's politics or analysis of ecological philosophy to see the politically significant and subversive nature of hunting – and it's a sure way to go out with a bang!

In closing, I hope that you, the reader, will not only enjoy the chapters in this book – thinking along with and/or against each author – but will also be better placed to tread the path of thinking critically about hunting. Seeking an answer to a riddle is the paradigm of the hunt, and this book's highest aspiration is to put you on the scent. Good hunting!

NATHAN KOWALSKY

PART I

THE GOOD, THE BAD, AND THE HUNTER

CHAPTER I

TAKING A SHOT

Hunting in the Crosshairs

Disclaimer: no real animals have been harmed in the writing of this piece. The safety is engaged – for now. In principle everything hunting related is *fair* game – there's no safe zone as the scope scans the horizon – but it is mostly our own convictions that are under peril here.

Looking Down the Barrel

We are going on a hunt here. Since we have not hunted together before, here's some background on me. I come from a family of hunters. Gramps and sons took to the hills in the Pyrenees armed with side-by-side guns.[1] Dad had two different-gauged sweet hunting-scene engraved shotguns: one for small game, the other for bigger animals like wild boar. I fantasized some day I'd get one.

The best shots we took with our air rifles were against "large mammalian game." My gun, a Norica .22, was a Howitzer that packed a punch compared to my friends' .177's. No, we didn't shoot dogs or horses. We played "war" and shot at one another – yup, we were foolish. I remember taking a shot at Manuel, his rotundity made him a better target, and wounding his hand at 150 yards. Zzzzing! His pellets flew by my ears as he chased while I ran away thinking how insane this was. And how fun. The thrill of this "play" set me on a hunting path...

But today I am not a hunter. I'm an "animal lover" who donates to Defenders of Wildlife. Shoot, what am I doing here then? Hold your fire and hear me out. I'm not your typical environmentalist either. In a sense I hunt: for truth, insight, and understanding. Not your usual quarry. But if you take me along as a scout, endure, and take the shot, you'll bag a different kind of game just as impressive as a 10-point buck. You won't be able to mount or eat our elusive prey, but it will give your kills a deeper meaning that will taste as rich as game compared to prepackaged super-market meat. However, this requires mercilessly shooting down much common sense and received wisdom about hunting. Are you game?

What are we aiming at here? Just as Socrates was bent on self-examina-tion, incessantly chasing himself, we're setting the Socratic crosshairs on hunting itself. The arduous terrain is peppered with rocky contradictions, tensions about to snap, ironies, and paradoxes (*apparent* contradictions that resolve into insight). Along the way you'll also take some insightful shots. Not to spoil the fun, you'll encounter these as I flush them out. The meth-odology, the way to carry this out, involves looking at the *how* and *why* of hunting. Rather than firing shells without a choke to see where the random pellets strike, this is about the well-placed one-bullet kill. This requires skill and patience. It's going to be tough and fun, as a hunt *should* be. One more thing: here we follow the *philosophical fair chase code* (PFCC): give opposing views a sportsperson's fair chance before trying to shoot them down.

Chambering the Philosophical Rounds

To excel at hunting you have to think not just as a hunter or predator, but also as prey. This very skill is the primer that sets philosophical thinking off: the ability to look at the world from different perspectives. Let's cycle the action and load another biographical round in the chamber to put you in my shoes.

> I'm about 10. For the first time I align the sights on an animal with intent to kill. My "hunting" resume is the usual one of vicious play-ground kids: skewering, burning, and crushing insect-like critters. But this is a bird, a "real" animal. Trouble is, I'm a WWF nature crusader. I mean, I pestered my father like a horsefly till he quit hunting. Yet, here I am, with a sweet, unsuspecting bird marked by the white dot. The heart pounding, I feather the trigger. Can I pull it?

The inner fight I encountered captures a vital *and* troubling tension inherent in hunting: the allure of asserting your superiority over another creature you pursue, and the realization that this implies killing it. We also take two birds with this shot as it captures the conflict *and* snatches a working definition (another PFCC tenet: define and clarify key concepts early). Aligning with this tension, some veteran hunters still have a residual sense of remorse once the rush of the hunt is over and they stare into dead eyes.

At this point the tracks we were following split into hunting for need, where hunters *truly* depend on killing animals for survival, and hunting for sport, the activity you, dear reader, very likely pursue. (Even if you eat what you hunt, you're at no risk of starvation should you not eat it.) The former doesn't face many ethical issues, but the latter attracts controversy like a doe in heat draws bucks. We're stalking the latter, so here the term "hunting" refers to the sporting kind.

Under what conditions, if any, is hunting for fun legitimate? This kind of challenge is what philosophers, as truth hunters, live for. It means confronting beasts most hunters prefer not to cross paths with: arguments against hunting. Worry not, they won't plead to be spared, trying to convince you to feed critters Disney-style by firing flowers. But this isn't about shooting tied-up animals either; it is about chasing better reasons for hunting so that spilled blood may be atoned.

My hands are stained red, just not in the way you may surmise...

Firing Blanks

Blanks? Blanks. That's what animal liberationists want you to shoot. Even better, spent shells, to avoid disturbing the animals. But their arguments sure are loud. Were they ammo, they'd be a magnum caliber with a nasty kick. Ironically, paradoxically, the reason to bring these folks here is to find better reasons to hunt. Before proceeding, another rule from the PFCC: don't simply reject or argue against the conclusions of opposing arguments that say "don't hunt." This looks at the gun from the wrong end (bad idea). We should look at the reasons they fire instead, the evidence that supports the conclusion. An open mind and a clear bore go a long way here.

Typically, those opposing hunting come with a side-by-side ethical shotgun, the rights of animals and their intrinsic worth in one barrel (as Tom Regan chambers it), and the suffering this inflicts on animals in the other barrel (with Peter Singer loading this one).[2] Actually, to down our quarry here we need only fire Singer's load because he bypasses two issues that muck up the other bore: the nature of rights and whether animals can have rights. For Singer these have "to be justified on the basis of the possibilities for suffering and happiness," and since animals have interests, at least in not being caused pain, this covers much of what matters to rights partisans.[3]

Singer shoulders the ethical theory of utilitarianism, built on the notion of our action's consequences. An action is morally right or wrong in relation to the amount of pleasure or pain it causes to those affected by it. Someone sharing ammo with you when you're out in the field is a happiness-producing action, whereas their using your dog for target practice is not. To recast this extra-light, yet keep the same firepower: it is wrong to hunt because of the suffering it brings animals. This makes *me* take the finger off the trigger.

The upshot: we should give equal consideration to the interests of all animals.[4] Fine. But for the record, the equal consideration of those interests is not the same thing as those interests being equal. It remains to be seen how they compare. We can flush out the difficulty of calculating animal pain versus human pleasure – especially if we scout out a context larger than individual animals and hunters, and consider the suffering this brings to other animals related to our prey and its role in the ecosystem, as well as how people's lives are affected by the hunter's activity (family members, hunting businesses, opponents). How do we estimate the pain and pleasure? Whereas the original argument seems to give minute of angle groupings, now even the best scope can't handle it. It's like trying to fend off a rhino with a cap gun. However, this is a "practical" difficulty that leaves the underlying issue standing: isn't there something wrong with causing suffering to animals for the sake of sport? The rhino is pissed.

We can discharge the following: animals *also* hunt and kill; they can do it, we can do it. True, as Woody Allen says in *Love & Death*, "nature is … spiders and bugs, and big fish eating little fish … animals eating animals. It is like an enormous restaurant."[5] But this won't cut it. Animals, acting on instinct and lacking cognitive capacity, don't know any better. We do. We can grasp the consequences of our actions. This means realizing that our fun rides on the suffering of other beings when there are alternative enjoyments available – even with guns and bows – which don't involve killing and maiming animals.

Another PFCC cue: a better strategy to deal with opposing views is to actually concede the point, then see if you can come up with a follow-up shot that blows it out of the water (should we be concerned with waterfowl). Let's agree with Singer that, because animals are not mere means but ends in themselves with interests of their own, we must not treat them as expendable for *trivial* purposes.[6] Now we need to show that hunting is not trivial – so much so, in fact, that it overrides the interests of animals in not being used as mere means or harmed on account of sport.[7] This is quite a challenge. Let's give it our best shot.

Loaded Words and Shooting Straight

But we can handload the cartridge with even more gunpowder.[8] You've heard and probably intoned it, "sticks and stones may break my bones, but words will never hurt me." Substitute Stone Age weaponry for *spritzers* and bolt-actions and we're set. In a genuine sense words hurt, since they're used to justify the skin-piercing bullets aimed at animals tagged as "pests." Besides, we're great at devising ways to avoid guilt-trips. Words that show contempt – "it's just a darn varmint" – or praise for the speaker's own prowess – "it was a bruisin' bruin" – cycle the conscience-easing action like it's custom serviced. However unpleasant this may be, as scrubbing bores always is, for the sake of a cleaner hunting ethos we should reflect on hunting tropes and their effect on the sport.

> The sight is on the bird. Breathe in, so cute; breathe out, I have it where I want it; breathe in, that'd be cruel; breathe out, just pull the trigger; breathe in, wonder if it has lil' baby birds; breathe out, it'd be quite a shot. My arms are tiring. Breathe … Crack! The pellet leaves. I can't wish it back.

Evolutionary psychology, which explains things in terms of whether they maximize our chances to procreate or not, supports the idea that language shapes how we view the world. I'm usually reticent to join their party (philosophically, they glass and interpret evidence too narrowly), but they present a persuasive case that should make us think twice before shooting off certain words. To pack this with as few grains as possible: gendered words ascribe different attributes to the same object across different languages. The word for "key," a female noun in Spanish, is described as intricate or lovely by Spaniards, whereas in German, the masculine noun has Germans describing it as jagged, or hard and heavy. Likewise language shapes what we see, since using the same word to cover more than one color, or more words to discriminate different hues, makes for faster or slower color recognition across different language speakers.[9]

To chase this toward our interests: if words shape how we see the world, and our word choices influence how we see animals, this has dire consequences for fauna. Referring to animals as pests, cuties, or beauties – prairie rats, sweet baby pandas, or gorgeous stags – may mean we shoot as many of them as possible, smooch 'em, or hunt them in a fair and honorable way. Often hunters speak of varmints derisively while praising game. Three-quarter bore expressions are pertinent here: "insults" passed off as neutral tags, such as varmint, vermin, pest; euphemisms like harvesting or culling; and hyperbolic renditions of animals and risk that speak of bruins, beasts, and monsters. These load the odds against the animals.

It can be argued that it's a fact that rodents are pests, or that coyotes are predators to be eliminated. But the argument's claw extractor isn't built for this; these reasons fail to grab the case, jamming the cartridge. For one, demeaning the animals actually brings the wrong emotional component (the positive one comes later). It puts rage in the machine, and anger and guns don't mix. Contrast varmint treatment with that of pets, referred to by "gentler" descriptions. Even when we must kill them because they are a threat, or there are too many, we devise *humane* ways to eliminate them. Because these animals suffer just the same, pest status is not a reason to disregard their suffering. Consistency requires equal treatment and a more humane way of disposing of them such as sterilization. But this means they'd be off limits for hunters. The issue is that language makes it easier to justify indiscriminate killing in ways we wouldn't condone for other animals, be they pets or prized game.

The other two categories follow suit. Hunters often refer to themselves as stewards of nature who *care* for the animals they hunt. Indeed, they do much good for the animals and their immediate environment. But terms like "harvesting" euphemistically disguise the fact that it's not conservation for the animals' sake but for the hunters'. It's about using animals to guarantee the joy of hunting – the vocabulary underscores their use as objects. If one *really* cared for the animals, one wouldn't hunt them. Since the last set of terms fits the pattern we won't ferret it out in detail, simply noting that speaking of bruins and brutes creates a mystique that takes out the best genes (true nature stewardship wouldn't do so; predators kill the weak, better serving the ecosystem).

JESÚS ILUNDÁIN-AGURRUZA

Let's shoot straight and call a thing by its name. We are not harvesting but killing when we hunt; it isn't a prairie rat, but a prairie dog; it's not a damned varmint, but a fox. And there is *nothing wrong* with that. These are not the kind of holsters you want for your concepts anyway. Ultimately this cheapens hunting, shooting at sitting ducks (at worst) or waddling ones (at best), not at challenging flying fowl. Here goes a follow-up shot. Even if the premises of the argument don't support the conclusion, the conclusion may still hold for other reasons. Let's grant that how we speak *and* think of the prey affects our behavior, resulting in a kind of controversial inauthentic hunting.

Paradoxically, this makes a stronger case for the hunting I believe is legitimate: a *meaningful* hunting carried out in ways and captured in words that don't belittle but honor animals.

Reading this may have been somewhat painful, but definitely a lot less so than having your behind perforated by a nosler-tipped round. You've been a sport staying with me. You can sigh with relief since now we'll argue for your side of things, and I'll take shots at myself instead of you. We're in luck. I just picked up the trail we're after.

The Virtuous Hunter

Something falls into the river. But I can't tell whether the waters have washed away the sweet bird or a chunk of branch. The elation gives way to remorse. To this day the bird's ghost haunts me: if I hit it, it flies on the sorrow I felt; if I didn't hit it, it's truly a ghost's ghost for haunting me with gratuitous guilt.

To get a tight grouping around the bull's eye: hunting as a sport requires that we willingly build it as a challenge. We make the hunt more difficult than it needs to be, curtailing our superiority over the prey to bring us as close to parity as possible while giving us the chance – not the certainty – to succeed. Michael, Robert De Niro's character in *The Deer Hunter*, exemplifies this by voluntarily embracing the one-shot kill ethos as his standard of excellence.[10] The interest lies in the *process* more than the result, as José Ortega y Gasset writes.[11] Of course, the kill is the goal (otherwise it's a travesty of a hunt). What marks the difference between an excellent hunt and a questionable one is *how* this is achieved and the reasons behind these actions, the *why*. The virtuous hunter follows an ethos, let's call it Diana's Code after the Roman hunting goddess, which points our thinking, actions, and weapons in the right direction. Here we argue for the non-triviality of hunting.

After much grueling philosophical tracking – comes with the turf – we've spotted our prey. The hunt for "the hunt" is finally on. Alert and ready, we *still* don't shoot. Hunting stands out among sports because it requires extreme self-control, what with the adrenaline pumping, the lure of the prey, and the very small window of opportunity, it's too easy to pull the trigger or release the string prematurely. Often the best skill a hunter has is being able to hold the shot or forsake it altogether. It takes true discipline. Hunters who, rather than risk a bad shot, let animals go that they've tracked for months before the season impress me. It's time to bring out the single-shot rifle of ethical theories, virtue ethics. This theory centers on hunters of virtuous character, who *aim* at being the best Nimrods possible:[12] *excellence* as hunters is the goal. Ortega concurs with this.[13] Virtues are the middle ground between vices and lead to this excellence. For example, courage sits between the vices of cowardliness and recklessness. Virtuousness depends on doing things for the right reasons: forsaking the shot to avoid just wounding the animal is virtuous, holding it to save a bullet ... well, the gun should go off and waste the round.

To hit the target we need good judgment, experience, deliberate thinking, and skills developed by habit. Indeed, at the heart of hunting is a *discipline* that requires developing those skills unique to hunting. You must cultivate *the skill of the kill*: unflinching, steely nerves; tracking and orienteering abilities; and, of course, superior marksmanship. This is built on hard work. Miguel Delibes, a Spanish award-winning novelist who says he was a hunter who became a writer,[14] celebrates the tough hunts of his youth, based on effort, sacrifice, suffering, and know-how.[15] This Spartan hunting is more meritorious – read virtuous – than the kind done on ATVs. We become soft otherwise. And this affects the value of the kill. Not all are worth the same.

Hunting practices are a diverse lot that fall on different places along the hunting continuum in terms of "virtuosity."[16] On the positive end, the virtuous hunter leads by example. Delibes pictures such a hunter in his *Diario de un cazador*: Lorenzo is a dedicated huntsman who shoots and talks straight, and owns up to his mistakes to avoid them in the future.[17] Hunting boar with spear, bear with bow, dangerous game up close and personal, or with a one-shot ethos, all follow Diana's Code and devise formidable and admirable challenges. Quality not quantity guides this. A central aspect of this superior kind of hunting is the ritual of honoring the

JESÚS ILUNDÁIN-AGURRUZA

kill and paying homage to it. It seems we could learn something from our Stone Age antecessors, who went out of their way to undo the violence of their deed by ritual veneration.[18] The cavemen were more sensitive and advanced than today's metrosexual crowd, let alone your average yahoo.

The ambiguous cases inhabit the middle of the range. My "hunt" was an example of novice hunting where no honorable kill was possible (for one, I shouldn't have shot the bird over the river, where the body was irrecoverable). There are questionable practices that virtuous hunters wouldn't use, such as electronic game calls. These give hunters an advantage over the animals and the sport itself, taking away any legitimate claim to a worthy challenge. In the words of another Delibes' character, Gualberto, as he comments on game calls, "it is as if on your wedding day your wife's old boyfriend waits for you with a blunderbuss behind a curtain. Is that hunting, boss?"[19] We might end up hunting with "smart bullets" that chase prey on their own ...

The vicious hunter operates at the negative end of the spectrum. Aerial kills from choppers, poaching, grossly "arranged" canned hunts and similar practices mark this shooter. A colleague witnessed a group of "hunters" corral a herd of elk into a small clearing just before hunting season; once it opened they formed a semi-circle with their vehicles and shot them all. Of course, this is not done in the open. Gualberto again: "I tell you boss, when a man has to hide to do something, it's cause the thing he does is not right."[20] I ask you, is that hunting, boss?

Time to take your hard-earned shot. When we chambered the philosophic rounds earlier I spoke of the tension inherent between the excitement of the chase and the act of killing. Of course, here the strain comes as a .50 cal. paradox. The more you appreciate the value of the life you take and observe Diana's Code, exerting yourself to make a true challenge of the hunt, the more valuable and genuinely enjoyable the hunt. It will also be all the more ethically legitimate. Conversely, the more you "belittle" matters – remember the issue of language? – the less valuable the hunt and all that follows. To add more spin to this, the greater the regret at extinguishing a living being for the right reasons and in the right way, the better you can feel about it! This doesn't mean you should go through a pack of Kleenex every time you hunt. Between the vices of being callous and a crybaby, there is the virtue of being sensitive. The virtuous hunter "feels" for the prey. Indeed, this is the best way to ensure an ethical hunt.

To give the coup de grâce, there is a sense in which the ethical treatment of animals is actually indebted to the virtuous hunters' ethos, for the latter *intentionally* limits what's allowable against the animal in the hunt.[21] This compassionate hunting depends on a genuine appreciation of animal life. One kills, but for better reasons. However, this doesn't mean wavering before pulling the trigger, because one cannot afford a flicker of doubt if one is to bag any partridges![22] Rather, it asks for an emotional connection afterwards – reflection. Hence the importance of giving due respect to the life just taken.

In short, the original question was whether we could justify hunting for the sake of fun in the face of animal suffering. Well, the issue isn't solved with a simple answer, "hunting is right" or "it's wrong." It requires a more nuanced answer that argues that hunting is acceptable for some people, some of the time, for some reasons. And at the core we find that the hunter's ethos, built on feeling for the animal, brings about ethical sensitivity and demands excellence from the *hunter of virtue*.

Parting Shot

I mentioned blood in my hands. I once killed a deer. On a bicycle! Talk about a skeleton in the closet (surely you didn't expect this!). I didn't run it over with monster tires or spear it *à la* Lancelot. Off the front of a training race, I encountered a herd of deer. Hesitating whether to stop or close to the finish, I pressed on. Caught between the road, parallel to their exit path, and an 8-foot metallic fence, they got spooked. With effortless elegance, even in panic, they jumped over the fence one by one. Except the last one. (Squeamish readers should skip the rest of this.) Its front leg hit one of the poles that held the fence in place. Its very attempt to get over actually drove the pole through the shoulder, impaling and dislocating it. Gaping wound. Muscle. Sinew. Bone. Blood. Gravity did its job. The deer fell on the other side, pitifully dragging itself away. Deer are resilient. Maybe this is another ghost and it survived? (Skeletons in closets, ghost stories, how fitting for hunting season and Halloween.) No, death's shadow followed it alright.

I'm aware this wasn't hunting; I wasn't *directly* responsible. But the point is, I've had my kill.[23] And given my empathetic temperament, that's plenty. However, had I been given the choice, I'd have preferred a one-shot deal that gave the deer a chance, where if successful I could honor it. I rely on other hunters, Virtuous Hunters, who respect their kills to

JESÚS ILUNDÁIN-AGURRUZA

help me atone for this. Then again, as a cruel and adventurous Spaniard – as the great philosopher Immanuel Kant so described my countrymen – maybe I should get over it.[24]

NOTES

1 I dedicate this chapter to them: Grandpa Juan "Atuna" Ilundáin-Muguiro and son Iontxo, both in the happy hunting grounds, and the rest of the pack, Jesúsmari (my father), Josetxo, and Pedro José. Their hunting exploits would have made Greek hunting goddess Artemis proud.

2 Tom Regan, *The Case for Animal Rights* (Berkeley: University of California Press, 1983); Peter Singer, *Animal Liberation* (New York: HarperCollins, 2002). There are also bolt-action, lever-action, and AR-15 platform arguments such as land ethic or ecofeminist critiques. For *other* arguments yet see Linda Jerofke's tasteful "Taking Stock: An Overview of Arguments For and Against Hunting," in Fritz Allhoff and Dave Monroe (eds.) *Food & Philosophy* (Malden, MA: Blackwell, 2007), pp. 221–35.

3 Singer, *Animal Liberation*, p. 8. His concern is "speciesm," treating other species in an unfair way.

4 Ibid., p. 231.

5 *Love & Death*, dir. Woody Allen (Metro Goldwyn Mayer, 1975).

6 Singer, *Animal Liberation*, p. 20.

7 Of course, hunting is not trivial for hunters, but from the point of view of animal suffering, all things being equal, the burden of proof is on the hunter.

8 Warning: this will make you uncomfortable; remember the PFCC and bite the bullet. It'll pay off in the end.

9 Sharon Begley, "What's in a Word? Language May Shape Our Thoughts," *Newsweek*, July 9, 2009. Available at www.newsweek.com/id/205985 (accessed July 31, 2009). There is a difference between language and thought that is ignored here. Language may simply reflect how we think of these. However, since the thinking at this level is dependent on language, this is probably a relation that goes both ways.

10 *The Deer Hunter*, dir. Robert Cimino (EMI films, 1978).

11 José Ortega y Gasset, *Meditations on Hunting*, trans. Howard B. Wescott (Belgrade, MT: Wilderness Adventure Press, 1995), p. 35ff. This short work, often cited in hunting circles in too poor a way, contains a plethora of insights for a flourishing life that merit a careful, deliberate tracking of all its pages. Following common practice, "Ortega" will be used hereafter.

12 Nimrod was the original badass "Mighty Hunter" of the Mesopotamians. A ruler who conquered plenty of cities, his reputation was tarnished in the Bible by association with the Tower of Babel.

13 *Meditations on Hunting*, pp. 98–9.

14 Miguel Delibes, *Mi vida al aire libre* (My Life Outdoors) (Madrid: Ediciones Destino, 1989), p. 201. Moreover, he says he was a hunter before he had a gun, as he hunted with stones as a child (p. 202).

15 Ibid., pp. 214ff.

16 Rather than hunting being absolutely right or wrong, there are better and worse reasons for hunting, and ways of realizing it, that line up on a continuum. This strategy of giving up black and white answers doesn't result in a relativistic "anything goes." It actually permits more precise and honest shooting. True, it brings some uncertainty at times, but it more accurately captures what's going on. Just as the gradients between different colors lack definite boundary lines, but we can tell a red from a yellow, there will be hunting practices that are clearly admirable, and others that won't even qualify as hunting. Context helps adjudicate difficult cases.

17 Miguel Delibes, *Diario de un cazador* (Diary of a Hunter) (Madrid: Ediciones Destino, 1995).

18 David Sansone, *Greek Athletics and the Genesis of Sport* (Berkeley: University of California Press, 1988), pp. 40ff. Although his book is about the definition of sport and Greek athletics, its first part has a truly insightful analysis of the phenomenon of hunting. Should readers be inclined to pursue this, they will find revealing ideas on why hunters display their kills and mount them, reasons beyond practical explanation for why they get rid of human scents, and many more enticing catches.

19 Miguel Delibes, "La caza de la perdiz roja" (Hunting the Red Partridge), in *Viejas historias de Castilla la Vieja* (Old Stories of Castilla la Vieja) (Madrid: Alianza Editorial, 1981), p. 140; my translation.

20 Ibid., p. 130; my translation.

21 David Inglis, "Meditations on Sport: On the Trial of Ortega y Gasset's Philosophy of Sportive Existence," *Journal of Philosophy of Sport* 31 (2004): 92.

22 Cf. Ortega, *Meditations on Hunting*, p. 98; Delibes, "La caza de la perdiz roja," pp. 122–5. It does bring you closer to not pulling the trigger. The ambivalence, whether from a self-avowed animal lover such as me, or a seasoned hunter with hundreds of kills, stems from the same source. We understand *The Deer Hunter*'s Michael better now when he goes from his one-kill ethos to taking the finger off the trigger at the end of the film. He's gained an appreciation for life and the tension has placed him on the other side. Hey, it happens even to the toughest.

23 I also have an impressive track record of killing all kinds of birds while driving (usually with my horrified wife in the car). But that's a story with a different lesson best left for another occasion.

24 Immanuel Kant, *Observations on the Beautiful and Sublime*, trans. J. T. Goldthwait (Berkeley: University of California Press, 1960), p. 100.

CHAPTER 2

BUT THEY CAN'T SHOOT BACK

What Makes Fair Chase Fair?

 About 25 years ago, I had an experience while hunting black bears in Ontario that affected my views on the essence of hunting and fair chase. As many of you know, spring bear hunting in Ontario was traditionally done over bait. On the first night of the hunt, I sat in my blind peering ahead at the bait which was approximately 50 yards away. I arrived at the bait around 2 p.m. The day was cloudy and rainy. By early evening, the heavy rain had let up and a steady drizzle and mist continued. By 8 p.m., the forest had become a misty canopy enshrouding all my immediate surroundings including the bait. At one point, for whatever reason, I sensed that something was behind me. My blind was a few yards in from an abandoned logging road. Knowing that a bear might circle a bait and even come into the blind I turned around very slowly, first my eyes, then my head. Behind me, approximately seven paces away (I walked it off afterward) sauntered a huge wolf. I looked at him and he looked at me. He sauntered quietly past me up onto an embankment overlooking the bait. We watched each other intently; then he turned and slipped off into the forest.

My dominant feelings were of wonderment, excitement, and intimacy. I felt a bond with that wild animal as I had never felt before with any living being other than a fellow human. I recall thinking to myself: there are no fences here ... we are the same ... we are both predators ... animals. I felt, for the first time in my life, my intimacy with the wildness of life itself. I felt my own radical animality. I felt I belonged to the wilderness, to the wild, as an intimate and participating member. I felt myself one with the wolf: a predator among predators. It was through this experience, so deeply felt, that I finally understood the essence of hunting: being a predator. All the artificiality of life evaporated as I looked at the wolf and the wolf looked at me. There were no fences, no artificial barriers between us. There was only the continuum of life and death. What follows in this essay flows directly out of this experience, coupled with my philosophical reflections on the nature of ethical discourse and inference.

I will begin the analytical part of this essay with a concern and objection. In the light of this objection, I will then present what I hope is a clear understanding of the nature and scope of fair chase.[1] First, my concern: one of the most serious mistakes made by hunters defending the morality of "sport hunting" is to define fair chase either in terms of a "contest" between an animal and the hunter, or a life and death struggle for survival between the two. The model for the morality of fair chase is thus what is normally found in athletic events in which there is an element of chance brought into play in order to make the contest "fair" to all the participants. So in the "sport of hunting," one celebrates the chance element of the hunt, namely, the animal's ability to escape or elude the hunter, either because of its superior instincts and natural abilities, or because the animal was not artificially confined and limited (for instance, by escape-proof fences), or because of the lack of significant disparity between the hunter and hunted.

The second model, which is of mortal "combat" between hunter and animal, is found primarily among big game hunters, though not usually among whitetail deer hunters, as it almost always contains the element of extreme personal challenge and/or danger. In this model, the hunted animal is perceived as a threat to the hunter and thus the hunter/hunted relationship is viewed as mortal combat in which there is parity of danger: for one or the other, the outcome will be final. This view is often implied or even expressly stated in the accounts given by big game hunters who encounter grizzlies in North America, or lions, Cape buffalo, and other large and "dangerous" animals in Africa. In this model of fair chase, the moral equation is the following: the greater the danger, the fairer the chase.

In my view, the athletic and combative models used to define and defend fair chase, and consequently the criteria entailed from such a model for hunting ethics, are inherently incoherent and potentially disastrous for the hunting community. Why? Because the moral principles

THEODORE R. VITALI

involved in such models entail the radical rejection of all hunting as intrinsically immoral! The reason is quite simple: if the animal hunted has a right to be hunted fairly – that is, if it has by nature the right to a fair chance to either escape or to avoid the hunter's attempt on its life – then it has a more basic right not to be hunted at all, since the right to be treated fairly is a result of the more basic right to be free of unjust aggression or manipulation without consent. It has the right to well-being and life. To argue, therefore, that fair chase entails fairness to the animal is to concede the argument from the outset. Whatever else may be true, whatever else fair chase may mean and entail, it cannot mean or require that for the hunter to hunt morally, the hunter must act in a way that is fair to the animal.

If what I have written above is true, then fair chase, if it is to have any moral subject at all, must refer to the hunter, not the hunted. Fair chase, in other words, has to require that the hunter hunts in a manner that is conducive to his or her own well-being and to the well-being of the community, both the human community and, by extension, the broader biotic community, not the animals hunted as such. Hunting, like all other human enterprises, must have as its primary or principal aim the well-being of the human community and the individual human beings who comprise this community. Everything else is derivative of this.[2]

This may be abhorrent to many moralists who seek a more egalitarian approach to the natural community, but nonetheless and despite the apparent abhorrence of the theory, it is still the only one that is ultimately rational. Members of every species seek to preserve themselves first and foremost, and in some species, their species as such. Hence the primary object of their efforts and endeavors is self-preservation in many and diverse ways. This is true of the human community as well and for every individual in the community.

For hunters to hunt fairly, therefore, the human community and the individual hunter must be the primary beneficiaries either directly or indirectly. When it comes to subsistence hunting, this is easy to see and understand. Subsistence hunters hunt primarily to stay alive, to live, though they may also hunt for the better quality of game meat over processed meat, and in some cases because of tradition and for the sake of self-reliance. I believe this is especially true in places such as Alaska. But most so-called sport hunters rarely if ever hunt to simply stay alive, even if they hunt for somewhat similar reasons as do subsistence hunters, namely, for the quality of the meat and the desire for greater self-reliance. Most sport hunters hunt for the experience itself, for the enjoyment or pleasure they derive from hunting. So the argument used by sport hunters that they hunt to eat is not sufficiently valid to warrant the moral legitimacy of hunting itself, namely, the taking of animal life. What then is entailed if non-subsistence hunting is to be justified?

According to Aristotle, the goal of all human activity ought to be, either directly or indirectly, human flourishing. Human flourishing requires that the individual live and thrive within the larger and more complex human community. Moreover, this community must exist and flourish within the even larger community in which it exists, namely, the biotic community. Human beings cannot survive, let alone flourish, in a world in which air and water are polluted, the land ravaged, the ecosystem distorted or destroyed. This is true not only physically, but psychologically and spiritually as well. Human beings belong, as a species, to a large, complex ecosystem in which all living beings share, compete in, and cooperate with each other – and at times and in certain circumstances kill each other – in forming an on-going life system or congeries of life systems. As members of this community and as direct and indirect beneficiaries or detractors of this community, human beings have serious obligations to foster the well-being of this entire community. The first moral obligation entailed by fair chase, then, ought to be that hunting should directly or indirectly contribute to the well-being of the larger biotic community. In short, for hunting to be moral, it should contribute either directly or indirectly to the conservation of wildlife and wildlife habitat, "to the integrity, stability and beauty of the biotic community."[3] In other words, hunting must play an integral role in wildlife management; hunting must be life-sustaining in the fullest and richest sense of the word. This is the necessary minimum criterion that must be met if hunting is to be ethical. Fair chase, then, must entail that hunting practices play an integral role in conservation.

The hunter observes or meets this criterion by observing hunting laws and regulations. Laws regulating hunting were promulgated and are continually amended to foster the well-being of the species being hunted and the overall biotic community, especially the relevant habitat. Conservation corps or wildlife commissions exist to study and assess the impact of hunting on wildlife, both those species being hunted and those otherwise affected by the hunting. Wildlife authorities exist to manage wildlife and habitat and thus regulate hunting insofar as hunting is a means to this end. When hunters observe laws and regulations while hunting, they either directly or indirectly foster conservation and thus actively participate in wildlife management.

THEODORE R. VITALI

With this in mind, it is easy to identify what is at least minimally required for hunters to be ethical – that is, to hunt fairly: to observe and obey all appropriate hunting laws, regulations, and, in most cases (though not necessarily all), local and regional customs. I caution about customs because some customs ought to be tolerated for social and political reasons though they are not the best practices. Again, it is up to wildlife managers, not the moralist, to assess how seriously damaging such customs are to the welfare of the herd or species.

Beyond the value of conservation, the hunter, apart from being an active participant in game management, must also gain something special by hunting that cannot be gained in any other way. What is this?

Because every animal's life is a good in itself and a good for others (the animal seeks its own survival and life and at the same time is "food" for others), the life of the animal is a good that must be respected as a good that cannot and should not be harmed, let alone destroyed, without sufficient reason. The basic principle applies here: do no harm. To kill an animal is to harm the animal, to destroy something good. It is clear that to do so for survival purposes or for the management of a very complex ecosystem are sufficient reasons to take the life of certain animals (e.g., culling deer herds that are damaging crops or even gardens in suburban neighborhoods), but in sport hunting these necessities are indirect and secondary, and in some instances remote. For the majority of hunters, the intention and motivation for hunting are sport, not game management. Thus, from the point of view of the individual hunter and the individual animal hunted (not hunters in general or the species in general), there has to be a reason for taking the life of a particular animal which is proportionate to the animal's life when food procurement and or game management are not the primary intentions of the individual hunter, even though the latter is still an essential good that must be present.

In my view, the hunter enters by his or her actions directly and consciously into the predator–prey relationship, a relationship fundamental to all living entities in this biosphere. My encounter with the wolf led me to experience, at a rather deep and intense level, this fundamental and most intimate relationship to the natural community: that of a predator engaged in life–death processes, the taking of life for the sustaining of life. Such an experience is clearly more than physical; it is spiritual, because it recalls the hunter to his most basic identity as a member of the natural (biotic) community, an animal among other animals, a predator among other predators. Only hunting and fishing (not catch and release) directly overcome the artificial relationship between human beings and their source of food, especially meat. Only hunting and fishing directly restore to the hunter or fisherman the depth of felt insight into one's own nature and its relationship to the natural community. This insight and experience are the good that warrants the taking of life through hunting and fishing.

The ethics of fair chase, then, requires these two elements: a careful and scrupulous commitment to conservation ethics grounded in the best biological sciences of the day, and a commitment to foster in oneself those disciplines that lead to greater reflection on – and respect for oneself as an active member of – the life–death continuum. This latter requires, in turn, conscious efforts to handicap oneself in the hunting experience in order to foster a greater immediacy and intimacy between oneself and the hunted animal so that as much as possible, a deeper relationship will grow between the hunter, the hunted, and the entire natural community – i.e., what Leopold described as *the land*, "our dependency on the soil-plant-animal-man food chain, and of the fundamental organization of the biota."[4] In the end, therefore, hunting is primarily a spiritual, not a merely physical event and this is its primary value and the proportionate reason for hunting.

As we have grown more accustomed to industrial food production, we have also become more detached from the larger biotic community and from ourselves as members of that community. We may still take nature walks, even long hikes in the forest, and we may be engaged in bird watching and wildlife photography, which are all wonderful hobbies and even avocations. But in all these latter instances, we remain "detached" from the life–death processes that define nature and our place in nature. We remain above the processes and to that extent, removed into an artificial space above and beyond the real world of nature and life. The hunter, on the other hand, participates directly in nature as a predatory member and as such directly impacts the natural community by taking life. The hunter's actions are immanent, not transcendent, and thus make the world different because of his or her actions. The hunter takes a life and consumes the flesh of the animal whose life he or she has taken. His or her actions are decisive, final, and complete. The good of the animal's life is ended and transformed into a good for the hunter and a good for the larger, more complex biotic community. The life process continues on as a direct result of his actions. And this is a good thing.

It is for this reason that fair chase hunting eschews any form of artificial hunting, such as the hunting of tamed or trapped animals, or of exotic species (especially those bred or penned for the purpose of canned hunting) that are foreign to the land. The hunter who hunts fair chase seeks to engage the animal within the animal's world – the land – and so relates to the animal in terms of the continuum between the land, the animal, and the hunter. If there is no appropriate relationship between the land, the animal, and the hunter, then the hunter cannot reach into and experience that fundamental relationship between him-/herself as hunter, the animal hunted, and the land that binds them together in an integral biotic (and, I would say, spiritual) community. To hunt an exotic deer, let alone an African lion or Asian tiger, in a confined area makes no moral sense to me at all. In such cases, there can never be the kind of spiritual intimacy between land, animal, and hunter that warrants and justifies the actual act of killing the animal.

Apart from such exceptional circumstances as canned or artificial hunts, one can easily see the emergence of this kind of intimacy between the hunter and the hunted as young and inexperienced hunters mature into seasoned and experienced hunters. Young hunters seek to dominate the animal hunted; older hunters learn to love the animal hunted. In the end, power is replaced by respect, domination by intimacy. At the outset of most hunting experience, young hunters generally make use of a fairly wide assortment of gadgets to help in the hunt. It is not uncommon to see a new hunter carrying a host of extra "utensils" to the hunt, including computerized range finders, elaborate multi- and often over-powered scopes, scent killers, even motorized vehicles. But one also notices as time goes on that this same hunter, having learned what was necessary and superfluous, carries less equipment and depends much more on his or her knowledge and skill. This becomes especially true of seasoned deer and bear hunters (in my experience) who cease using high-powered, scoped rifles for more primitive weapons, including black powder muzzle loaders and especially archery. In the latter case, one often sees a hunter change from a compound bow to a recurve or even a long bow. In many cases, this is done because the hunter wants to exercise much more skill and stealth in the hunt and also to come "closer" to the game, to challenge him-/herself to achieve even greater intensity in the experience and the relationship between him-/herself as hunter and the hunted animal. For the experienced bow hunter, the intimacy between hunter, hunted, and land is crucial and obvious.

One of the finest hunters I have ever known, Milo Burcham, taught me this lesson as I hunted with him for elk and mule deer in Montana a few years ago. Milo had acquired such competency with both rifle and bow, and in calling in and taking elk, that he handicapped himself to the point where he hunted during the first part of the season only with a recurve bow, hardly any real camouflage, and with the intention to hunt an area no matter how strenuous the effort, even if it meant backpacking into an area in order to maximize his chancing at a large bull. While using a compound bow in the past, he hunted only for larger six-point bulls, although after taking up a recurve, he considered any elk a trophy. It so happens, however, that he took his largest elk by any means, a seven-point bull, with his recurve. Only towards the end of the hunting season, if he had not achieved his goal, would he take any legal elk with rifle or bow.

One day, while hunting with him on a deserted and abandoned logging road on the side of a steep mountain, Milo caught sight of a mule deer at the other side of a rather huge canyon. I have no idea how far that distance was but I could barely identify the mule deer with field glasses. Using a spotting scope to examine the deer, he pointed out that this muley would be a fine animal to take. In sheer wonderment I asked why he even cared about this animal; the deer was across an impossible canyon and so far beyond any possibility of being hunted, let alone taken, that it seemed to me not even worthy of a further thought, let alone a serious effort. He looked at me and said that we would climb to the top of the ridge, move along the entire rim of the mountain, camp out, and try to find him the next morning. I said to him that even if this were possible, what would we do with him if we were to get him? "Oh," he said, "we'll quarter him and pack him out." How long will that take, I asked? He said, "Probably two days."

I am an old Missouri and Kentucky deer hunter. I sit in a tree stand overlooking a network of deer trails, watch a crossing for two or three days, and shoot the first legal deer that comes across my path. The thought of stalking a deer for two days in a deep forest on the top of a mountain saddle and hauling the deer out on my back went far beyond anything I had ever thought possible or desirable. As it turned out, we didn't pursue the deer, not because Milo didn't think I could do it, but because the deer moved on into a heavily wooded area that made it next to impossible for us to ever find him. Milo gave up on the deer, not on me (though he should have).

I give this example because it provides a glimpse of where the subjective and relative sides of fair chase come into play. For someone like me, a very average hunter with very average hunting skills, a good stalk may amount to long hours of patient waiting sitting in a tree stand overlooking various deer trails. It may and likely entails scouting for deer sign, good shooter preparation for the sake of a successful and clean kill, good emotional and psychological discipline to remain silent and alert for many, many hours in one sometimes uncomfortable place, and the skill to track,

THEODORE R. VITALI

find, and clean a fallen animal. But to Milo Burcham, clearly a superb hunter, such a hunt would not bring him any closer to his basic human and animal nature as a human predator than going to the grocery store. For Milo, far more is demanded. Milo has to stalk that far distant muley or that huge bull elk under extreme circumstances. His skills are honed to achieve that level of hunting and thus are required for his hunting experience. Hence, in my view, Milo is morally obliged to hunt at such a level. Most hunters, including myself, are not. We achieve the best experience possible for us by normal means of pursuit. Some of us, upon achieving greater skills at taking our game, should, morally speaking, begin to handicap ourselves at some point in order to foster greater intensity of experience, and thus, greater intimacy between ourselves and the animal hunted. That is why, I believe, one should continue to develop one's hunting and shooting skills leading to the gradual abandonment of artificial helps in stalking and taking game. For the relatively young, the use of sophisticated weapons is important because the hunter must seek to kill the animal cleanly and as painlessly as possible. Therefore, the young and inexperienced hunter is morally obliged to use the most efficient means of taking the game. But as the hunter develops his or her skills, he or she ought to begin to simplify his or her hunting methods, gradually reducing the more technically sophisticated weapons for the simpler.

Finally, the pleasure a hunter derives from the hunting experience, including the killing of an animal, ought to be the result of an action well done. This means it must be virtuous in every sense: fully human, conscious, reflective, humble, and respectful of the animal. As I stated above, most hunters grow into this as time and experience temper youthful enthusiasm and thus help engender in the hunter deep love and respect for the animal hunted. The morality of the hunt is inseparable, in the end, from the spirituality of the hunt, and that spiritual dimension constitutes the primary value which justifies the hunter hunting, not for physical subsistence, and not for conservation, but for moral, psychological, and spiritual renewal as he or she enters ever more basically and immediately into the life–death continuum of the natural community.

This is what fair chase ultimately means and entails.

NOTES

1 The phrase "fair chase" commonly refers to the morality or ethics of hunting wild game. It refers, more precisely, to the ethical character of the pursuit

(chase) itself, namely, its "fairness" to either the animal hunted (the usual interpretation) or to the hunter and the hunting community (as I will argue).

2   Aquinas, following Augustine, makes this very claim: all things work for the good of the whole except that the human good is a good unto itself, a good to which all the rest is ordered (Aquinas, *Commentary on St. Paul's Letter to the Romans*, chap. 8, lect. 6).

3   Aldo Leopold, *A Sand County Almanac* (New York: Oxford University Press, 1949), pp. 224–5.

4   Ibid., p. 178.

THEODORE R. VITALI

CHAPTER 3

A SHOT IN THE DARK

The Dubious Prospects of Environmental Hunting

 Hunters are often perceived to be environmentalists, as they are a major political force for protecting various ecosystems that support the game they pursue.[1] Take Ducks Unlimited Canada (DUC) as a case in point. It is a not-for-profit environmental organization that has 7,100 established habitat projects across Canada, where habitat is provided for waterfowl and 600 species of plants, insects, and animals.[2] The organization was founded in 1938 by sportsmen[3] who enjoy killing the waterfowl in these environments.[4] I want to show that there is a tension between (1) the obviously environmentally minded and commendable pursuit of preserving habitats and (2) the preservation of habitats to enable one to engage in the sport of killing members of species that live in these habitats. To do so, I will explore the relationship between hunting and environmentalism.

I will argue in this chapter that many standard defenses of hunting as an environmental practice fail. First, I will discuss the view that hunting allows humans to take on their natural role in ecosystems. Second, I will address the claim that hunting is the ideal method for learning to appreciate nature and morally relate to it. Third, I will call attention to the paradox of ethical hunting. The tenets of the sportsman's code lead to a commitment not to hunt at all. Last, I will return to the tricky DUC Case, which we will be better equipped to handle following a sustained reflection on the relationship between environmentalism and hunting.

Taking On Your Natural Human Role
by Killing Non-Human Animals

It can be argued that hunting is natural and preserves the balance of nature. Some contend that the natural human role in ecosystems is as predator and consumer of non-human animals. Others claim that hunting is a way to preserve the balance of nature. I will counter these views through a discussion of the crippling, negative impacts of attempts to manage game animal populations on non-human animals, and current technological advances in hunting tools. Less a reminder of one's membership in the biotic community, hunting is more a testament to humanity's ability to dominate.

First, let's get clear about what claims of "naturalness" amount to. "Natural" is a ubiquitous term that is often used to smuggle in claims of moral correctness. Proposing that hunting is a natural activity and that it is therefore a morally permissible activity is highly problematic.[5] We can also say war is natural; this does not mean we actively advocate pursuing it or that we consider it a good state of affairs. We could say humans naturally manifest violence and greed; this does not mean we try to encourage these traits in our children. To say a thing is natural does not make it morally right. Claims to the moral rightness of hunting cannot depend on the claim of naturalness.

Unable to appeal to the naturalness of being hunters or the naturalness of predator–prey relations between human and non-human animals, one might instead contend that hunting keeps the balance of nature in check. The viability of this claim is called into question through the negative impacts hunting has on species' well-being. For example, Lewis Regenstein notes that "Hunters and other forms of 'wildlife management' can adversely affect the evolutionary development of animal species: by seeking out and killing the largest and strongest animal of the herd (e.g., the 12-point buck or the bighorn ram) the hunter removes the best of the breeding population."[6] Hunters do not pursue the weak and the old. By destroying the animals most likely to survive harsh winters through removing the most genetically fit animals, how are hunters aiding the species? Moreover, given the central role individual members can play in their larger communities, the destruction of one member may have unpredicted negative impacts: "The loss of the leader of a wolf family, for example, can traumatize and disorient the pack for a long period of time, and affect its ability to survive and reproduce."[7] Again health and fitness may resultantly decrease, calling into question whether hunting contributes to the balance of nature.

Hunting is often defended as a method of population control. The role of hunting in regulating populations today is often predicated on the initial flaws of attempts to regulate populations.[8] The over-hunting of predators is often the cause of the problem of now overpopulated species. A good example is with regard to deer populations:

> A claim frequently made by hunters is that they are the conservationists, and are helping "balance the ecology" by preventing the overpopulation and starvation of wild animals. They conveniently ignore the fact that, in the few cases where deer actually do overpopulate, it is often because hunters have helped eliminate the deers' natural predators, such as wolves, mountain lions, and coyotes.[9]

Thus we can see that ecosystem health is likely best preserved by allowing species to self-regulate in the environments they inhabit.[10] Peter Wenz argues that predators other than humans are often destroyed by hunters to ensure that they will have sizable enough game populations. As a result, "the modern hunter disrupts rather than helps maintain natural balances in the ecosystem."[11] To ensure hunters do not decimate prey animal populations, "predators of those populations are decimated, such as the wolf, formerly a predator of deer in Wisconsin."[12] The 1973 Senate Commerce Committee issued a report "recommending new legislation to protect endangered species. It stated that 'the two major causes of extinction are hunting and destruction of habitat.'"[13] There is something very wrong if we consider one of the two major causes of extinction – hunting – to be an effective method of population control.

Moreover, modern limitations on hunting and the creation of more efficient and lethal tools for hunting change the dynamic of hunting considerably. Aldo Leopold laments:

> a common denominator of all sporting codes is not to waste good meat. Yet it is now a demonstrable fact that Wisconsin deer-hunters, in their pursuit of a legal buck, kill and abandon in the woods at least one doe, fawn, or spike buck for every two legal bucks taken out. In other words, approximately half of the hunters shoot any deer until a legal deer is killed. The illegal carcasses are left where they fall. Such deer-hunting is not only without social value, but constitutes actual training for ethical depravity elsewhere.[14]

The illegal kills, which are left to rot, help to illustrate another problem with some forms of modern hunting: today hunting is usually about sport, not survival. Further concerns arise when we consider the modern technology used. Leopold, a seasoned hunter himself, marked a net trend pointing "clearly toward more and more mechanization, with a corresponding shrinkage in cultural values."[15] If the mechanization for hunting is too sophisticated, the façade of fair chase crumbles. Given modern weaponry coupled with game reserves, the success of hunts is greatly increased. A sense of equal membership in the biotic community is hindered by hunters having highly efficient and damaging technology at their fingertips.

Discover Nature by Killing Non-Human Animals

Another defense of hunting is that it is an excellent method for learning about nature. Henry David Thoreau maintains that through interacting with nature via hunting one gains respect for one's prey and is led to discontinue the practice of hunting. Such a view fails to account for more fruitful methods of facilitating respect for nature, such as becoming a naturalist.

Thoreau suggests hunting is a good way to introduce the young to nature, and he maintains that after this education humane hunters will leave off killing. He recalls such an introduction to nature himself:

> I sometimes like to take rank hold of life and spend my day more as the animals do. Perhaps I have owed to employment and to hunting, when quite young, my closest acquaintance with Nature. They early introduced us to and detain us in scenery which otherwise, at that age, we should have little acquaintance. Fishermen, hunters, wood-choppers, and others, spending their lives in the fields and wood, in a peculiar sense a part of Nature themselves, are often in a more favorable mood for observing her, in the intervals of their pursuits, than philosophers or poets even, who approach her with expectation.[16]

It is certainly true that those in direct contact with nature witness intricacies more readily than those who are not. Thoreau is correct in proposing that the teaching of ecosystem appreciation at an early age is elemental to producing an adult who has a bond with nature. It is crucial to cultivate an appreciation for the complex interworkings of the natural world.

But shooting at the very entities that compose nature is a rather strange way of doing this. Put simply, killing is not generally the best form of learning about others and manifesting respect for them. Consider an analogous argument applied to another natural species, namely, *Homo sapiens*. Entertain the absurdity of the following statement: I learned to respect human life and understand my relation with it by tracking *Homo sapiens*, learning of their surroundings and their behavior patterns, and then killing them for food.

Thoreau's hope is that the student of nature "goes thither first as a hunter and fisher" until later, provided they have the "seeds of better life" in them, to identify the hunted creatures as proper objects of poetry or natural study "and leaves the gun and fish-pole behind":[17]

> We cannot but pity the boy who has never fired a gun; he is no more humane, while his education has been sadly neglected. This was my answer with respect to those youths who were bent on this pursuit, trusting that they would soon outgrow it. No humane being, past the thoughtless age of [girlhood or] boyhood, will wantonly murder any creature which holds its life by the same tenure that [she or] he does.[18]

Thoreau's trust that humane humans exposed to hunting will soon outgrow it is far too idealistic. Raising hunters with an ethic that should eventually override the desire to hunt is not a wise way to educate our youth if a move away from hunting is the desirable end. Such an approach is counterproductive because the goal (not hunting) is pursued through encouraging contrary behavior (hunting). As an educational model one rarely first encourages the behavior believed to be non-ideal, in the hopes that a realization of its wrongness will grow out of performances of the non-ideal behavior. Analogously, consider the wrongheadedness of educating someone about the wrongness of theft by first encouraging them to learn the craft of thievery and then hoping that with time they will realize they should leave off this enterprise. It is a fault of our society that hunting is "oftenest the young [woman's or] man's introduction to the forest, and the most original part of [herself or] himself."[19] The introduction to the forest should be a far less destructive one.

Hunting is often thought of as a way for humans to create or renew awareness of our too often forgotten relationship with nature. However, there are many options other than destroying animals as sport or for food that can serve equally well for getting people immersed in nature: hiking, backpacking, camping, photography,[20] wildlife research,[21] becoming a naturalist, sketching, and participating in citizen science,[22] to name a few. Such pursuits provide an opportunity to commune with nature in ways hunting does not, facilitating relationship and learning without killing. These activities also serve as counters to the claim that people who are against hunting do not want to get their hands dirty, wish to remove themselves from nature, and do not realize the fundamental truth of life is kill or be killed. Mucking about in a bog exploring the members of the ecosystem involves getting dirty, being in and of nature, and relating directly to it – the relation just is not one of killing. In response to the kill or be killed mantra, humans alone have the capacity to be ethically informed consumers. Some humans, that is, not those faced with limited access to non-animal food sources due to poverty or geographical location, need not kill non-human animals to survive comfortably.[23] The death of others to ensure human survival is inevitable given our membership in the food chain and wider ecological systems, but there are choices regarding what sort of death is involved (be it of plants or animals). Although some hunters may know more intimately where the flesh that they eat comes from and pay closer attention to how those ecosystems function, a naturalist can have an equally intimate relationship with non-human animals and knowledge of ecosystem function.

The Paradox of Ethical Hunting

We must recognize that there are differently motivated hunters. Some hunt respectfully and depend on their prey for survival. Respectful hunting that is necessary for survival is morally permissible. All organisms are entitled to pursue their own survival. In circumstances outside of survival there is a hunting code of ethics meant to ensure ethical hunting practices. Paradoxically, however, premises of this code lead to the conclusion that hunting is morally wrong.

Hunting was once necessary for survival. In those circumstances, of course, hunting is permissible; we have a right to survive. Such hunting gains moral dimensions if it is done respectfully,[24] which minimally involves following the basic code of hunting ethics that I discuss below. To understand the attempt to hunt ethically, we must look at both the methods of killing non-human animals and the motives initiating the killing. Eugene Hargrove writes:

🦌   LISA KRETZ

Tribes often had customs according to which they asked the forgiveness and understanding of wild animals that they killed for food. Such customs or traditions, however, did not survive in Western civilization, in which a tradition of sport killing of wildlife for pleasure, not food, developed instead. The hunter, according to this tradition, derives enjoyment from the killing [of] animals without any feeling of guilt.[25]

Hargrove over-generalizes here, painting all hunters with the same brush. There are hunters that hunt for the sheer pleasure derived from it. E. Donnell Thomas responds to hunting naysayers with: "In short, we have become a society of secular Puritans, reading evil into just about anything that anyone could possibly do just for the hell of it."[26] There are hunters that hunt to have an experience in nature that involves predatory relations, but may well also involve remorse. Consider Thomas McGuane's reflection that: "Nobody who loves to hunt feels absolutely hunky-dory when the quarry goes down. The remorse spins out almost before anything."[27] The point I wish to take from Hargrove is that to the extent that hunting is a recreational pursuit where pleasure is derived from the act of predation and killing, it is not a morally sound act. This is because unnecessary harm is caused to an animal (pain, death, maiming), potentially their kin (an animal with young), and potentially to the species (removing the fittest members). Killing unnecessarily is immoral because it is an act of unnecessary destruction; others are harmed without good reason. We must ask what the specific reasons are for hunting today, being mindful not to borrow romantic historical notions that no longer apply. Aldo Leopold shares in Hargrove's concerns about modern hunting:

> Take a look ... at any duck marsh. A cordon of parked cars surrounds it. Crouched on each point of its reedy margin is some pillar of society, automatic ready, trigger finger itching to break, if need be, every law of the commonwealth to kill a duck. That he is already overfed in no way dampens his avidity for gathering his meat from God.[28]

There is ample reason to question idealized notions of hunters communing with wilderness, taking from it one buck with one shot, in the great glory of nature.

Now I will focus on ethically concerned hunters who follow the sportsman's code. These hunters are faced with the self-defeating nature of the code. Brian Luke outlines the primary rules of the sportsman's code: "SC1. Safety first; SC2. Obey the law; SC3. Give fair chase; SC4. Harvest the game; SC5. Aim for quick kills; SC6. Retrieve the wounded."[29] Of note is that "the code as a whole entails a strong principle calling for the minimization of the harm done to non-human individuals."[30] This is evident through rules to lessen the pain inflicted by hunting (quick kills, retrieving the wounded), therefore showing a concern for the animals themselves. A hunter is no more successful in achieving a kill by killing quickly as opposed to, say, torturing the animal; either way, the animal ultimately ends up on her/his plate. The concern present in the code for limiting animal suffering shows concern for the animal itself.

According to Luke, this concern for the animal's well-being, when brought to full fruition, would eventually cause one who upholds the code to give up hunting altogether. The end result is the valuing of an animal for its own sake (rather than for its sake relative to human consumption and/or desire for an entertaining recreational pursuit). Luke tells the story of a hunter who fatally wounded an elk and pursued it for 30 consecutive days to retrieve it:[31] "Viewed in this way, rules SC5 and SC6 are not abstract injunctions to minimize suffering in the aggregate; rather they represent the hunter's sense of personal responsibility for the suffering of the specific individual that they shot."[32] This case serves as evidence that the hunter's code contains concern for the well-being of the animal itself; hunters following the code wish to avoid causing unnecessary pain. "Of the six parts of the sportsman's code," only SC1–3 can be given a reading solely concerned with the hunter's well-being; the rest of the code presumes "a recognition of the intrinsic value of individual animal lives and a sense of personal responsibility for minimizing one's imposition of animal suffering."[33]

SC5 and SC6 are what lead to the essential contradiction of the sportsman's code. "The commitment to avoid causing unnecessary pain implies leaving healthy animals alone, not just shooting them more carefully, the rules hunters have developed to prescribe *how* to hunt ethically presume principles that pointedly raise the question of *whether* to hunt at all."[34] It follows from SC5 and SC6 of the code that on the face of it hunting is wrong.[35] Hunters' ethics are paradoxical because "hunters become more ethical by hunting in a way that is sensitive to the animal's interest in avoiding pain and continuing to live; nevertheless, this very sensitivity and respect for animals entails that hunting is not justifiable, that even true sportsmen are not acting ethically."[36] In response to the paradox one can choose to embrace it, renounce the code, or renounce hunting.[37] One could also claim that although one has an interest in minimizing some suffering, this interest need not expand to a desire to end all

LISA KRETZ

unnecessary suffering. However, to the extent that hunters adopt a code of ethics that manifests care for those they kill, they will have to provide independent argument as to why the care they show stops short of a limitation on killing the non-human animal. Furthermore, the harm inflicted can reach beyond the particular animal killed; it can apply to its young, mate, and the entire pack if the role of the animal killed was a vital one for their success as a group.

Hunting and Environmentalism

Now I will return to the claim that hunters are indeed environmentalists. I have argued against the views that hunting preserves the balance of nature and that hunting is an ideal introduction to nature. I have also described the paradox of ethical hunting. DUC is a hunting group lobbying for the preservation of wilderness that manifests a desire to ensure the survival of the species it hunts. One problem with its stated aims is that the places to be "preserved" are specific and limited. Also, to save a thing *for use* is not the same thing as saving it for its own sake. Ecosystem preservation for making certain species available for recreational killing results in a game reserve, an area where a crop of organisms are made available for human consumption. Although habitat preservation is achieved by DUC, the motivation is primarily for hunting – it is not an act that manifests an appreciation of species and ecosystems for their own sake. The underlying motivations of environmentalists, those who recognize the inherent worth of species and ecosystem health, differ from those of hunters. When environments and particular species are saved for hunting purposes, it is to ensure game production for future slaughter. The desire for non-human animals as human food/entertainment is the central concern. Although the practical actions advocated by hunters and environmentalists may overlap at times, the underlying motivations are importantly different. Hunting is often done at the expense of species fitness. Also of worry is the fact that only environments that produce desirable game for sport are "worth" saving. Moreover, it has been shown hunting is not the best means for generating respect for non-human animals.

In summary, claims about the naturalness of hunting are deeply problematic. There is much contrary evidence against the claim that hunting preserves the balance of nature, including harms to species fitness via hunting, hunting being one of the primary causes of extinction, and the failure of hunting as an effective method of population control. Current hunting technology is so effective that hunting is less a reminder of humanity's role in a healthy web of life, and more a testament to humanity's ability to dominate. Claims that hunting is the best method for learning about nature are met by the absurdity of applying this line of reasoning to learning about, say, human animals. I presented alternative methods for respectful engagement with nature and gathering knowledge. Ethical hunting is paradoxical. Components of the sportsman's code make evident a concern for the animal itself. This concern, if brought to full fruition, would result in the cessation of hunting. It turns out that the assumption that hunting and environmentalism automatically go hand in hand is fraught with difficulty.[38]

NOTES

1   I wish to flag here at the outset that my discussion of hunting in what follows applies primarily to hunting as practiced in North America within a Western tradition. My critique applies only to this group. Indigenous hunting, and the practices associated with it, would require a far different philosophical analysis.

2   Ducks Unlimited Canada, "Dedicated to Wetland and Wildlife Conservation." Available at www.ducks.ca/conserve/index.html (accessed November 26, 2009).

3   I follow suit with common terminology such as "sportsman" and the "sportsman's code" but I'd be negligent not to note the gendering of hunting language, and how pronounced it is. This is a topic worthy of independent study which, unfortunately, time and space do not allow for here.

4   Ducks Unlimited Canada, "Our Position on Hunting." Available at www.ducks.ca/aboutduc/beliefs/hunting.html (accessed November 26, 2009).

5   That one cannot derive an "ought" from an "is" was first argued by David Hume in his *A Treatise of Human Nature*, ed. David Fate Norton and Mary J. Norton (New York: Oxford University Press, 2002), p. 302.

6   Lewis Regenstein, *The Politics of Extinction: The Shocking Story of the World's Endangered Wildlife* (New York: Macmillan, 1975), p. 16.

7   Ibid., p. 14.

8   I take this as a manifestation of hubris regarding human abilities to manage the complexity of ecosystems.

9   Regenstein, *The Politics of Extinction*, pp. 28–9.

10   I should qualify this by saying we should, of course, seek to remedy or minimize the destruction that occurs through human involvement (e.g., the

havoc that can ensue following the introduction of invasive species). Doing this well requires great humility, though.

11 Peter S. Wenz, "Ecology, Morality, and Hunting," in Harlan B. Miller and William H. Williams (eds.) *Ethics and Animals* (Totowa, NJ: Humana Press, 1983), p. 193.

12 Ibid.

13 Regenstein, *The Politics of Extinction*, p. 4.

14 Aldo Leopold, *A Sand County Almanac and Sketches Here and There* (New York: Oxford University Press, 1968), pp. 178–9.

15 Ibid., p. 181.

16 Henry David Thoreau, *Walden and Civil Disobedience* (New York: Harper and Row, 1965), p. 157.

17 Ibid., p. 159.

18 Ibid.

19 Ibid.

20 Wildlife photography as an ethically superior alternative to hunting is discussed by Jonathan Parker in chapter 13 of this volume.

21 This is a suggestion made by Aldo Leopold in *A Sand County Almanac*, p. 184.

22 Dr. Cathy Conrad is a central force for advancing citizen science in Nova Scotia. See Cathy Conrad and Andy Sharpe, "Community-Based Ecological Monitoring in Nova Scotia: Challenges and Opportunities," *Environmental Monitoring and Assessment* 113 (2006): 395–409. For an illustration of community-based monitoring in action see the Community-Based Environmental Monitoring Network, www.envnetwork.smu.ca/welcome.html (accessed November 26, 2009).

23 The moral justification for adopting a solely plant-based diet is derived from (1) the desire to minimize the negative environmental impact of obtaining protein from non-human animals – see Francis Moore Lappé's *Diet for a Small Planet* (New York: Ballantine, 1971) – and (2) the desire to minimize pain.

24 I am here thinking of Karen Warren's description of respectful hunting in "The Power and Promise of Ecological Feminism," in Michael E. Zimmerman, J. Baird Callicott, George Sessions, Karen J. Warren, and John Clark (eds.) *Environmental Philosophy: From Animal Rights to Radical Ecology* (Upper Saddle River, NJ: Pearson Education, 2001), pp. 322–42. She recalls a story of a Sioux elder whose son was sent to learn "Indian ways" from his grandparents (p. 338). As I read the account, it is one where the hunting is necessary and thus morally permissible. The boy was taught "to shoot your four-legged brother in his hind area, slowing it down but not killing it. Then, take the four-legged's head in your hands, and look into his eyes. The eyes are where all the suffering is. Look into your brother's eyes and feel his pain. Then, take your knife and cut the four-legged under his chin, here, on his

neck, so that he dies quickly. And as you do, ask your brother, the four-legged, for forgiveness for what you do. Offer also a prayer of thanks to your four-legged kin for offering his body to you just now, when you need food to eat and clothing to wear" (p. 338). This sense of reverence seems essential for manifesting adequate respect.

25 Eugene C. Hargrove, "Foundations of Wildlife Protection Attitudes," in Eugene C. Hargrove (ed.) *The Animal Rights/Environmental Ethics Debate: The Environmental Perspective* (Albany: State University of New York Press, 1992), p. 154.

26 E. Donnell Thomas, *To All Things a Season* (Belgrade, MT: Wilderness Adventures Press, 1997), p. 6.

27 Thomas McGuane, "The Heart of the Game," in *An Outside Chance: Essays on Sport* (New York: Penguin, 1982), p. 230.

28 Leopold, *A Sand County Almanac*, p. 166.

29 Brian Luke, "A Critical Analysis of Hunter's Ethics," *Environmental Ethics* 19 (1997): 25. "SC" is shorthand for "Sportsman's Code."

30 Ibid., p. 26.

31 Ibid., p. 32.

32 Ibid.

33 Ibid.

34 Ibid., p. 33.

35 Ibid.

36 Ibid., p. 39.

37 Ibid.

38 I wish to thank Nathan Kowalsky, Darren Abramson, Wayne Myrvold, and Michelle Willms for their comments on earlier drafts.

CHAPTER 4

HUNTING LIKE A VEGETARIAN

Same Ethics, Different Flavors

Sixteen years after becoming a vegetarian, I shot my first deer through the heart. That might strike you as decidedly odd. Perhaps more so when I mention that I'd become a vegetarian – and then a vegan – partly because I abhorred violence and suffering. Guided by compassion, by concern for animal welfare, and by feminist critiques of domination, I objected both to the slaughter of my fellow creatures and to their confinement in meat operations, dairy farms, and egg factories, the bending of their lives to serve human ends.

Each autumn, seeing deer hunters – always men, it seemed – headed into the New England woods with rifles, shotguns, or bows, I'd wonder what kind of sickness possessed them. That they, like most Americans, ate flesh was bad enough. That they went to such lengths to pursue and kill their own meat on the hoof was incomprehensible. Did they find some kind of sadistic pleasure in it? Did their lust for big-antlered trophies blind them to the barbarism of their pursuit? Repentant, I looked back on my own boyhood fishing and frog hunting as an unfortunate, pre-moral phase – before I'd truly begun to think and feel.

Other concerns underpinned my vegetarianism as well. I knew, for example, that people around the world starved to death every year. I knew, too, that many pounds of corn went into producing each pound of grain-fed beef. I could see no reason to perpetuate this pattern of first world gluttony. Humanitarianism clearly pointed toward forgoing meat and dedicating more agricultural land to the production of food for hungry humans. Likewise, I'd learned that meat industry workers are often underpaid and poorly treated. And even if they were paid well and treated well, must not the constant cruelty and killing they engage in do them some kind of harm? Must not the common practice of "thumping" runt piglets – grabbing them by the hind legs and smashing their heads against concrete floors – harden people's hearts and distort their notions of morality?

I also objected to the ecological impacts of meat. According to a 2006 United Nations report, 30 percent of the earth's land surface is dedicated to livestock production, with one out of every five acres of the world's pastures and rangelands degraded as a result of overgrazing, compaction, and erosion. The livestock industry contributes heavily to both water usage and pollution and is a driving force in deforestation, particularly in Latin America. It's implicated in climate change, too, accounting for 18 percent of human-caused greenhouse gas emissions, more than all the world's fuel-guzzling passenger cars, buses, trains, and planes put together. Combined, these factors make the global livestock industry a serious contender for the grand prize of ecological devastation: Leading Cause of Biodiversity Loss.[1]

I was determined to be mindful about my diet's consequences for the world and for the many beings who inhabit it. I aimed to confront those consequences with eyes open, to take responsibility, to choose the path of least harm. I was committed to finding a respectful, holistic way of eating and living, a kind of right dietary citizenship.

I was mindful, too, of the consequences for my own integrity. On all the grounds noted above, I'd concluded that killing animals was an unnecessary evil, so a sense of moral wholeness and alignment, of values put into action, could only come from a meat-free diet.

This dual attention – to both inner and outer consequences – is, I think, nearly universal among strict vegetarians.

Consider religious vegetarianism: as a longtime agnostic, my sense of dietary morality didn't stem from religion. Yet it resonated with the world's major traditions of religious vegetarianism, particularly those rooted in India – Buddhism, Hinduism, and Jainism. Their teachings on compassion and *ahimsa* (non-violence) address both the outer consequences of flesh-eating (animal suffering) and its inner effects (negative *karmic* impact and the stunting of human spiritual growth). Though abstention from meat is less prevalent in Judeo-Christian-Islamic traditions, many people have extended these religions' teachings – including the various versions of "thou shalt not kill" – beyond the human species, pointing to the consequences for both killed and killer.[2]

Consider, too, how secular proponents of vegetarianism link flesh-free diets with harmony and wholeness, suggesting that eating animals deforms us both inwardly (morally) and outwardly (socially and ecologically). They refer to the broad ethical, humanitarian, and environmental concerns noted above. They cite research associating animal abuse with inter-human violence.[3] They point to the connection drawn by ecofeminists between the subjugation of animals (and of nature in general) and the oppression of women.

And they invoke emblematic phrases that reflect the same concerns. Here are but a few examples. Regarding the consequences for other beings in the world: "To my mind the life of a lamb is no less precious than that of a human being. I should be unwilling to take the life of a lamb for the sake of the human body."[4] More inwardly: "To abstain from the flesh of animals is to foster and to encourage innocence."[5] And, perhaps most powerfully, the outer and inner drawn together: "Not until we extend the circle of compassion to include all living things shall we ourselves know peace."[6] "While we are ourselves the living graves of murdered animals, how can we expect any ideal conditions on the earth?"[7]

Such thoughts, whether framed in secular or religious terms, challenge us to reconsider the distinction between our inner and outer worlds. Is there a real separation between the two? Or is this a dualistic illusion, an artificial boundary drawn where I imagine that "I" end and "other" begins?

Of course there are many people who give a simpler explanation for avoiding flesh foods: they want to stay healthy. It's why I first cut back on meat, recognizing that excess beef and pork did my body no favors, especially when laden with antibiotics and pesticide residues. But all the strict vegetarians and vegans I have known – people who have completely eliminated flesh foods from their diets, rather than merely reducing their intake – have been motivated by deeper reasons. They have intended, above all, to do no harm.

When I squeezed the trigger, the buck jumped – a small, quick, hunched movement – then leapt forward, arcing among the trees. Something in his bounding gait told me I wouldn't need to shoot again. A moment later, going full tilt, he collapsed and plowed into the forest floor. The moment felt surreal.

Three autumns, I'd hunted deer without success. I'd begun to doubt that I'd ever make a kill. If I ever did, I imagined there would be a flood of mixed emotions, sorrow and elation and awe and gratitude all jumbled together. Now that it had happened, now that this whitetail had gone down and stayed down, my feelings were obscured by a veil of shock.

Hardly believing this was real, I walked to where the buck lay in the frosty maple leaves, crouched down beside him, and looked closely at the texture of his coat, brown finely flecked with black, and at his elegant head, his great ears and slender, symmetrical antlers, a simple fork on each side. I breathed in his heavy musk. Shaken, I put a hand to his now-still ribs.

After a few minutes, I fetched my knife and made the first tentative incisions. Through hair and hide. Then through abdominal wall. I pulled the buck's guts out onto the dry leaves. In the freezing air, his blood was hot against my hands.

My journey toward hunting began with vegetables.

During my years as a vegetarian, I'd become increasingly aware of the impacts of agriculture on the planet's ecology and on individual animals: the topsoil lost every year, the fish and other aquatic life killed by fertilizer runoff, the birds killed by pesticides, the countless rabbits and rodents minced by grain combines, the thousands upon thousands of deer shot by farmers to protect all manner of crops, the habitats destroyed by clearing land for agriculture in the first place, and so forth. I'd realized, too, that plenty of underpaid, poorly treated workers were tending North America's fields and orchards.

Whenever possible, I opted for organic foods, thus minimizing my diet's chemical footprint. I ate close to home, too, buying food grown by small-scale, local farmers: no massive machines or mistreated laborers working the fields, no need to truck the produce cross-country, a minimum of plastic packaging. Though much of my food still came from afar – greens and fruit in winter, tofu and other products year round – "local and organic" were my watchwords, signifying harmlessness, an ethical panacea.

If all harm could be attributed to faraway giants of industrial agribusiness, my faith might have lasted longer. But take Joey, the kindly organic farmer whose veggies travel less than a mile to the produce display of the crunchy local food co-op. You couldn't ask for a gentler, more conscientious steward of the land. Ask him about deer, though, and he'll tell you: "I've got a few guys on call. When there's too much damage, they come and plug one and we share the venison." Or ask about woodchucks: "I smoke-bomb their burrows constantly. Preemptively. A tunnel in a sandy bank right next to a kale field? Someone's going to move into that!"

Time and again, my wife Catherine and I had purchased Joey's greens. Time and again, we'd picked strawberries from his fields. It had never occurred to us that Bambi and Chuckie were getting plugged and bombed to make that food available to us.

Even in our own garden, it was impossible to keep the wild entirely at bay. Our tall, rugged fence did keep out the deer and, for years, the woodchucks, too. Insects were another matter. We didn't mind the flea beetles nibbling small holes in our greens. But, if we let them, cabbage moth larvae would decimate our broccoli. Cucumber beetles would strip and kill our newly sprouted squash seedlings.

Once we'd seen the damage they could do, we took action. I sprayed the broccoli with *Bacillus thuringiensis* I got from Joey; the larvae ingested the bacteria and died. Preferring not to use more serious pesticides, I hunted down the cucumber beetles one by one, squishing them between thumb and forefinger. Beetle-squishing was, I knew, beyond the pale of veganism, the strictest practice of which – out of concern for the bees – prohibits eating honey.

I was murdering insects. Joey was murdering woodchucks. His rifle-toting friends were murdering deer. All to keep veggies on our dinner table. Regardless of what I was actually putting into my mouth, the consequences of my diet weren't turning out to be as pure and harmless as I'd planned. I couldn't look away, feigning innocence, pretending not to know what occurred.

At the time, Catherine was studying holistic health and nutrition. A few of her instructors – former vegetarians themselves – offered words of caution about long-term veganism: be careful to get key nutrients. And our doctor, a Buddhist naturopath, reviewed an analysis of my blood chemistry and suggested I could use more protein.

We eased into it slowly. Local, organic yogurt. Then eggs from cage-free hens. I started noticing changes. I had more energy, felt more alive. My allergic sensitivities diminished. Perhaps these things had other causes, perhaps I could have achieved them in other ways – I'm no expert on nutrition – but it seemed to me that they were linked to our shifting diet.

Next came wild-caught fish and locally raised chicken. Their consistency and flavor felt alien. Over the previous decade, even meat substitutes that approximated the textures and tastes of flesh had seemed strange to me. But once the initial unfamiliarity passed, I craved them, ate them hungrily.

It made me think of a winter camping trip in the Adirondacks. A few years earlier, a friend and I had been there for a few days in February.

As we prepared dinner over our camp stove one frigid evening – eager both for the immediate warmth of the food and for the caloric fuel – my companion added butter to the pan. I watched ravenously. Except for cream in the occasional cup of coffee, it was the first animal product I'd consumed in years. Had I been alone, I might have grabbed the frozen quarter-pound stick, peeled back the wax paper, and started gnawing.

Catherine and I wanted the creatures we ate to have lived happily and died swiftly, mercifully. And we still wanted our diet to be minimally harmful to the earth, minimally wasteful of feed grain and other resources. So we bought local poultry whose provenance we knew. As I sit here typing, our freezer is home to several chickens raised by a young couple we know, also longtime vegetarians; when she got pregnant and started dreaming about roasted birds, they adjusted their diet and before long found themselves raising meat animals. Compared to a factory farm, their grassy, treed backyard is chicken heaven.

But still, after a decade of vegetarianism the transition to eating flesh made me uneasy. The habitat destruction and animal casualties incidental to agriculture were collateral losses, regrettable and unintended. The deaths of the creatures I was eating now weren't incidental to anything. Each had died specifically so that I could ingest and digest part of its body, extracting elements of its tissues and adding them to mine. While fruit and grain could – in theory, at least – be plucked from tree, bush, or stalk by relatively gentle means, and while vegetables politely declined to bleed, these individual fish and birds had met some intentional, violent, twitching end.

Soon, I returned to my boyhood pastime of fishing. Eventually, I started hunting.

Killing, in itself, did not attract me at all. But if I was going to eat flesh, I needed to look directly at the living animal and take responsibility for its demise. Reflecting back on it now, I think of feminist vegetarian Carol Adams' "absent referent," a term she borrows from linguistics. "Behind every meal of meat," Adams argues, "is an absence: the death of the animal whose place the meat takes. The 'absent referent' is that which separates the meat eater from the animal and the animal from the end product."[8] It was an absence I couldn't stomach. I had to face the animal and its death.

"I've long had an odd thought," writes Christopher Camuto, "that no one who hasn't killed, skinned and butchered at least one animal on his or her own should be allowed to buy meat in a grocery store."[9] Though I'd hesitate to impose that requirement on others, I felt obliged to meet it myself. I couldn't go on killing by proxy, eating chickens without any real sense of what that meant, keeping the truth at bay just as I had in my vegetarian days, eating tofu and rice – and Joey's greens and strawberries – without seeing, or wanting to see, the whole picture.

But why turn to hunting deer? If a confrontation with killing was all I wanted, I could have raised chickens myself, or simply volunteered to help a chicken-raising friend on slaughter day, wielding the hatchet and seeing how it felt. Why take up a rifle instead?

The answer is that I was after something more than a simple face-to-face reckoning. For years, I'd hiked through the woods as a curious, concerned conservationist. Nothing wrong with that. But I wanted to feel more a part of the land, to see differently, to sharpen my attention, to feel more like a participant in nature and less like a spectator. I wanted to engage with and better understand the local ecosystem, the wooded ridges and valleys that the white-tailed deer and I both call home. I sensed that hunting might help me establish a different relationship with the land, a sense of belonging, a kind of communion.

Communion through hunting? A few short years earlier, the notion would have stirred suspicion in my mind and heart. In response to it, I might have turned to ecofeminist Marti Kheel's scathing critique of the "holist hunter" and the "holy hunter," men who use the language of ecology and spiritual identification with nature "to camouflage and to legitimate violence and biocide,"[10] to mask their psychosexual urge to dominate and kill.

Now, though, I knew hunters – both men and women – whose respect for nature was no mask. Their compassion for animals and their concern for the health of the planet were undeniable. They took to woods and fields, as hunter-feminist Mary Zeiss Stange has put it, "for the same inner reasons they always have: for food, of course, but also for connection, and for knowledge about what it means to be human in our complex and increasingly fragile world."[11]

If my reasons had revolved merely around killing, then hunting wouldn't have served the purpose well. As I soon learned, you can spend hours, days, and seasons in the forests of Vermont without ever squeezing a trigger, often without even seeing deer. They number only 10 or 12 per square mile.

In three autumns of deer hunting, I did everything but kill. In the timberland behind our house, I mapped deer trails and old stone walls. I found where bears feasted on wild berries and field corn, and where bucks' antlers had rubbed saplings bare. I watched porcupines and squirrels and woodpeckers going about their lives. I said silent hellos to the chickadees and nuthatches who chirped and flitted around me curiously.

In fresh-fallen snow, I once tracked two does, noting how their route eased across the land, crossing an old railroad bed where the terrain was gentlest. A few miles off, on my friend Richard's woodlot, I learned to expect that there would be a few scrapes – patches of leaves pawed up by bucks as the rut drew near – toward the bottom of a little valley where several deer paths converged.

My ethics, the values that turned me into a vegetarian, had not changed. All that had changed was my perspective, the angle from which I saw the world and applied those values.

In hunting, I was aiming to be mindful about the outer consequences of my diet. I was aiming, someday, to confront one of those consequences – the death of animals – with my eyes open. Killing an animal myself – mindfully, swiftly – seemed to be the most conscientious path, perhaps even the path of least harm. And I was aiming to better understand the land and my non-human neighbors. I was on the same quest that led me to vegetarianism, the quest for a respectful, holistic way of eating and living in relationship with the world, for right dietary citizenship.

My inner aim remained the same, too: integrity. Having concluded that I needed some animal protein in my diet and that some harm to animals was inevitable in even the gentlest forms of local agriculture, moral wholeness and alignment could only come from taking responsibility for at least a portion of the killing.

Earlier, I suggested that this dual attention – to both inner and outer consequences – is common among vegetarians. I won't make a parallel claim on behalf of most hunters. I don't know how many hunters share these sensibilities. Some clearly do not. When I overhear a hunter say that he goes to the woods to shoot rabbits for the sheer challenge of it, with no intention of eating them, or when I'm told about a moose shot in deer season and left to rot just because some guy wanted to kill something, I experience the same old revulsion. I still wonder what kind of sickness possesses such people.

I do know, however, that this dual attention is central for some hunters, including a few I know well.

After I finished gutting the deer, I gathered up my pack and rifle. Down the ridge a couple hundred yards, I found a man sitting on a fallen tree trunk – my friend Richard. Dressed in a plaid wool jacket and looking far

TOVAR CERULLI

younger than his 60-some years, this longtime student of Buddhism might have been simply meditating on the forest, but for the .300 Savage across his lap.

I walked up, came to a stop, and raised my hand for him to see. A bit of blood remained on my fingers and knuckles, despite the maple-leaf scrubbing I'd given them. Richard's brows lifted above deep-set eyes and a gentle smile spread across his broad, angular face. He nodded.

"I heard the shot," he said.

During a weeklong meditation retreat, Richard had once asked his teacher about Buddhism's first precept: to refrain from harming other sentient beings. As they talked, it had come out that Richard was a meat eater and a hunter. His teacher had been flabbergasted. By the end of their conversation, Richard had committed – with a hundred fellow students as witnesses – to trying vegetarianism for a year.

One year had turned into two. He didn't eat meat, buy meat, or hunt. He paid even more attention to his food, to where it came from, to what impact it had. "It was a good practice," he once told me. "I got sensitive to things. All critters are just trying to make a living."

Developing more awareness and compassion, he'd found he couldn't take killing as lightly. If a housefly annoyed him with its buzzing, he didn't need to swat it. He began to notice things he hadn't before. When he live-trapped mice in his root cellar and then released them on the far side of the beaver dam across the road, he wondered: was he just feeding them to the mink who hunted there? When he planted his garden, wasn't he killing creatures with every shovelfull of dirt he turned?

In the end, Richard had found that he felt hypocritical being a vegetarian and not acknowledging that he was still causing harm to other creatures. He'd decided that, for him, the solution was to try his best to balance things, to accept the harm, to refrain from causing it unnecessarily, to avoid wasting anything. "The deer nibble on my garden and I nibble on them," he told me. "Everything is chewing on everything else, yet there's a harmony in it."

Richard may have worked all this out to his satisfaction, but I had not.

Together, we dragged the buck over steep, bony ridges and down through a sugarbush to where my truck was parked by Richard's house. I thought about all the time and effort I'd expended over the past three autumns. All to what end? To have a large mammal dead on the ground?

It helped that it had been quick. Holding the deer's torn-in-two heart in my hand, I knew oblivion had come swiftly. It was precisely the shot I'd been hoping for. He probably felt only shock in those few seconds before the lights went out. It was easier than most other ways a deer's life was likely to end: in cold and starvation, across a car's front end, at the teeth of four-footed predators.

Yet that swiftness did nothing to alter the raw fact: I had killed this graceful creature. Now that I had taken his life, I wasn't sure I wanted it. A great hollow grief had begun to well up inside.

I thought of the long hours of grisly work ahead of me. Though the 60 pounds of local, organic, forest-fed, truly free-range meat would feed me, Catherine, family, and friends through the winter, I didn't like the idea of transforming this beautiful animal into a skinless carcass, then into dismembered quarters, then into chunks of steak, small pieces of stew meat, and a pile of venison ground up in the hand-crank grinder I'd bought for the purpose. I knew I'd be slow and uncertain with the knife. Only once, three years earlier, had I helped with the butchering of a deer.

I could have paid someone else to cut up the buck; plenty of people offer the service locally. But I wouldn't. Butchering was part of the point. In facing the emotional and moral troubles of the entire killing-and-eating process, I aimed to shake myself free from another – and, in my view, more perilous – emotional and moral danger: forgetfulness. It would, I felt, have been too easy, too seductively comforting, to keep a sanitized distance from the sources of my sustenance.

With my Buddhist friend's help, I hauled the buck over the rough terrain. And I wondered: now that I had killed this deer – now that the "absent referent" had become such a palpably present being – would I hunt again?

When the answer surfaced from my inner turmoil a day or two later, I was still standing at the kitchen counter, boning knife in hand.

The next fall, my second deer dropped where he stood, consciousness snuffed out in a flash.

NOTES

1   All claims in this paragraph come from Henning Steinfeld et al., *Livestock's Long Shadow: Environmental Issues and Options* (Rome: UNFAO, 2006), pp. xxi–xxiii. The calculations are disputed. Some claim that livestock production accounts for as much as 51 percent of anthropogenic greenhouse gas emissions; see Robert Goodland and Jeff Anhang, "Livestock and Climate Change," *World Watch* (Nov/Dec 2009): 10–19. Others, including ranchers, point out that different methods of raising livestock have very different

ecological impacts; see, for example, Nicolette Hahn Niman, *The Righteous Porkchop: Finding a Life and Good Food Beyond Factory Farms* (New York: HarperCollins, 2009).

2 The Seventh-Day Adventist Church provides an interesting Christian case. Today, the Adventists' public promotion of vegetarianism focuses on physical health. But church co-founder Ellen White also wrote of "the moral evils of a flesh diet. ... Think of the cruelty to animals that meat-eating involves, and its effect on those who inflict and those who behold it. How it destroys the tenderness with which we should regard these creatures of God!" Ellen G. White, *The Ministry of Healing* (1905; repr., Whitefish, MT: Kessinger, 2005), p. 315.

3 See, for example, Andrew Linzey (ed.) *The Link Between Animal Abuse and Human Violence* (East Sussex: Sussex Academic Press, 2009). For a contrasting view, see Emily Patterson-Kane and Heather Piper, "Abuse as a Sentinel for Human Violence: A Critique," *Journal of Social Issues* 65, no. 3 (2009): 589–614.

4 Mohandas K. Gandhi, *An Autobiography: The Story of My Experiments with Truth* (1957; repr., Boston: Beacon Press, 1993), p. 235.

5 Howard Williams, *The Ethics of Diet: A Catena of Authorities Deprecatory of the Practice of Flesh-Eating* (1883; repr., Chicago: University of Illinois Press, 2003), p. 31. This is a translation of a phrase that Stoic philosopher Lucius Annaeus Seneca attributed to his teacher Sotion.

6 Though this line is often attributed to Albert Schweitzer, I have been unable to determine its true origins.

7 Isadora Duncan, *My Life* (New York: Liveright, 1927; repr., 1996), p. 221. Because Duncan wrote these words in the context of discussing George Bernard Shaw, versions of the phrase are misattributed to Shaw himself. A poem entitled "Living Graves" is also attributed to him, though I believe its author remains unknown.

8 Carol J. Adams, *The Sexual Politics of Meat: A Feminist-Vegetarian Critical Theory*, 10th anniv. ed. (New York: Continuum, 1990, 2000), p. 14.

9 Christopher Camuto, *Hunting from Home: A Year Afield in the Blue Ridge Mountains* (New York: W. W. Norton, 2003), p. 288.

10 Marti Kheel, "License to Kill: An Ecofeminist Critique of Hunters' Discourse," in Carol J. Adams and Josephine Donovan (eds.) *Animals and Women: Feminist Theoretical Explorations* (Durham, NC: Duke University Press, 1995), p. 87.

11 Mary Zeiss Stange, *Woman the Hunter* (Boston: Beacon Press, 1997), p. 8.

CHAPTER 5

WHAT YOU CAN'T LEARN FROM CARTOONS

Or, How to Go Hunting After Watching *Bambi*

Warning: Plot Spoiler!

For my fifth Christmas (this would be Christmas of 1968), my parents gave me and my older sister an LP of the *Bambi* soundtrack. A few days later, my Mom put the record in the player so we could listen. The album came with a large picture book, and we kids flipped through the pages, wide-eyed, as we followed the sound. We heard the opening chorus of "Love is a song that never ends" and later the "Drip, drip, drop, little April showers." We heard the stags charging through the meadow and followed along, taking in the pictures. And then we heard the shotgun fire, and young Bambi calling out "Mother! Mother!" My sister and I wailed. We stopped only to catch our breath, and then we wailed some more. We shut off the record player and tried to comfort ourselves. Dad returned from a long hard day at work a short time later. He was disgusted that a Christmas gift could send his children into such despair and his home into such chaos. Too late did he learn that *Bambi*, of all things, was not appropriate for children.[1]

Hunters need to read the work of their critics carefully, not only in order to counter their arguments, but also to learn about the nature of hunting and to incorporate their insights into our own accounts. So now, as an adult, I want to see what *Bambi* was saying by looking at how the animators at the Walt Disney Studios constructed the movie. What exactly is the criticism of hunting, and how were they able to make that criticism so powerfully? What did *Bambi* get right, and what is clearly wrong? To help, I will also look at Matt Cartmill's criticism of *Bambi*.[2] While Cartmill puts his finger on some fatal flaws in *Bambi*, his corrective also falters. Finally, I turn to the writings of Richard Nelson for a hunting story that incorporates the strengths of both Disney's *Bambi* and Cartmill's insights.

Mediums: The Seen and the Felt

Disney loosely based *Bambi and the Great Prince of the Forest* on a book by Fritz Salten, entitled *Bambi: A Forest Life*. The different mediums both required and allowed the filmmakers to tell the story in a different way. The message is more than the medium, however. Disney did not shy away from a creative reworking of the material, such that the two versions tell different stories.

The change in mediums does partially determine Disney's message. Salten's book must carry the story through descriptions and dialogue. Disney's film, by contrast, "is an essentially silent movie: a wordless, rhythmical ballet performed to an orchestral accompaniment."[3] The Silver Anniversary edition of *Bambi* gives viewers access to comments made in the planning meetings for the film. Those comments show Disney animators keen to push the envelope of their current understanding of an animated motion picture.[4]

Prior to Disney, cartoons could be only cute and funny. The characters were flat, two-dimensional line drawings, and the stories – short and funny – matched the characters. In the world of cartoons, the laws of physics apply selectively, no injury is serious, and death is unknown. Anything and everything is funny in the form of a cartoon, even extreme forms of violence. (*Itchy and Scratchy* illustrates this principle on *The Simpsons*.) For these reasons, you can't learn from a cartoon about the character of a saint or a hero, and you can't learn about the realities presented in epics, tragedies, or religious narratives. This aesthetic of "cute and funny" operates as a norm for cartoons, and animators had to fight like Yosemite Sam to develop something different.

Disney tried to challenge the position that cartoons could portray only the cute and funny. *Snow White* (1937) and *Pinocchio* (1940) enabled viewers to experience real beauty in a cartoon. Likewise, Disney found that a strong villain on a big screen with a good script, animation, and music allowed a cartoon to portend even tragedy. With *Fantasia* (1940) the studio tried to match the depth and power of Bach, Tchaikovsky, Dukas, Stravinsky, Beethoven, and Schubert with animation on the big screen. They learned the power of music as a tool different from either dialogue or animation. The animators applied these lessons to *Bambi*. Disney animators and story editors discovered the difference between "what is felt" and "what is seen."[5] Their notion of "the felt" relates closely to the concept of the "sublime" used by philosophers. What is "seen" is the cute or the beautiful; it is determined by the perfection of its form and the recognition of that perfection by a viewer. The "felt" or the "sublime," by contrast, concerns our *inability* to catch sight of the form. The object may be too large or too powerful. It may disorient us or make us feel small. Yet, if we can stand our ground in the midst of feeling overwhelmed, we experience sublimity. Classic examples of sublime objects (that is, objects which evoke sublimity in us) include clouds, the ocean, cliffs, storms, and death.[6]

The Disney animators recognized that they were trying to present the sublime through a cartoon. They dropped as much dialogue as possible out of the film. Likewise, they chose to communicate as much as possible through music. In *Bambi*, two "characters" and one event benefit from these methods and take on the aura of the sublime.

Bambi opens with a pan of a dark, sometimes out-of-focus, moving multi-plane shot of the forest. The animators understand that the forest is itself a character in this story, and they want it to be "mysterious," merely hinted at; they want it to be felt rather than seen. The forest is sublime.

The animals, by contrast, remain cartoons. Disney animators gave them realistic body movements compared to earlier cartoons. Still, they have been humanized and characterized with huge eyes sporting human irises, shortened noses, rounded heads, facial dexterity, minimal shading, and, of course, speech. The animals in *Bambi* may each be accompanied by a uniquely assigned instrument and theme, but they are flat characters, fully presented to vision. They remain within the aesthetic of earlier cartoons; they are cute.

The second character to be felt but not seen is Man. The Disney editors took every image of individual people out of the final version. (Only a shot of a distant hunting camp remains.) Instead of showing a specific individual, the film indicates the presence of Man "by ominous, lurching music."[7]

Bambi's mother is shot and dies offscreen. The listeners know she died because we heard the music, we heard the shot, and we hear Bambi's cries of "Mother!" The old stag's "Your mother cannot be with you any-more" merely confirms what we already know. The animators knew they were making the scene more powerful by *not* showing Bambi's mother falling. "We're going to make quite an impression."[8] They sure did. Because the audience could feel rather than see the central characters and the central event, the movie had "the force of a sledgehammer ... despite its pervasive and repellent cuteness."[9] These thematic elements, made possible or necessary by the medium of animation, transformed Salten's original version of the story. Disney Studios also made other alterations that make Salten's *Bambi* and Disney's *Bambi* into different, even competing, stories.

Ted Steven states it baldly in a planning meeting: "We should get away from the book."[10]

Competing Messages: "Man was in the Forest" vs. "There is Another"

Salten's story, written in the aftermath of the Great War, takes death as its central theme. Nature is red in tooth and claw. Predators kill and eat, prey are killed and eaten. Salten stages a dialogue between the last two leaves of autumn, now brown and withered, as they anxiously anticipate falling to their own deaths and joining the millions of other leaves already down. When they finally fall and float to the ground, the reader feels it as a tragedy. While humans seem to be either gods or devils, they too die, as Bambi sees at the end. Bambi voices the theological moral of the story: "There is Another who is over us all, over us and over Him [Man]."[11] The reign of this One above the circle of life and death reconciles Man and the forest.

Disney's *Bambi*, produced during the preparations for and beginning of World War II, presents Nature as a calm and peaceful harmony (except for the winter scene where Bambi's mother cares for him by feeding him bark from the trees). All of the animals are friends; crotchety "Friend Owl" looks down from his perch with grandfatherly affection on the gathering of rabbits and mice. Larry Morey asserts in a planning meet-ing: "They should all be friends." Story editor Perce Pearce agrees: "There's nobody swooping down and eating someone else."[12] In the realm of nature, there is no death, only birth and life. Disney isolates and focuses Death onto one character, Man. Pearce, again: "their one common enemy is Man. That's the conflict there – and keep it simple."[13] Simple, indeed. Death disappears from Nature. In Disney's *Bambi*, the animators portray the two leaves falling only as a beautiful transition of autumn into winter. All dialogue about anxiety in the face of death disappears, and in its place ... music. And Man is always the devil, never a god. The most piercing line in the film comes from Bambi's mother as if pronouncing judgment on a sin: "Man ... was in the forest." In contrast with Salten, Disney offers no resolution of the conflict between Man and Nature, Death and Life: "It is about surviving in the forest."[14] This is the reason Roger Ebert describes Disney's *Bambi* as "a parable of ... nihilism and despair"; it paints reality as a "world of death and violence."[15]

In the end, Disney did not successfully change the aesthetic of cartoons as a medium; *Bambi*'s presentation is not adequate to the sublime realities of Nature, of Man, and of Death. While the death of Bambi's mother does come off as a tragedy, the film accomplishes this only by placing Man and Death offscreen and by communicating through music rather than animation. I have often wondered how my own reaction to *Bambi* depended on hearing it like a radio broadcast rather than seeing the actual film. Further, Warner Brothers' "What's Opera Doc?" (1957) insists that if you animate the whole thing, the cartoon aesthetic overcomes powerful music (Wagner's *Ring* cycle) and the presentation of hunting and death.

Nevertheless, Disney Studios successfully constructed *Bambi* to make the viewer *feel* that hunting is immoral; more generally, the film portrays the unseen Man as a cosmic murderer of Nature. This thesis becomes clear as we compare the book to the film. My five-year-old reaction was appropriate after all.

Challenging *Bambi*

Disney Studios have had little trouble persuading children to feel in prescribed ways, and they were successful beyond belief in making *Bambi* into a cultural icon. Disney did not invent the criticisms of hunting and Man, but it did plant them deeply in the hearts of children all across the land. "Hunters regard *Bambi* as the most powerful piece of antihunting propaganda ever produced, and they are probably right."[16]

Bambi's success has placed hunters in an embarrassing spot. First, of course, it forces them to argue against a cartoon. No one wins an argument with a cartoon. (This includes me.)

But it is more awkward and more serious than this. Cartmill notes that while hunters may criticize *Bambi*, they still seem susceptible to *Bambi*'s critique of hunting. He surmises that this is because they share a "symbolic framework" with *Bambi*. Both *Bambi* and hunters make a strong distinction between Man and Nature. Some hunters see Nature as a foe to be conquered; many others see Nature as sacred and good, but both Disney and hunters agree on this symbolic framework.

Cartmill proposes to outflank both Disney and the hunters by rejecting that shared assumption. But he is primarily after the hunters. Without the assumed split between Man and Nature, hunting will wither away. That is, if we do not make any distinction between Man and Nature, then there is no morally relevant difference between killing a human and killing an animal. If there is no moral difference between killing animals and humans, then there is no difference between "hunting" and "murdering." "Hunting" must dissolve as an intelligible concept. He concludes: "no doubt people will go on killing friendly and unfriendly animals for various reasons. But no matter what sort of animals they kill or how they do it, they will have ceased to hunt."[17]

On what basis can the split between Man and Nature be denied? Cartmill suggests two possibilities. First, science. The results of science recognize the continuity between humans and animals. At least since Darwin, science has firmly located man within nature. So, Cartmill firmly states: "It is a fact of nature that human beings are animals."[18] (We needed Darwin to learn that?!) Also, the methods of science *require* that it look for commonalities between humans and non-humans, because science explains individual instances as expressions of a general law. Human distinctiveness cannot qualify as even a possible topic in science.[19] So, all sentient life is equal, and must be placed on a level plane. Man is not higher than Nature and Nature is not higher than Man. We cannot say how humans are different from non-humans; there are no hierarchies of life. We are all "lumps of one universal stuff."[20]

Cartmill also raises a second possibility for unifying Man and Nature. The ethical theory of utilitarianism insists that humans and animals are alike in at least one respect: both have the capacity to feel pleasure and pain. Since pleasure is good and pain is bad, we have a moral duty to produce by our actions the greatest amount of pleasure over pain. But since animals can feel pleasure and pain, we must take account of the ways our actions affect them. Cartmill asserts "that the suffering of sentient animals is something that is intrinsically undesirable."[21] Hunting would seem to be incompatible with utilitarianism. More strongly, utilitarianism could provide an ethical basis for denying any real difference between hunting and murder.[22]

Both science and utilitarianism, then, recognize a continuity between humans and non-human life, and this continuity makes any distinction between murder and hunting impossible.

Bambi's Counter-Charge

Cartmill's challenge leaves Walt Disney with plenty of room to turn around for a counter-charge. Disney could say that Cartmill has misdiagnosed the power of *Bambi*. As I have already shown, *Bambi*'s persuasive force lies not only in its symbolic framework (the "Man/Nature" dichotomy), but also in the presentation of its characters and its storyline. Hunters have a hard time responding to *Bambi* for aesthetic reasons, because the characters and the criticism of hunting are *felt* rather than articulated verbally or visually. While Cartmill substitutes science or utilitarianism for Disney's symbolic framework, he provides neither a counter-story to *Bambi* nor alternative characters. More strongly, he explicitly rules out the sublime.

We might say that Cartmill's symbolic framework is little more than a cartoon. Cartoons are by nature and by design flat and entirely visible, hiding nothing. So also the objects of science are fully laid out for the vision of science. For the utilitarian, sentient life-forms appear in only one dimension: the capacity to feel pleasure and pain. Since science does not recognize any hierarchy of life-forms, there is no hierarchy of life-forms. Cartmill places all life on an equal – which is to say a flat – plane in which differences are abolished. There is nothing science cannot see. He considers, only to dismiss, all the romantics, transcendentalists, and religious types who insist that there is something "more" than scientific vision. (They are all just afraid of science, he thinks.) Disney's animators, by contrast, recognized that not everything can be made visible without making it into a joke. Their genius was to recognize that a cartoon is the denial of the sublime and to present the sublime nonetheless.

We have before us, then, two criticisms of hunting: Disney's *Bambi* and Cartmill's deconstruction of hunting in the name of science and utilitarianism. Disney's *Bambi* raises Man, Nature, and Death above the level of a cartoon through a sophisticated use of animation and music, but its simplistic oppositions ultimately tie it to the cartoon it is. Cartmill provides a sophisticated criticism of the binary opposition in *Bambi*, but he is unable to draw *any* distinctions, and he insists on accounts of Man and Nature that are entirely seen and not felt. Neither criticism by itself is convincing, but both provide resources that hunters should incorporate in a more adequate account of hunting. We need an account of hunting which gives voice to the experience of the sublime in hunting and recognizes a strong continuity between humans and non-human life. Richard Nelson's *The Island Within*[23] can be read as a direct and specific response to these needs.

Re-gifting *Bambi*

With *The Island Within*, we return to Salten's medium of words in a book, a narrative punctuated with philosophical musings. The first chapter opens with a quote from Grandpa William, a Koyukon hunter, who gives voice to the Koyukon tradition of hunting: "A good hunter ... that's somebody the animals *come* to."[24]

Grandpa William does not represent Cartmill's tradition of the industrialized, utilitarian West or of a European hunting tradition bent on conquering Nature. The Koyukon tradition does not, like *Bambi*, make a sharp dichotomy between Man and Nature. Rather, humans, land, plants, and other animals all belong to one community. Humans are not lowered to "lumps of one universal stuff"; life is not flattened to a two-dimensional visual plane. Instead, the Koyukon believe that "all of nature is spiritual and aware, that it must be treated with respect, and that humans should approach the living world with restraint and humility."[25] They believe that "no animal should be considered inferior or insignificant and that humans should never place themselves above any part of nature."[26]

Far from making hunting into an incoherent concept, this inclusive community places hunting at its center. The community is interdependent and harmonious, and hunting names one of those interdependent and harmonious relations. This is why the Koyukon hunter cannot be the careless poacher presented by Disney and even Cartmill. Concepts of "respect" and "gratitude" belong at the center of the Koyukon understanding of the relation between the hunter and the hunted.

In order to introduce these concepts, Nelson takes the reader with him and his border collie on a hunting trip to an island off the Northwest coast. He attempts to accomplish with verbal descriptions the same feat Disney performed with orchestral scores and animation that only hints at the true reality. That is, Nelson wants us to feel the trip rather than see it, and his words offer us a glimpse of that which we cannot find in a cartoon. The chapter moves back and forth between minute, beautiful details and overwhelming, sublime, saturated phenomena. He marvels at classic examples of the sublime: rain, wind, death, and the nature of luck. He writes on his experience of a storm: "Someday a storm like this might catch me on the water and carry me away, but I love it all the same. What better way to vanish than into the dark flailing breath of a north Pacific storm? I float toward sleep, drawn away from the fears in my mind by the comforting tempest outside. The great storm contains me."[27]

As he walks through the virgin forest, he is overwhelmed by the size and majesty of the trees.

> Their trunks soar upward and vanish amid clouds of boughs that shiver down their burden of rain in big silver droplets. Standing beside a giant spruce, I stare into its swaying heights and try for some comprehension of its mass. I feel like shouting aloud, for the sheer pleasure of being in the midst of life on such a scale, trees that have survived centuries of storms, pestilence, and the crashing down of neighbors. Perhaps it's better that I keep quiet, mindful of being as insignificant here as mite crawling through a field of tall grass.[28]

Nelson also reflects on his own conflicted emotions about hunting. He refuses to shoot a doe still accompanied by a young one. Finally, after a few near misses, Nelson shoots a deer and recovers it.

> Overwhelmed with gratitude and emotion, I feel myself crying inside. It is a buck deer, full and fat and heavy muscled. It is a buck deer and the island that made him – the muskeg, the forest, the high mountain meadows, the amber ponds and clear streams. It is a buck deer and the gray sky and rain, the rare sunshine, kelp eaten from the shore in the pinch of winter. It is a buck deer and all the seasons of four years or five, the bleating of fall, the supple does that moved beneath him and carried his fawns, and the moonlight and stars, the wind, the fretting of the sea we stand beside. It is a buck deer and it is me, brought together as flesh poured out over the island's rock.[29]

The Koyukon harmony with their environment is not the undifferentiated life of Cartmill's science. Wind, rain, waves, and trees are each characters – enormous, sublime characters – with their own characteristics and with roles to play in a story. They are moral characters.

Just as surely, the island is not Disney's Nature, because it is full of eagles and owls "swooping down on somebody." Nelson is not Man, since he occupies a different universe than the careless poachers caricatured in *Bambi*. *Bambi*'s hunters would not be crying inside. Nelson's buck is not Bambi. Though, like Bambi, Nelson helps us to feel our way through the hunting story, he teaches us to feel differently about hunting. He does not settle all of our questions about hunting, but he draws us into descriptions that point a way forward in thought and in action. Nelson's work makes it possible to hunt after *Bambi*.

Tomorrow I'll grab my bow and go walking in the woods.

NOTES

1 If Disney advertised *Bambi* then as they do now, he was right to feel betrayed. Here is the way Disney describes the movie on Amazon.com: "The forest comes alive with BAMBI, the critically acclaimed coming-of-age story that has thrilled and entertained generations of fans. ... This grand adventure is full of humor, heart, and the most beloved characters of all time – Bambi, the wide-eyed fawn, his playful pal Thumper, the lovable skunk Flower, and wise Friend Owl."

2 Throughout this essay, I engage with the work of Matt Cartmill, "The Bambi Syndrome," in *A View to Death in the Morning: Hunting and Nature Through History* (Cambridge, MA: Harvard University Press, 1993), pp. 161–88.

3 Ibid., p. 174.

4 *Bambi: Platinum Edition*, DVD, dir. David Hand and Wilfred Jackson (1942; Walt Disney Home Entertainment, 2005).

5 Ibid.

6 A more complete but also accessible account of sublimity can be found in Sheila Lintott, "Sublime Hunger: A Consideration of Eating Disorders," in Fritz Allhoff and Dave Monroe (eds.) *Food & Philosophy: Eat, Think, and Be Merry* (Malden, MA: Wiley-Blackwell, 2007), pp. 60–2.

7 Cartmill, *A View to Death in the Morning*, p. 175.

8 *Bambi*, "Bambi: Inside Walt's Story Meetings," 42:44.

9 Cartmill, *A View to Death in the Morning*, p. 178.

10 *Bambi*, "Bambi: Inside Walt's Story Meetings," 5:05.

11 Fritz Salten, *Bambi: A Life in the Woods*, trans. W. Chambers (New York: Simon and Schuster, 1928), p. 286; cited in Cartmill, *A View to Death in the Morning*, p. 165.

12 *Bambi*, "Bambi: Inside Walt's Story Meetings," 7:46.

13   Ibid.
14   Ibid., 1:05:00.
15   Cartmill, *A View to Death in the Morning*, p. 178.
16   Ibid., p. 162.
17   Ibid., p. 244.
18   Ibid., p. 243.
19   Ibid., pp. 220, 226.
20   Ibid., p. 220.
21   Ibid., p. 240.
22   Cartmill appeals to utilitarianism only as a "consensus ... in the industrial-ized West" (ibid.). That is, he is not claiming that utilitarianism is founded on a kind of science that can quantify pleasure and pain, as some utilitarians have. Cartmill seems content to conclude that hunting and utilitarianism are inconsistent. I am extending his use of utilitarianism to connect with his main argument that from a scientific perspective, hunting is no longer an intelligible concept.
23   Richard Nelson, *The Island Within* (New York: Vintage Books, 1989).
24   Ibid., p. 3.
25   Ibid., p. 9.
26   Ibid., p. 23.
27   Ibid., p. 10.
28   Ibid., p. 12.
29   Ibid., pp. 31–2.

PART II

THE HUNTER'S VIEW
OF THE WORLD

CHAPTER 6

HUNTING FOR MEANING

A Glimpse of the Game

Close at hand, instead of boar spear and lance, I had my pen and notebook. When a thought occurred to me, I jotted it down, so that if I came back with empty hands, they should at least be full of tablets. There is no reason for you to despise this sort of study; it is wonderful how the mind is aroused by the activity and motion of the body. All round you are the woods, and solitude, and the deep silence that is observed in hunting. From now on, whenever you hunt, you have my full permission to bring your notebooks as well as your snacks and canteen. You will learn by experiment that Minerva roams the mountains as well as Diana.
Pliny the Younger, first century CE[1]

Weighing the Value of Meat

One February day when she was eight years old, my daughter Sabina and I were sitting on a bench in New York City's Union Square watching squirrels digging up nuts. We were not discussing hunting, so it seemed abrupt when she suddenly announced that she didn't want me to hunt squirrels. I said, "Wait a second, but it's okay for me to hunt deer?" "Yes," she said, which obliged me to respond, "Isn't this a contradiction?" She paused only briefly before declaring with complete confidence, "With a small animal, you only get a little bit of meat from one life." Then she boldly stared at me to see what I'd say to this philosophical pirouette, and the truth is that I was silenced by the fact that an eight-year-old should have such intellectual power within her, the power to leap over the sort of contradiction that most meat-eating anti-hunters seem bafflingly comfortable to inhabit.

In defense of contradictions, though, that same year later found us bearing fishing rods on a trail outside of Wisdom, Montana, when Sabina suddenly grabbed my arm, pointed and whispered, "Dad! Look! There's a grouse! Grab a rock and kill it!" Before I even had time to look for a suitable rock, she pulled a jar of Powerbait from her pocket, offered it to me, and I pitched it at the grouse. It was a fat blue grouse, far more meat than a typical gray squirrel. We later enjoyed it over the fire along with our trout, puffball mushrooms, miner's lettuce, and wild strawberries.

I have only a few thoughts in trying to square my daughter's two responses, the squirrel response highly conceptual, the grouse response a hunter's, thoroughly but not thoughtlessly visceral. For starters, it is philosophically relevant that we were in New York City in the first instance and Montana's Pioneer Mountains in the second. But regarding Sabina's logic, while she has eaten plenty of game meat from the time she was a toddler, she had never eaten squirrel before, and this may have freed up space for her calculus regarding the quantity of meat and the value of life. Then again, regarding both her squirrel logic and her response to that grouse, she is clearly mindful of the death in hunting and yet has finely nuanced rather than fundamental qualms about it, adores venison yet loves deer, as any thoughtful hunter does.

Stalking the Essence of Hunting

What does it mean to be a "thoughtful hunter"? In his 1942 *Meditations on Hunting*, José Ortega y Gasset writes:

> When one is hunting, the air has another, more exquisite feel as it glides over the skin or enters the lungs, the rocks acquire a more expressive phys-iognomy, and the vegetation becomes loaded with meaning. But all this is due to the fact that the hunter, while he advances or waits crouching, feels tied through the earth to the animal he pursues, whether the animal is in view, hidden, or absent.[2]

This is not closer-to-nature romance but experiential insight. When I hunt, my mind oscillates between, on the one hand, being thoroughly outside myself – directed at the tree, at the rustling leaves, at the damp moss, at the breeze (I am the breeze), at the panther prancing with purpose toward its destination, at the coyote racing straight toward blaze-oranged invisible me, at the deer through its tracks – and then, on the other hand, the stream of simple thoughts provoked by the clarity of being outside of one's self and a poignant emptiness. I'm aware that my feet are as cold as the day, and I ask myself, "What am I doing?" I am hunting. What is hunting about? The answer is in the question: hunting is about hunting, nothing more, nothing less. Plus – and there is little room for this quasi-thought in the field, just a backdrop – I might kill, gut, and drag a deer, bringing home meat that will go into my body and into the bodies of the people I love. When I experience that pleasurable not-quite-a-thought, I don't need to remind myself how many vegetarians I know who enjoy occasionally eating wild turkey and elk, and how much life follows a hunting death, the bodies of game animals becoming human bodies, deer literally transubstantiated into women and men. But the meat is not the essence of hunting. Or, to paraphrase Heidegger in our search for the essence of hunting, meat may be a correct answer but it is not the truth. The truth is that hunting is a mode of revealing. Ortega writes:

> In itself, life is insipid, because it is a simple "being there." So, for man, existing becomes a poetic task. ...That of inventing a plot for his existence, giving it a character that will make it both suggestive and appealing. ...The fact is that for almost all men the major part of life consists of obligatory occupations. ... So here is the human being suspended between two conflicting repertories of occupations: the laborious and the pleasing.[3]

These are interesting images, but they are also very general until Ortega makes the idiosyncratic and somewhat startling claim that "the most appreciated, enjoyable occupation for the normal man has always been hunting. This is what kings and nobles have preferred to do: they have hunted."[4] Well, kings and nobles are not normal men, responds Thomas Paine from a different European perspective, noting: "To read the history of kings, a man would be almost inclined to suppose that government consisted in stag-hunting, and that every nation paid a million a year to a huntsman."[5] But Paine was clearly not a hunter, so he might not have appreciated the little-known fact that Poland's Bialowieski National Park, a World Heritage Site adjacent to the Belarus border, contains a herd of

European bison that would have become extinct had not nobility preserved it in order to hunt.[6] But it is not just about nobility, and Ortega pushes further, adding that "it happens that the other social classes have done or wanted to do the same thing."[7] This is confirmed by exemplary historical references, including the fact that "Hunting and fishing rights were among the first demands made by German peasants during the Peasants' War of 1524–5 and by French peasants in the early stages of the French Revolution."[8] Later in the book Ortega will even suggest that the truest hunters are poachers. Meanwhile, he has represented hunting as waywardly fundamental. Wayward because it is a pleasure. Fundamental because of what Ortega is imagining is its universal allure. The text is sometimes spiced with an array of ethnocentric, classist, or simply dated observations, yet he sets off on a path that is also defined by a series of strong, confident, and controversial claims worthy of consideration.

The first significant observation that Ortega makes in his attempt to track down the essence of hunting is that the difference between "sport" hunting and "utilitarian" hunting is incidental, because, he suggests, these are "transient" purposes that remain outside the essence of hunting: "The different ends attributed to hunting do not essentially determine the operation which is its substance."[9] Hunting, then, is not to be thought of as an instrumental activity, a counter-intuitive thought if ever there was one; counter-intuitive, that is, if one thinks of objectives in a reductive manner. Yes, bringing home the meat is part of the story, and the story would not function without the meat, nor without the coextensive death that yields it. And yet, again, the meat is not the truth, and the death is conjoined with life.

Same As It Ever Was

It is impossible for me not to think historically, not to think through the philosophical orientation points offered us by philosophers such as Machiavelli, Marx, Nietzsche, and Foucault. Yet I am enough of an existentialist that I am compelled to inhabit and experiment with double thinking, to consider, on the one hand, the sense in which being human is a fluid response to shifting conditions yet, on the other hand, the simultaneous sense in which life is always the same (repetition with a difference). So, for example, I have always found great clarity in Marx's insight regarding technology, a reference especially relevant here since the example he uses is a weapon: as Marx observes in *Wage Labor and Capital,* the invention of the firearm does not simply provide a more effective way of accomplishing the same purpose that earlier technologies did, not just a more efficient version of a rock, a spear, a bow, a cross-bow.[10] No, the introduction of the firearm transforms the very nature of the army, changes the social relations and activities coextensive with a military apparatus: that is, the firearm changes what an army *is*. Now, we all get Marx's point, and of course he is right. And we certainly under-stand what Heidegger means in indicating a fundamental difference between the windmill and the hydroelectric dam, between a world that gifts us and a planet challenged as "standing reserve."[11] Technology is always a mode of revealing. We know where these sorts of historical thoughts go, straight to the bleak landscape before our eyes, a bleakness of a form and scale never anticipated by our ancestors.

Historical thinking is as generally vital to philosophy as is its more specific sense of its own history. Yet, so is historical thinking's twin, the existential thought that life is always the same. This second thought plays out in Ortega, when he claims that hunting cannot "be defined by its particular operations, its techniques," which leads to the conclusion that "hunting cannot substantially progress."[12] These thoughts push in a direction entirely different from the examples given by Marx and Heidegger, causing me to linger with Ortega.

Developments in weapon technologies "do not count as essential changes,"[13] writes Ortega. Thus no particular technique can claim pri-macy in relation to the essence of hunting. Here we are on the track of a truth which I can confirm by reflecting on my own experience. I hunt primarily with modern center-fire and archaic muzzleloading rifles, but in the tutelage of my father I learned long ago that hunting ptarmigan or other grouse with rocks is fundamentally the same activity, as is hunting rabbits with a slingshot. The basic difference is simply one of range, a difference that is so unsubtle that it lends itself readily to an over-empha-sis that effaces a whole other register of hunting nuances. A game warden once stopped a friend of mine who was carrying a spear when they crossed paths in the woods. The warden considered giving him a ticket for deer hunting without a license, but didn't since he came to the rather bizarre conclusion that Mark was not actually hunting; maybe he was laughing too hard to notice how lethal the homemade spearhead was, and maybe he couldn't bring himself to see that Mark's intentions were serious, and that his hunt was accompanied by a hope and a prayer, as all hunts must be. Mark went home empty-handed, a universal experience familiar to any hunter. It is worth noting that spears are still not on the list of weapons prohibited by the State of New York for big game hunting, and thus while Mark tends to favor a lever-action carbine, his spear remains outside the artifices of the state hunting machine.

Invoking another technology, when I visit ancient buffalo runs in Montana, I picture hunts repeated at the same sites over hundreds and hundreds of years, linking communities over eons; my hunt is a meager homage to the runners and hazers stampeding the herd above – as if in the sky – and to the blood-spattered women below, laughing and chatting as they butcher twitching bison. Shifting continents, while the mighty Athenians also chased deer and boar, they mostly hunted hares with dogs and nets, which is why Plato also refers to nets and enclosures in *The Sophist*, where, as in *The Republic*, philosophy is depicted as the hunter, and where, if you read that dialogue in a particular way, the prey – the sophist – repeatedly slips away, including at the end. Medieval and early modern hunters drove deer and boar into enclosures, then attacked them with lances. These are all very different techniques or tactics, but what they share in common is repetition of field practices with the strategic objective of slaying animals.

I flag wildly different hunting technologies and techniques for two reasons.

First, at least a portion of the current widespread antipathy toward hunting might, understandably, be the association between hunting and guns. It's my best guess that unless one has been raised with guns, they are steely abstractions. I am always stunned by people who, distracted by firearms, think that modern hunting consists of simply walking into the woods, aiming at an animal, pulling the trigger, then next thing you know there's blood on your hands. *This is an image of hunting minus the hunting.* Fear of or concern about guns might also lead to the misguided thought that the .30–30 – a deer-hunting classic – belongs to the same family as the 9 millimeter pistols favored universally by criminals and soldiers, and, by extension, even possibly the same family as cheap plastic landmines and Predator drones. But the .30–30 is not part of any family other than hunting; it is a hunting rifle, simple as that. I am not sure if it is even possible to commit a crime other than poaching with one. Hunting is violent, but it is neither criminal nor warfare. This despite the fact that traditionally, hunters were warriors who used the same weapons for two different practices, a historical reality that may complicate philosophy's efforts to understand hunting.

Second, and whatever one thinks of Ortega's other claims, he is right that killing is neither the exclusive purpose nor thus the essence of hunting.

Stated more forthrightly, and gauged against my own experience, he is right in suggesting that, "To the sportsman the death of the game is not what interests him; that is not his purpose. ...The hunter seeks this death because it is no less than the sign of reality for the whole hunting process. To sum up, one does not hunt in order to kill; on the contrary, one kills in order to have hunted."[14] Trophy hunting aside, even most non-subsistence hunters think of eating wholesome game meat as part of the purpose of hunting, which is of course premised on the death of an animal but is ultimately about life, and not just about "life" generally but about a rigorous practice and a good life, including a healthy diet. If my thoughts continue to return to meat, it is because the meat is the *sign* of the hunt, the singular sign, but not the essence, since the essence will among other things refer us to our ancestors who modern hunters continue to echo, echoing those whose hunting enabled us to be here now, hunting the condition of our being, a deep thought that can be rejected only by thinking ahistorically, by ignoring the ghosts of the hunters behind us (and so a unique kind of historical thinking is implicated in the thought that hunting cannot progress).

I find it strange that humans have reached the point at which the last remaining hunters have to explain or defend themselves, and I also suspect that much anti-hunting involves a romanticized image of "nature," an image deprived of the advantages of what is revealed by hunting. Strange it is, too, that the word "humane" is just a dressed-up version of the word we use for ourselves.

"Hunting," writes Ortega, "is not an exclusively human occupation, but occurs throughout most of the entire zoological scale. Only a definition of hunting that is based on the complete extension of this immense fact ... will get to the root of this surprising phenomenon."[15] Ah, but unlike the wolf or cougar, "we" have a choice or at least we'd like to think we do; we certainly don't have a choice not to choose and that's where things get interesting. Ortega registers this, and he notes that hunting includes an intrinsic disparity between hunter and hunted, which leads to a definition: "*Hunting is what an animal does to take possession, dead or alive, of some other being that belongs to a species basically inferior to its own.*"[16] This definition would be blatantly problematic were it not qualified by the thought that, "Vice versa, if there is to be a hunt, this superiority of the hunter over the prey *cannot be absolute*. Here is where the matter begins to be really subtle and interesting."[17] Indeed. There would seem to be very little critical thinking in the zoological hierarchy Ortega has apparently repeated, yet here he loosens his commitment to or complicates that hierarchy by observing that the hunted animal must have its *chance*.[18] The prey doesn't have any choice but to be prey, but it does have a chance, which is signaled by the fact that it is alert in advance to the hunter, as if the chances are that it would be hunted, and the chance is simply and always there in the form of any natural predator, including the human.

I glass the herd from a mile away, and while the does continue grazing, the buck is already staring right at me. As any stalking predator would do, I scan the terrain for a stealthy route that will render me invisible and get me closer, and I vanish from his sight and run the better part of the mile, finally crawling on my belly and poking my head up behind a rock, hoping that the herd is still there. This time it is, but the buck makes me out instantaneously and the herd is suddenly running (the pronghorn is the second fastest land mammal on the planet, its 40 m.p.h. capability exceeded only by the cheetah, now extinct versions of which are probably what taught the antelope its speed). The herd has vanished. I catch my breath. Then, following a practiced guess about where the herd has gone, I continue hunting, and maybe I locate them and maybe I don't, always the same story, the predator's return to the field.

In my experience, if success is measured by what is carried home, hunts are often unsuccessful. Frequently, the hunt happens but nothing has died. This is the reality, a *natural* death haunting the hunt whether or not an *actual* death occurs: predator and prey are partners in the dance of life, animal to animal.

The End of Hunting

"Life is a terrible conflict," writes Ortega, "a grandiose and atrocious confluence. Hunting submerges man in that formidable mystery and therefore contains something of religious rite and emotion in which homage is paid to what is divine, transcendent, in the laws of Nature."[19] Here, captured finally in the clumsy locution "laws of nature," is where Ortega is getting at something fundamental, particularly if in place of "religious rite" we substitute "rites of respect" or maybe simply "rites." This is neither ideology nor speculation; in *Homo Necans*, Walter Burkert cites archaeological as well as upstreamed ethnological evidence that the line between hunting and ritual, including ritual sacrifice, is permeable: "At a site in Siberia," for example, "twenty-seven mammoth skulls were found set up in a circle around a central point where a female statuette lay buried beneath a pile of bones and partially worked tusks."[20] Practices such as bone arrangements and the raising of animal hides were connected with the ritual in which "hunters are said to have expressed clear feelings of guilt with regard to the slaughtered animal ... [a] ritual that betrays an underlying anxiety about the continuation of life in the face of death."[21] Me, as a hunter, I don't think that "guilt" is the right word, nor is "regret," but the animal's death does linger. In any event, "The bloody 'act' was necessary for the continuance of life, but it is just as necessary for new life to be able to start again."[22]

All of that sounds like ancient history, and the central question for us now would seem to be, where is hunting today, when over half of the world's population lives in cities, where the only thing resembling game tends to be pigeons, rats, and then those squirrels?

As someone who spends so much of his life in cities and not nearly enough out in the field, and as someone who lives in degraded times, I am barely a hunter, a point partly about the clumsiness of my ritualistic repetition of our ancestors. Yet it remains true that "The general lines of the hunt are identical today with those of five thousand years ago,"[23] true, too, that " 'Natural' man is always there, under the changeable historical man," and then that " 'Natural' man is first 'prehistoric' man – the hunter."[24] I find this further elaboration of a double analysis quite compelling. Subjectivity continually mutates while existence never changes, with the added thought that the hunter represents that other plane, a plane less of continuity than of eternity now nearing its end. "By hunting," writes Ortega, "man succeeds in effect in annihilating all historical evolution, in separating himself from the present,"[25] that or – I'd add – separating himself from the historical present in order to inhabit an eternal return. The violence of hunting aside, and also beyond the modern resistance to acknowledging death in all forms, this annihilation is perhaps one reason why urban people, including many cosmopolitan environmentalists, are so uncomfortable with hunting; beneath the veneer of modern weaponry, hunters smell archaic and thus out of joint with the time. Yes, hunting has long been infused with layers of artifice. In modern times, these layers include scientific state-run wildlife management systems, unreasonable travel arrangements, all that sexy blaze orange clothing, and so on. Yet those layers of artifice are "outside of hunting itself,"[26] outside, that is, what we philosophers struggle to conceptualize as the essence of hunting.

Hunting may be saturated with "codes" – it is organized by them – but it is a practice, not an idea, an ethics, not a morality. I say this thinking about the fact that my grandparents were hunters and that this – the thought of what they inherited that I in turn inherit – influences who or what I am, me as a hunter, as does the memory of them and of every hunt. It is not the "idea" that my grandparents were hunters that makes me one. That is not the nature of my choice to be a hunter. Choosing to hunt means hunting for meaning, and some of this has to do with not recovering the past, but with breaking through time by engaging in a practice without which none of us would be here. In addition to the cold ground, the sky, the breeze, the birds, the seemingly interminable waiting, it is in part about engaging and reenacting our ancestors and the way that they provided for life, including our lives, by paying extraordinary attention in the field and by killing other animals.

Regarding Ortega, his words may have diminishing truth as melting ice challenges traditional hunters, and as modern hunters – people like me – are themselves an endangered species. Regarding humanity, Ortega observes that "He has always lived with the water at his throat."[27] But never before as what is to come; while the water is rising, the future will be thirsty for all creatures, predator and prey alike. There is no return, and we will continue to hunt for meaning, until, dying of thirst, we drown.

NOTES

1 Quoted by J. K. Anderson, *Hunting in the Ancient World* (Berkeley: University of California Press, 1985), p. 100.
2 José Ortega y Gasset, *Meditations on Hunting*, trans. Howard B. Wescott (New York: Charles Scribner's Sons, 1985), p. 123.
3 Ibid., pp. 24, 26.
4 Ibid., p. 27.
5 Thomas Paine, *Rights of Man* (Harmondsworth: Penguin Books, 1985), p. 236.
6 It is worth pondering the thought that the Wilderness Society and similar private organizations now perform a function not entirely different from that of nobles in earlier times.
7 Ortega, *Meditations on Hunting*, p. 27.
8 Roger B. Manning, *Hunters and Poachers: A Cultural and Social History of Unlawful Hunting in England 1485–1640* (Oxford: Clarendon Press, 1993), p. 17.
9 Ibid., p. 43.
10 Cf. Karl Marx, *Wage Labor and Capital* (New York: International Publishers, 1933), chap. 5.

11 Cf. Martin Heidegger, "The Question Concerning Technology," in *Basic Writings*, ed. David Farrell Kress (New York: Harper and Row, 1977), pp. 311–41. "Standing reserve" means that we not only subjectively view but also objectively treat the planet as if it were just a big battery there to fuel human activity.

12 Ortega, *Meditations on Hunting*, p. 45.

13 Ibid.

14 Ibid., pp. 96–7.

15 Ibid., p. 46.

16 Ibid., p. 47.

17 Ibid., p. 49.

18 Ibid.

19 Ibid., p. 98.

20 Walter Burkert, *Homo Necans: The Anthropology of Ancient Greek Sacrificial Ritual and Myth*, trans. Peter Bing (Berkeley: University of California Press, 1983), p. 14.

21 Ibid.

22 Ibid.

23 Ortega, *Meditations on Hunting*, p. 107.

24 Ibid., p. 116.

25 Ibid., p. 117.

26 Ibid.

27 Ibid., p. 113.

CHAPTER 7

GETTING BY WITH A LITTLE HELP FROM MY HUNTER

Riding to Hounds in English Foxhound Packs

For a number of years I have been participating in a tradition that has been part of the English countryside for around 300 years. I have been riding as a member of English foxhound packs. This opportunity came about as a result of my anthropological research into foxhunting. I participated as a rider in order to appreciate a cultural experience; to hear the stories and find out about a way of life. However, my role drew me into a collaboration with an unanticipated character in this network: the "made hunter," a horse shaped and seasoned for the chase.[1] These horses acted as my equine gatekeepers into this foxhunting world. Their knowledge of the social and physical environment was superior to mine. They knew the game and they knew the country, so I relied on them and I learned from them, just as novices to hunting have done for centuries. This account is based on a combination of observations from archival foxhunting texts and reflections from my own relationships with these horses. It describes the experiential fusion of the human/equine partnership, narrates the transitional process of learning to trust a horse's judgment, and observes that the relationship between horse and rider is a timeless collaboration.

However, before I kick on, I must apologize to foxhunting purists. My title refers to participation in foxhound packs as "riding to hounds," but many would, quite justifiably, take issue with my use of this term in relation to my account of careering around the English countryside while clinging grimly to my horse. Riding to hounds is the formal phrase used to describe the activity of the section of a hunt known as the "Field." In mounted foxhunting, the Field is a group of riders, led by a Field Master. This section of the hunt constitutes what I suppose could loosely be called participating spectators. These riders follow the pack of hounds and the Huntsman, who is in charge of the pack, in order to watch them hunt a fox.[2] The participation of the Field is not really meant to be an excuse to blast across the landscape on a horse. Riding to hounds ought to involve a focus on both the hunting environment and the skills exhibited by the hounds and the Huntsman. Indeed, Victorian hunting author Scrutator makes a point of distinguishing between correct and incorrect terminology, and behavior, in this respect. In a scathing and lofty assessment of the Field he declares, "Riding to hounds and riding after them are far from being one and the same thing."[3] The former, he explains, is characterized by an expert attention to and an appreciation of the finer points of venery.[4] The latter, carried out by the majority of the Field in his eyes, entails an uneducated, philistine pursuit in the general direction of a pack of hounds. I know which category he would place me in. Particularly in the early stages, my participation in the Field operated according to a basic needs hierarchy. In a Maslowian sense,[5] it was a case of cling on to the horse and keep up. However, all those who follow hounds have to begin somewhere. Like others before me, this elemental stage was essential if I were to make any progress towards appreciating the nuances of a foxhunting environment.

Saddle Up and Swallow Your Pride

Archive foxhunting texts provide reams of advice for newcomers, supposedly designed to minimize calamity, social disgrace, and embarrassment. Charles Richardson, writing over a hundred years ago, leaves the adult novice with no illusions as to the consequences of adapting to the chase: "Every season produces whole batches of recruits to hunting who are of mature years, and such people are, as a rule, more in need of advice as to their conduct than are the infantile beginners."[6] He continues with the equally incisive observation that urbanites, such as myself, are particularly likely to be untutored in the finer points of hunting etiquette. Such people, he announces, have "not been in a position to learn what may be called the rudiments of the chase." His final pronouncement on this matter is particularly deflating: "These novices in all that pertains to matters of venery unless they are lucky enough to escape notice, are very likely to be a source of mirth to their better-informed neighbours." However, I began to feel that, rather than enabling one to avoid these embarrassing *faux pas*, this type of caustic commentary merely heightened awareness of the degree of amusement and disruption that one has more than likely generated. I could envisage these whiskery old hunting gentlemen sniggering at my ineptitude through the fusty and moldy pages of these antiquarian books. Yet, although their observations may be harsh, they are not without foundation. During my novitiate I had time to reflect upon sociologist Erving Goffman's sage advice that, in order to be a successful ethnographer, one must be "willing to be a horse's ass."[7] He certainly had a point. During my fieldwork in the hunting field I spent many hours perched above one and there were numerous times when I definitely felt like one.

It is true to say that I am not a particularly stylish or accomplished horsewoman. Indeed, R. S. Summerhayes, in *Elements of Hunting*, sums up my pre-hunting level of ability as though he had met me. In his introductory text to foxhunting, initially written 80 years ago, he makes this assessment: "I must assume, which is probably true, that you are no great performer, but able to handle any reasonably mannered horse with satisfaction to yourself and no harm to him."[8] I did not fall into the category of Anthony Trollope's elegant "embryo Diana,"[9] who lends grace to a day's sport. I needed all the help that I could get. But I *did* manage to get by with the aid of a helping hoof from my equine partners. However, the maxim "horses for courses" is certainly applicable where foxhunting is concerned, because only a certain type of horse can take on the onerous responsibility of an untutored human. Richardson notes that, once in the hunting field, all horses tend to be overcome by an "extra ebullition of spirits."[10] Likewise, Summerhayes cautions that the experience of foxhunting can transform the most trustworthy and angelic horse into an absolute devil. Venatical voices from the past warn newcomers to avoid all manner of types of unsuitable equines. Apparently, "harness nags," "queer horses,"[11] and "flash gentlemen"[12] are to be shunned at all costs as they will inevitably lead the rider to offend against the unwritten laws of foxhunting etiquette. However, these authoritative authors all sing out in harmonious praise of "the made hunter."

The Made Hunter: Product and Agent

A hunter is not a definitive breed of horse. It is an animal, used for foxhunting, which may conform to a range of shapes, sizes, and types. However, the term *made* hunter refers not so much to the horse as a physiological entity as to the abilities and aptitude of a horse that has learnt its skill and trade in the hunting field. It has earned its colors; it knows its job. The "made" part of this term is interesting. At first glance it would suggest that these horses are little more than a crop to be harvested. There is an inference of equine passivity, which is reminiscent of a divided, dualistic conception of nature and society. The idea of "making" these animals implies that they are creatures that can be "shaped" and "manufactured," according to cultural requirements, while playing little part in the process themselves. Yet, this inherent sentiment would appear to be contradictory. It appears to be too restrictive to effectively encompass the active qualities that make the "made hunter" a horse that is a valued asset in the hunting field.

Although it is a speculative point, it is possible that the term may simply exist as a remnant of a modernist outlook, which accompanied the origin and development of modern foxhunting. The sport and culture of foxhunting emerged, in England, during the eighteenth century and grew in popularity throughout the nineteenth century. These were years defined by industrial, scientific, and social revolutions, which yielded grand narratives, rationalist paradigms characterized by a belief in technical and cultural progression and advancement. Mankind could shape the world and gain increasing control over nature and society.

Inevitably these horses were, and still *are*, "cultural products"[13] and commodities. They are trained and tested for aptitude and can be sifted and graded in terms of how they should accord with differing preferences and regional requirements. Yet, although the term "made hunter" is part of hunting discourse, foxhunting culture affords the animal much more respect than this term would suggest. At no point during my research did I encounter an outlook that disregarded the importance of the participation and agency of the horse. Indeed, such a perspective would sit at odds with the way in which these animals are currently viewed, nor did it feature as a theme in archive hunting texts. To those who are closely involved with these horses, their sentience and acuity have long been acknowledged.

Hunting landscapes, or hunt countries as they are called, place idiosyncratic demands on animals. Riding to hounds is not like riding in an arena. It involves a fecund, visceral engagement with a living landscape. Consequently, the best hunters are prized for their sharpness, as this quality is needed to deal with the unpredictability of the terrain. A skilled hunter will be able to use its "fifth leg." This term refers to the ability of the animal to get itself out of trouble and cope with the seemingly impossible. The horse has to be able to work things out and react quickly even if you can't – particularly if you can't. The need for a hunter to be mentally alert was a quality noted in the nineteenth century by the 8th Duke of Beaufort. He declared that this attribute was more important than physical assets: "People talk about size and shape, shoulders, quarters, blood, bone and muscle, but for my part give me a hunter with brains. He has to take care of the biggest fool of the two, and think for you both."[14] An equally important attribute in these animals is "heart" and an enthusiasm for the chase. Lieutenant-Colonel Geoffry Brooke advises that it is possible to overlook certain physical deficiencies in a hunter if he is "honest" and possesses "the heart of a lion."[15] Likewise, when asked what quality he liked best in a hunter, Brian Fanshawe, former huntsman of the Cottesmore Hunt, referred to attitude, reflecting that "The good ones really love it. They become part of the ... team. ... [T]hose horses appreciate their job is to stay with the hounds, and they get over the most extraordinary obstacles to get you there."[16]

Horses and Humans: A Foxhunting Partnership

Certainly, a day's hunting will confront horse and rider with "extraordinary obstacles" encountered in an unconventional manner. Initially, I was fazed by what appeared to be the recklessness of riding to hounds. There are so many variables that make it a much more chaotic and unpredictable equestrian experience than anything that I had encountered before. The Field would career over hard rutted tracks, plough through deep mud, canter over tarmac, and jump off and onto roads. Pile-ups, rabbit holes, blind ditches, jumps with branches at head height, lashing hooves, darting hounds, vicious thorned hedges and wire are just a few of the myriad, maverick elements that require extra vigilance. Indeed, I began to appreciate why early public opposition to foxhunting was based not on issues of animal cruelty but on moral objections that the dangers associated with the chase exhibited a disregard for *human* life.[17] This latter point is evident in Peter Beckford's *Thoughts on Hunting*, which first appeared in 1781. Beckford takes issue with "those who may think the danger which attends upon hunting a great objection to the pursuit of it,"[18] but then this element is one aspect of its appeal. Yet, I must confess that there were occasions when, from my perspective, an exciting frisson became distorted into icy fear. It was like accepting a lift from an attractive and engaging stranger, who morphed into a leering and malevolent Mr. Hyde, driving at full speed with all the doors locked.

One early near miss brought it home to me that this form of riding was going to be different from the other solitary, sanitized endeavors of my pre-hunting life. As my hunter and I sped along, just a few strides out from jumping a hedge, we were met by a hurtling human/equine combo flying directly across our path. The hijacked pilot yelled out some unintelligible and desperate cry as she thundered towards the obstacle. Whether this was aimed at me, her renegade horse, or was a howl for divine intervention, I couldn't tell, but we were on a collision course. As I was carried ever closer towards a point of impact, dithering about my course of action, my hunter knew what to do. He did not carry on regardless, or panic and decide to refuse. With unchoreographed synchronization, he checked his pace just enough to allow the other horse to clear the jump, but kept the momentum to leap it himself. As we landed on the other side, with my arse still in the saddle and heart still in my mouth, I blessed his sharpness and grit. However, I was informed that these experiences are to be embraced, not shunned. At one meet with a new Hunt,[19] I confessed my nervousness to fellow Field member, Maggie, in the pub, before we set off. I hoped to find reassurance. "I know what you mean," she mused, "but an old hunting lady who I know advises giving yourself a good scare at least once a week." She paused, swilling her whisky around nonchalantly in her glass, before she imparted the rest of this sagacious statement: "Apparently, it reminds you that you're still alive." I managed a weak smile of affirmation, nursed my glass of port, and reflected that this was quite true. I had become much more aware of the fact that, actually, I quite liked being alive.

However, these made hunters got me through these challenges, working things out where I hadn't a clue, judging pace and ground, even knowing where we were when I was disoriented. Yet, I was always mindful of the need to trust their experience. I was repeatedly instructed by foxhunting veterans to leave the horse to "work it out for himself." Again, advice from the Victorian era suggests that this has long been the case in foxhunting. Scrutator explains that "A made hunter ought to have perfect liberty of his head ... a horse that knows his business in the

Field would carry a good rider much more safely to the end of a run, even with loose reins, and without whip or spur."[20]

What these observations from across the centuries point to is the bond needed between rider and a competent hunter. The anthropologist Tim Ingold notes that "humans and animals relate to one another not in mind and body alone, but as undivided center of intention and action, as whole beings."[21] He observes how issues of trust and domination enter into human and non-human relationships, which exhibit differing "terms of engagement." Riding a hunter in the manner advocated involves elements of domination, but a degree of mutual trust is essential and the "sharp horse" must be permitted to use the qualities that make him a good hunter.

Katy, a member of the Field who hired out her horses for hunting, reflected that some accomplished riders, unfamiliar with riding to hounds, could not enter into this relationship. They did not respect the horse's abilities and superior experience and tended to over-ride her hunters, curtailing their skill. Katy observed that this lack of faith could upset the animal so that the rider might experience an unnecessarily difficult day, fighting a battle that he or she need not have begun. "He was holding him up too tight," she commented of one such rider's effect on her horse. "Wound him up it did. Should have given him his head." Katy also seemed irritated that her horses had been made to feel anxious when they were performing as they should. Repeated fractious incidents of that nature could ruin the most capable of horses by destroying its trust in the rider and itself. Similar Victorian observations refer to the folly of those who would "fret a sober animal."[22] The 8th Duke of Beaufort suggests that the tendency not to interfere with a good hunter is a reason why his female contemporaries coped so well in the hunting field. However, there are no traces of nascent feminism in his musings, as he speculates that their success in this matter might possibly be the result of either social graces or a delightful, charming, and unenlightened serendipity:

> How often we hear a woman praised for her hands; how often hear it said that the gentler sex have naturally better hands than we men. Partly, no doubt, this is because they are the gentler sex, because they have not the strength to pull and haul a horse about that we, alas! have. But mainly it comes from this, that they are content to leave their horses alone. Mounted, as they mostly are, and certainly always should be, on thoroughly trained and experienced hunters, they are satisfied to leave everything to the horse; it is his business to carry them, theirs to be carried. Whether this happy state of confidence arises from their superior tact, or from ignorance, matters nothing.[23]

Increasingly, I began to see that, although riding to hounds appears to be a comparatively unrefined form of riding, it involves more forethought than would first seem apparent. As I have explained, the riding can be fast and the terrain demanding. However, because of this, the contract in this human/equine partnership includes a clause that a rider must exhibit a sensitivity to the animal's efforts. Lord Bentinck's nineteenth-century missive to his inexperienced Huntsman reminded him of the folly of ignoring this duty. He raged: "the very men who encourage you to gallop and jump unnecessary fences are the men who will bring you to your doom. ... I have seen you tire two horses in a day, which of itself proves want of science and want of knowledge, and want of proper intellect and observation of the chase. Let me see no more of it."[24] I could hear the same sentiments expressed over 160 years later, as fellow Field member Caroline related the maxim "Never trot when you can walk, never canter when you can trot, never gallop when you can canter." She made this point one day after a field master led the way, jumping over a large ditch. "Why waste your horse unnecessarily?" she asked rhetorically, walking her hunter calmly over the land bridge a few yards away. She was correct. I learned that there was always a time when a horse would need its energy to launch itself over a necessary obstacle, and tired horses tend to make mistakes.

Foxhunting Resonances

As the hunting seasons moved on I began to be drawn into an altered relationship with the environment. Riding as part of a hunt engenders a bonded, sentient experience. It took me from an alienated, fragmented urban environment into the fourfold relationship of hunt, landscape, horses, and hounds. The made hunters played a role in heightening my awareness of these elements. They literally *incorporated* me into this hunting world. This experiential fusion led me to reflect upon the embodied nature of foxhunting.

The twentieth-century philosopher Maurice Merleau-Ponty explained that our self-perception needs to be understood in relation to our ongoing movement in the world. There is, he argued, no detached "inner-man." We are not divisible, static, or separate objects, but are involved in a holistic, reflexive, "kinaesthetic" engagement with the environment.[25] He explained: "By considering the body in movement, we can see how it inhabits space (and moreover time) because movement is not limited to submitting passively to space and time, it actively assumes them, takes them up in their basic significance."[26] Similarly, Ingold emphasizes the importance of our "dwelling" in a landscape. Our interaction with the world is not divisible from it. We do not act upon a surface but dwell in our environment in a sensual, fluid, and integrated manner. Moreover, we experience and know our environment in a vital dynamic capacity. In the same vein, Michael Carolan draws attention to our embodied, mobile, and intimate experience of a landscape, which affects our participation with and perception of that space. He observes: "mind is body; consciousness is corporeal; thinking is sensuous. In short, our understanding of space is more-than-representational. It is a lived process ... (we think as bodies)."[27] Clearly, this embodied interaction is multifaceted, occurring in many varied spheres of engagement. Indeed, Carolan recounts an interview during which a farmer told him of the different ways in which he knew his land. This even included the sensation of experiencing the contours and textures of the earth as it filtered from the tires of his tractor through to his body.

Patently, we do not engage with our environment in a static manner, nor do we relate to the world in realms that separate mind, body, and environment. Moreover, we incorporate space in all manner of modes, which have their own paces and rhythms. On horseback, this manner of dwelling is lifted to another level as the rider takes on the senses and the physicality of another living creature. But this augmented experience is not a mechanistic extension of the kind described by the farmer in his tractor. The horse is not simply a vehicle; it is a sentient, powerful, excitable, and often stubborn creature with its own manner of being in the world. The height, speed, and the senses of the horse resonate within the rider. You feel the animal's exertions and heartbeat and you experience its nervousness and excitement. Certainly, when there is a harmonious synergism, it is a transformative and symbiotic experience. Towards the end of one season it dawned on me that the horse and I were attuned to the point where I simply had to think where I wanted to go and Robby, the little gray hunter, went there.

A perspective from a horse is different and feels different to that of being on foot. The "muscular consciousness" entailed in experiencing a landscape becomes elevated. Through riding to hounds, the comparatively puny human frame takes on the power of the horse. You are *propelled* over ditches and *fly* across the land. It is within this context that I began to experience the hunt country not simply through my own physical being but through the "corporeal poetics"[28] enjoyed during these "centaur hours."[29] Riding as part of a hunt engendered a collaborative fusion and an elaborated experience, which molded, amplified, and defined my interaction within the hunting landscape.

However, the hunt country is a confusing world for a newcomer. There are no traffic lights, fixed signposts, written instructions, or paved routes to send you on your sanitized way. Yet again, the made hunters helped me to become integrated into this unfamiliar new sphere, acting as my translators and guides in this fascinating, foreign world. They knew the calls on the hunting horn, yet I did not. They understood the subtle signals encoded within the noises and actions of the hounds and Huntsman. They relaxed in the lulls, yet watched and listened intently when something significant was happening. Nostrils and ears would twitch and they would fidget around for a better view. They would become impatient and start shivering with anticipation, ready to move off when they recognized the correct cues. They would tell me that something was about to happen, or suggest that I was missing something.

It didn't take me long to notice how a made hunter could find extra energy when hounds started to "speak."[30] Even though Harvey was a young horse, and reasonably new to hunting, I could tell that he enjoyed it. He was one of those horses that would read what was happening intently. One day, I pointed out to Dan, who owned Harvey, that the hunter was flagging a little towards the end of the day. "*He's* alright," Dan observed with a grin. "He's pacing himself. He knows what's what. You wait until he hears hounds speaking. He'll be off then." Dan was correct, but then Harvey was a sharp horse who had a heart for hunting. And yes, he *was* beginning to save himself, holding just a little more back, until he knew that he really needed it. When he heard hounds speak, yes, there *was* an extra bounce in him. But, again, I was only just beginning to learn what those who ride to hounds have known for generations. Yoi-Over, an ex-Huntsman writing in the early twentieth century, explains the effect that the music of hounds, or the "Bells of the Chase," has on both rider and hunter. Their peal provides a stirring soundtrack, which elevates the tempo of a hunt. It is, he declares:

> Music that "drives the funk out of yer..." Music that takes the stones off the back of your hunter directly it reaches his ears, ... music that will draw your horse on till he can barely lift one hoof afore another, yes lure him to lift them without whip or spur.[31]

The "veneric play,"[32] to which he later refers, fuses the characters, integrating the individual and the social. The human and animal collective of the Hunt become bound together with the fragile and mutable nuances of the hunt country and everything therein. Through foxhunting I became drawn into this uniquely embodied relationship with place that can only occur within the context of these "foxhunting spaces." However, this drama has been a long-running show in which the made hunter must always occupy a leading role. The activity of participation within mounted packs creates a bond of experience, not just amongst those who ride to hounds now, but amongst all those who have ever done so. There is a temporal extension in this experience, a vital continuity that has to remain tangible in an increasingly "distantiated"[33] and virtualized world. And if foxhunting is still around in another 300 years, I would feel happy to chime in with my venatical predecessors, from these faded and yellowing pages. We would all still be telling the new recruit the same thing. Get yourself a good made hunter, trust his judgment, give him his head, knock back a stiff whisky, kick on, cling on, and begin to enter your new, ancient world. We suspect you'd enjoy it.

NOTES

1 In foxhunting the word "hunter" is only used to refer to a horse, not a human. "The chase" is a term used to refer to foxhunting and the canines in the pack are never called dogs, but hounds.

2 In 2005 traditional foxhunting was banned in England and Wales. Foxhunting can still continue within the confines of the law, but this means that hunts must abide by a range of confusing and complicated compromises. The intention of Hunts is to continue hunting, according to the legal constraints, in the hope that the legislation will be repealed. In order to resume traditional hunting in the future, and maintain that tradition, Hunts operate as closely as they can to their original methods, while staying within the law.

3 Scrutator, *Recollections of a Fox-Hunter*, 2nd ed. (London: Philip Allen, 1925), p. 81. Scrutator is the pseudonym used by this author.

4 Venery is an alternative word for hunting and also for sexual activity. However, the former meaning derives from the Latin word *venari*, which means to chase or hunt, and the latter from the Latin *veneria*, which refers to sexual desire or love. Although some contend that hunting and sex may well have a number of connections, this account uses the term venery to refer to hunting only!

5 Abraham Maslow developed a model of a hierarchy of human needs. According to Maslow, before higher needs such as self-actualization can be reached, basic needs must be met. In my case survival was a fundamental Maslowian requirement that governed my early foxhunting experiences. See Abraham Maslow, *Motivation and Personality*, 2nd ed. (New York: Harper and Row, 1970).

6 Charles Richardson, *Practical Hints For Hunting Novices* (London: Horace Cox, 1906), p. 72.

7 Erving Goffman, "On Fieldwork," *Journal of Contemporary Ethnography* 18, no. 2 (1989): 128.

8 R. S. Summerhayes, *Elements of Hunting*, 2nd ed. (London: Country Life, 1950), p. 2.

9 Anthony Trollope, *Hunting Sketches* (London: Hutchinson, 1933), p. 34.

10 Richardson, *Practical Hints*, p. 26.

11 Ibid., pp. 54, 4.

12 Summerhayes, *Elements of Hunting*, p. 3.

13 Bob Mullan and Garry Marvin, *Zoo Culture* (Urbana and Chicago: University of Illinois Press, 1998), 4.

14 Duke of Beaufort and Mowbray Morris, *Hunting* (London: Longmans, Green and Co., 1885), p. 206.

15 Geoffry Brooke, "Horses," in Sir Charles Frederick, *Fox-Hunting: The Lonsdale Library*, Vol. 7 (London: Seeley, Service and Co., 1930).

16 Brian Fanshawe, interview by Carolyn Abel, in *Foxhunting: Past, Present and Future* (Leicestershire: Melton Carnegie Archive, 2006).

17 See Italo Pardo and Giuliana Prato, "The Fox-Hunting Debate in the United Kingdom: A Puritan Legacy?" *Human Ecology Review* 12, no. 1 (2005): 143–55.

18 Peter Beckford, *Thoughts on Hunting*, 4th ed. (London: Methuen, 1918), p. 272.

19 "The meet" is a term used to refer to the venue where a Hunt meets.

20 Scrutator, *Recollections of a Fox-Hunter*, p. 86.

21 Tim Ingold, *Perception of the Environment: Essays on Livelihood, Dwelling and Skill* (London: Routledge, 2000), p. 75.

22 Richardson, *Practical Hints*, p. 54.

23 Beaufort and Morris, *Hunting*, p. 207. I am not in total agreement with the duke's rationale for female competence in the hunting field. However, his observations about the actual conduct of women riders still appear to be pertinent. I asked one horse owner how he felt about hiring his animals to foxhunting novices. He replied: "The girls are never a problem, but the lads can pull them about a bit."

24 Lord Henry Bentinck, in R. B. Fountain, *A History of the Burton Hunt: The First 300 Years* (n.p.: The Burton Hunt, 1996), p. 41.

25 Ingold, *Perception of the Environment*, p. 203.

26 Maurice Merleau-Ponty, *Phenomenology of Perception* (London: Routledge and Kegan Paul, 1996), p. 102.

27 Michael S. Carolan, "More-than-Representational Knowledge/s of the Countryside: How We Think as Bodies," *Sociologica Ruralis* 48, no. 4 (2008): 409.

28 Ibid.

29 Roger Scruton, *On Hunting* (London: Yellow Jersey Press, 1996), p. 69.

30 "Speaking" is the term used to refer to what might generally be called the "baying" of hounds. However, it is a more nuanced term than this definition would suggest. It means the noise that a pack makes when it has located a scent. Many other esoteric terms are used, in hunting, for the wide range of noises made by hounds. Indeed, the sound made by packs is highly valued, to the extent that it is referred to as hound "music."

31 Yoi-Over, *Bells of the Chase* (London: Hutchinson and Co, n.d.), p. 31. Yoi-Over is a pseudonym, based on a foxhunting call. By "our of yer," Yoi-Over means "out of you."

32 Ibid.

33 See Anthony Giddens, *The Constitution of Society* (Cambridge: Polity Press, 1984) and Anthony Giddens, *Runaway World*, 3rd ed. (London: Profile, 2002). In this particular context I have used distantiation to refer to what Giddens describes as time-space distantiation and the stretching of social relations. This can occur in a number of ways, under a number of circumstances. However, in an increasingly globalized world, there is a greater ability and tendency for social interaction to be conducted under less tangible, more distant, and potentially alienating circumstances. In a fundamental sense, the activity of foxhunting stands apart from this trend, as it relies upon being embedded physically, cognitively, and sensually in the environment. It cannot be uprooted and virtualized in the manner that many other types of interaction may be.

CHAPTER 8

TRACKING IN PURSUIT OF KNOWLEDGE

Teachings of an Algonquin Anishinabe Bush Hunter

Context: Hunting from an Anishinabe Perspective

Applying a traditional Anishinabe[1] perspective to the philosophy of hunting inspires a deep look at the relationships between human beings and the creatures of the earth that sustain us. In order to begin to appreciate the Anishinabe approach to hunting, it helps to have a more general understanding of the traditional indigenous perspective, where the reference to "traditional" does not necessarily refer to "old" and unchanging. As Russell Barsh reminds us, "what is 'traditional' about traditional knowledge is not its antiquity, but the way in which it is acquired and used."[2] At the same time, there are certain core dimensions of knowledge that run like threads through the generations, transmitted through storytelling, song, and dance.

Although there are many cultural differences between indigenous peoples worldwide, most – if not all – traditional indigenous worldviews express a broad view of community that involves reciprocal relationships of care between family members: "It is the story of all life that is holy and is good to tell, and of us two-leggeds sharing in it with the four-leggeds and the wings of the air and all green things; for these are children of one mother and their father is one spirit."[3]

Traditional indigenous peoples interpret the world from a holistic and integrated perspective of knowledge that combines an epistemological perspective with a moral perspective.[4] The epistemological perspective sees all of creation – humans (past, present, and future), animals, fish, birds, insects, plants, the water, the land, the air, the trees, the sky, the clouds, the rain, the mountains and the rocks – as *belonging* to the same *family*, in relationship with one another. The moral perspective sees all family relationships in terms of responsibility and reciprocity: giving and taking. In order to maintain good family relationships between all members, it is necessary for all interactions to reflect reciprocity. Taking too much or giving too much destroys the balance that must exist in the family.

A central bond that ties members together in their family relationship is spirit. This fundamental belief contributes to both the moral and epistemological perspectives. The belief that life exists in various dimensions and forms – not only the physical, but the mental, emotional, and spiritual as well – allows Native people to appreciate the connections between all family members and to know about the characteristic ways that each member contributes to the family.

It is from this perspective that the Anishinabe philosophy of hunting emerges. According to this integrated perspective, it is understood that certain animals participate in the family relationship by giving themselves for the sustenance of human family members. The human family members respond by accepting these gifts, as we would expect anyone to accept a gift from her kin: with gratitude and respect. Both of these attitudes are evident in careful harvesting practices, which require knowledge of animal characteristics and patterns, and of how much and when to harvest so as not to take too much or at the wrong time. A significant aspect of the Anishinabe concept of hunting is learning how to connect with the other creatures of existence through experience. In this regard, in their description of the old days, Raymond Pierotti and Daniel Wildcat recall how Native people "understood themselves as predators, part of the world of prey, and connected to prey in a profound experiential sense."[5] At the same time, Native people recognized that the "lives of human beings ... often depended on taking the life of the animal, and [that] the act of giving up its life so that humans could survive was ... a profound sacrifice for the animal."[6] In recognition of this sacrifice, and in gratitude, it is the traditional way to hold feast ceremonies in honor of the prey, and to practice an ethic of not wasting anything from it.

For hundreds of years, the Anishinabe have been sought out as hunting guides due to their comprehensive knowledge of the patterns of the

JACOB WAWATIE AND STEPHANIE PYNE

"natural" world. This knowledge includes an awareness of the particular animal's experience of existence, and the ability to realize the depth of the relationships that exist between humans and the rest of creation. Anishinabe understandings of "hunting" can be transmitted through storytelling, an age-old and sacred means of transmitting knowledge and transforming awareness. Teaching in this way provides learners with clues, while allowing them to actively figure things out for themselves.

Teachings on Hunting

It is recounted in the Algonquin legends that all species – including "man," the human species – created their own languages. The human species developed a means to express the meanings that people had come to understand: their semantic acknowledgment of reality. The birth of a language created meanings for each word and transmitted a code that conceptualized an ideal. It is from this perspective that we come to the word "hunt," which

FIGURE 8.1 Jacob Wawatie (Mowegan), teacher, elder, and director of Kokomville Academy. Photograph © Alice Beaudoin. Reproduced with permission of Alice Beaudoin.

simply means to seek and find, and does not necessarily imply that the hunted must outrun or be smarter than the hunter. Taking this simple view of the origins of hunting allows us to go down a different path of understanding the way in which the word "hunt" has developed its meaning.

A long way back, humans were somewhat blank to the environment. They had yet to experience and interpret the temporal and spatial dimensions of life on Mother Earth; they had yet to come into "cognitive contact with reality."[7] Despite this "blankness," the humans had been gifted with many abilities by all of the creatures in the world, so they were able to learn, survive, and thrive in their new environment. Kokom[8] Lena Jerome Nottaway told a short version of the Algonquin human creation story, which describes how humans came into the world and received these gifts. The story reminds us that we are part of a whole and that we must coexist as equals with all of creation, respecting everything that the Creator has granted us for our existence.

Many winters ago, before there were any humans on earth, the animals were gathering food for the fall feast. The trees did their part by supplying the wood for the cooking fire; the fish, by bringing water for the tea. There was plenty of food for everyone, with extra for the spiritual offering baskets. Everyone was there to enjoy the food, but they also came because the land was going to sleep for the winter and they had to say goodbye until spring. Most of the birds flew south where the weather was warmer but some stayed to keep an eye on Mother Earth while she was sleeping. Some animals hibernated for the winter months. Some of the trees threw leaves on the ground to cover Mother Earth and keep her warm. The insects began crawling under leaves and fallen tree stumps. The fish kept the water moving so the lakes and rivers wouldn't freeze too thick. The rest of the animals took their turns to watch over Mother Earth while she was sleeping for the winter.

Soon the snow started to fall and covered Mother Earth with another warm blanket so she wouldn't get cold. Every living creature went to sleep for a good long rest. During this winter sleep they were disturbed by a strange dream that kept them awake for part of the winter. In this strange dream they saw a standing figure made of mist or fog with no specific features to define it. Throughout the winter they slept, tossing and turning restlessly until spring when the warm weather returned.

When spring arrived the birds came back to their summer place and the animals crawled out of their holes, stretching their legs. The insects buzzed around to wake up the others who were still half asleep, the trees reached up toward the warm sun, and the fish started splashing in the water, which was beginning to warm up. Mother Earth was so happy to see her children cleaning up and preparing for the spring feast. There were so many fresh, hot foods on the table. As they were eating they began to talk about their dream. The big white pine said, "I had a strange dream this winter. There was this thing in front of me that did not have a solid body. It did not move or say anything."

The other creatures listened as the big, white pine told about his dream. They had all had similar dreams during the long, cold winter months. They all wanted to talk about their dreams. The wise old bear quieted the others and said, "It is a sign of the creator telling us another creature will soon be living with us. To welcome this new creature we will go to the sacred fire tonight for a ceremony." Every single creature went to the river where the ceremonial fire was being made. Most of them were curious about what was going to happen.

The bear drummed and chanted the sacred song of the creator. Then the bear walked over to the fire and said, "If this creature is to live among us I will give him the gift of wisdom – wisdom to lead his children to a bright future." As he put his tobacco into the fire the smoke began to rise and there it lingered above the fire just as it had in their dreams. The creatures oohed and aahed in amazement of what they were seeing. The bear returned to the fire as the figure disappeared into thin air.

The eagle hopped up to the fire and lifted his sacred tobacco and said, "To this creature I will give the gift of vision so he may see where he came from and where he is leading his children." He dropped his tobacco into the fire and the smoke rose. Again it lingered in the air, this time a bit longer than the first time. Then the sturgeon flopped over to the fire and said, "I give this creature the gift of strength so he may overcome the obstacles of life." He flipped his offering into the fire and flopped over to the nearby river. He saw the creature beginning to take shape and then vanish again into thin air. Next the ant walked over to the fire. Lifting his grain of tobacco the ant said, "I give the creature the gift of understanding so he will be able to work with others."

Suddenly four big, tall legs towered over the ant. As the ant looked up to see what it was, again it disappeared. The ant walked back to the circle, amazed at what he had seen. Then the big, white pine leaned over and spoke in a low, low voice, "To this creature I give the gift of self-respect so he may stand tall, and strong when hard times arise." The white pine sprang back after he dropped his tobacco into the fire and watched the figure hovering over it. The thunder roared, "To this creature I give the gift of voice so he may be heard by his children."

Each of the animals, the elements, trees, birds, fish, and insects had a special gift for the creature. Each time they gave him their gift the figure became more and more solid. The last of the creatures was the louse. He had to holler to be heard, "To this being I will give the gift of understanding that we are all part of this creation."

FIGURE 8.2 This prayer blanket is laid down in feast ceremonies when the people remember and give thanks for the kind and useful gifts they were given by the other creatures of Mother Earth. Image reproduced with permission from Jacob Wawatie (Mowegan).

Then the solid figures of a man and a woman walked out of the fire with tears in their eyes in appreciation of the gifts they had been given by all creation. They spoke in unison, "We thank you for all the gifts that we have just received and hope that they will be used wisely for the well-being of our children. We will cherish these gifts and may we pass them down to our children and our children's children. Migwetch!"[9] As the ceremony ended, the man and woman greeted each of the creations and shook their hands to thank them individually for the wonderful gifts they had received and to promise that these kind and useful gifts would always be remembered.

It is with this understanding of the relationship between humans and other creatures that the Anishinabe understand "hunting." One way to appreciate this understanding is by continuing the story to tell about Nathan, the first son of the two people who walked out of the fire. As we follow Nathan in his journey through life, growing and venturing out into

JACOB WAWATIE AND STEPHANIE PYNE

the world, we will begin to see how Nathan used the gifts passed down from the creatures of Mother Earth to evolve in his understanding of hunting.

Nathan was born one summer day and showed his first sign of being a good hunter: gasping for air, breathing in and giving his cry of triumph, "Alleluia!" Nathan wanted to live and take another breath, and another. When his second breath came, his cute little mouth began to move and he puckered his little lips. Then his neck began to move, he locked onto a scent, and going in for the kill, he clasped on and locked in: food, success. Nathan had found his mother.

As Nathan began to grow, he learned to manage his sheltered environment on a daily basis and to do the things that were necessary to achieve a sense of well-being. Nathan had mastered the first stage of understanding and applying his knowledge and understanding of hunting as an innate attribute of all species to pursue existence within an environment. After a certain age, Nathan had grown too big to be feeding on his mother. He had learned well how to sustain himself by relying on his mother who had provided him with an inexhaustible pantry and a personal malleable toy. Now it was time to move on. Nathan began to realize that the pantry must have been getting filled from some place. The great open space was his to explore – a living space with a multitude of events, the matrix of Mother Nature. Nathan stood by the entrance of his shelter inhaling the sight before him and contemplating its magnitude. With one last look back at the breast of life, he took his first step forward across the threshold into a new sphere of existence within the providence of Mother Earth.

One early spring morning, Nathan sat listening to the leaves blowing softly through the branches. The birds sang their soothing song, awakening from their nightly forty winks. This was a space of time when all living creatures are awake, even the night creatures that roam the nights who are just settling down. The break of dawn is an intense moment in the environment, which generates the movement of interconnected relationships in every single milieu: the birds, the fish, the trees and plants, the animals, the water, the wind and the rocks, and of course, human beings – the myriad of life.

Nathan listened to the orchestra of nature, and began to appreciate the different sounds and rhythms of each audible apparatus within the environment. He instinctively directed his attention to identify the source of each noise. This gift of perception had been given to his parents by the rabbit and, through them, was passed on to him. He thought about this and he was grateful for the gift. With his rabbit ears, Nathan noted how at certain moments, an outbreak of excited sounds could be heard, and he could see them spreading like a blanket across the land.

On the trail of life that led away from his shelter, Nathan moved out into the surrounding forest. Discovering a diversity of flora emanating life, he began to notice how certain plants grew in certain places, telltale signs of their unique ecological settings. As he moved further into the territory along the waterway, Nathan observed how the water source attracted the growth of the canopy. Since Nathan was a part of the ecological and biological setting that he was encountering, his presence stirred reactions, which were sounded in the orchestra of Nature. As Nathan walked along the winding trail under the canopy, he instigated the movement of creatures that shy away from human presence. He was learning about the relationship between plants as they are dispersed throughout the different ecological settings, and about the various creatures that are attracted to them. Along the waters, the attraction of the spirit of the water enticed all species, and within the waters was a world of its own. Nathan had begun to learn about what is out there and to understand how each ecological setting contributes to the interactions of the creatures of the forest.

Day after day, Nathan followed the trail that led away from his shelter. He followed the seasons and learned from the weather, which inspired a deeper understanding of the ecological settings. He began to understand the changes that occurred through the land with each moon. His maturing knowledge of the environment grew, and with it came a sense of well-being. Nathan had a sense of what he needed to know about what is out there, and an understanding of how each ecological setting contributes to the interactions of the creatures of the forest. This gave him a sense of satisfaction within his own space of time.

Nathan spent a lifetime following the trail that led away from his shelter. He had acquired much knowledge since he first went into the forest, and had come to understand many things along that trail, including hunting and fishing. He had learned how to see and listen, and to perceive how all was related.

One day Nathan followed a moose and observed the food chain that occurs on the land. He perceived the effect of the seasons, the winds, and the weather and became aware of the physical, mental, emotional, and spiritual setting of the creature. He had followed the trail of the moose throughout the seasons, for the moose had much to offer in terms of goods. On the pathway to learning about the benefits of the moose, Nathan had learned to read the tracks of the moose to determine many things, including its size, age, and gender. For example, the shape of the tracks gave him subtle hints about whether they belonged to a male or a female, where the male imprint was distinctive because of an external swing in his gait.

Nathan had seen the moose eat different kinds of shrubs among the diversity in the boreal forest. In the spring, the moose would start eating the little buds from mountain ash, alder, poplar (aspen), white birch, but seldom from the evergreen. When the moose did eat from the evergreen, it was a sign that the moose was ill. The moose – like all animals, including the carnivores – would also eat the leaves of the poplar in the spring. These leaves provided a form of inoculation against the viruses that were being awakened by the melting of the snow.

Nathan found that most parts of the moose were edible and he created recipes for cooking them. Here are some examples:

- The nose: cut the nose off the head of the moose. Singe the hair completely from it and boil until tender.
- The tongue: cut off the tongue up to the beginning of the windpipe. Boil until tender.
- The head, eyes, cheek, and meat of ear section: cut up the head to fit into a big pot. Boil until meat falls off the bone or until tender.
- Hooves: cut off the hooves to the first joint (shin). Boil one to two minutes. Soak each hoof in boiling water to help remove it from the inner fleshy tissue. Hit the hoof with a solid hammer-like object to loosen and remove inner section. Boil inner section until tender.[10]
- Large intestines (tripe): used to make smoked sausage. Clean. Season to taste (salt, pepper). Turn inside out. Smoke with black spruce and green branches (needles included). The smoking process is finished when the tripe is firm and smoke dried. Boil until tender.
- Marrow of the jaw and leg bones: usually roasted by the fire. Crack bones open when ready.
- Four stomachs: clean and boil until tender.

Besides the food benefits of the moose, Nathan found the moose had many other uses. The skin could be used for shelter, clothing, straps, tools, weapons, bed covers, and toys. The hair of the moose could be used for matting the floor of the doghouse during cold weather. The bones could be turned into jewelry, tools, and toys. The antlers were used in the skinning process, and to make tools, musical instruments, jewelry, toys, and glue.

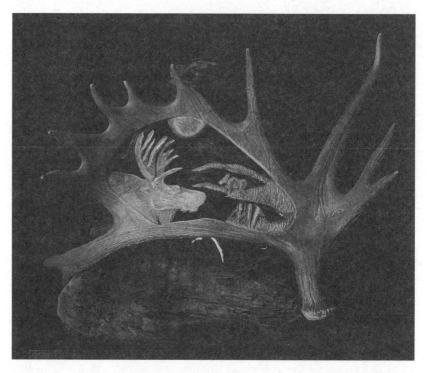

FIGURE 8.3   This moose antler carving was crafted by Jacob Wawatie. In addition to telling the story of the interconnectedness of all things, the carving provides a means of expression through which the moose's spirit is carried on. Photograph © Alice Beaudoin. Reproduced with permission of Alice Beaudoin.

Nathan had learned to respect the moose's need to disperse across the land. He had walked in the moose's pathway. He had witnessed the moose's quest for comfort, even through the harshest of weather, and he had read the silent hints left behind by the moose through the changing seasons. With this knowledge, Nathan was able to live in balance with the moose that shared his territory, taking neither too few nor too many from any one area.

Through his knowledge of the moose's food sources and how the moose related to its ecological setting, Nathan was able to zero in on the moose's domain. He had learned the best time to get his moose: when it was fat, which gave him the sign that it was healthy. He also came to understand the moose's biological processes and genetics, which changed through the different seasons of the moose. After Nathan had killed a moose, he would make a feast ceremony to thank the spirits who had contributed to meeting his needs. On his path to understanding, Nathan had come to understand the universe of each creature in the same way he had come to know the universe of the moose, and every spring and fall he would have a feast ceremony to honor all of the creatures who had contributed to his existence.

After many journeys along the trail that led from his shelter, Nathan had become an old man. His parents had long since passed, and it was his turn to share the knowledge of his journeys before he too passed over to the next world. So Nathan made a hunting song in the old language to express some of what he had learned:

Pekatc mosek nidjanisidok	Walk softly my children
Kigibideckwa kegadjigwesi	He'll hear and come, the homo sapiens
Ninadimadin pemadiziwin	Smell for life
Kibikiyone kegadjigwesi	He has blocked nose, the homo sapiens
Midjim nehete nidjanisdok	The food is dispersed my children
Kegadjigwesi odikwahabadan	The homo sapiens is watching it
Madjibiyek nidjanisidok	Move away my children
Kegadjigwesi kinosinewgonan	The homo sapiens is following us
Nadigam minikwen nidjanisidok	Drink from the shore my children
Pabamokojiye kegadjigwesi	He paddles around, the homo sapiens
Kitijimitok nidjanisidjik	Make plenty of tracks my children
Pabamosehi kigadjigwesi	Make them walk, the homo sapiens
Opimimeckode pimemopitok	Run along the side of the hill
Tcaginigehik Kigadjigwesi	Make him tired, homo sapiens
Madjibiyek nidjanisidok	Move away my children
Kegadjigwesi kinosinewgonan	The homo sapiens is following us

Tah tah!

Then Nathan sang his song to remember the steps he had undergone to understand the moose – a sacred creature in a sacred world. As he sang, Nathan entered the moose's world as he had done day-to-day, moon-to-moon, and season-to-season in the days of his youth. Through his song, Nathan gives us some basic knowledge to work with in order to understand how to harvest our prey. It is a story of mother moose singing and teaching her children about the forest. The story gives the setting of the animals. It is a hunting song with no direct clues; but in a subtle way it teaches people where to go and lets them still do some work on their own. It lets them come to their own awareness.

FIGURE 8.4 Lena Jerome Nottaway, Jacob's grandmother, carrying a moose's nose. Lena taught Jacob to hunt moose, and he remembers her as "a cute little thing, but she was a firecracker who could be heard when she whispered. Kokomitcetc migwetc [thank you, Little Grandmother]." Photograph © Michael Greenlar. Reproduced with permission of Michael Greenlar.

Hunting and Awareness

In the end, Nathan "the hunter" came to understand hunting through the skills and abilities gifted to him by the very creatures he was hunting – gifts which he remained ever grateful for – and he passed some of that

  JACOB WAWATIE AND STEPHANIE PYNE

understanding along to the next generations in the form of a song. Nathan's hunting song not only provides clues for the hunter to locate prey. Through language, rhythm, and melody, the song also inspires an awareness of the experiences of other creatures, reminding us that all life-forms are linked together in an intricate web of interconnected relationships.

The story recounted in this chapter shares not only a traditional Anishinabe understanding of hunting, but also a traditional Anishinabe approach to expressing this understanding. Many of the lessons are not direct and obvious. In keeping with the traditional approach, clues are given to entice and challenge the learner to reach his or her own awareness.

From the Anishinabe perspective, it is difficult to consider hunting in isolation since it is only one window of a much larger picture. Hunting is linked to understanding through experience and language. More than simply a quest for game, hunting is a quest for understanding that involves seeking out the ways and the languages of the other creatures and entities of Mother Earth. It involves becoming aware of the many interactions between these creatures, and of how to interact with these creatures in a way that acknowledges and remembers the original gifts they gave to humans ...

... As Nathan lay inside his shelter breathing in his final few breaths, the frog's chirping came to his ears and told him that the moose was just now beginning to call.

NOTES

1   In keeping with the conventions of anglophone and francophone Algonquins in the western part of Quebec, the authors prefer the simpler spelling of "Anishinabe" over against the double-vowel "Anishinaabe" spelling characteristic of the Odjibwe and Algonquin peoples of Ontario [Ed.].

2   Russell Lawrence Barsh, "Indigenous Knowledge and Biodiversity," in United Nations Environment Program (UNEP), *Cultural and Spiritual Values of Biodiversity* (London: Intermediate Technology Publications, 1999), p. 74.

3   Black Elk, quoted in Laurie Anne Whitt, "Indigenous Peoples, their Environments and Territories," in *Cultural and Spiritual Values*, p. 73.

4   This is not to say that all indigenous people ascribe to their traditional perspectives, but that there is a certain extent to which various indigenous cultures can be identified with – and identify themselves with – particular traditional worldviews, which are often enshrined in their traditional languages.

5   Raymond Pierotti and Daniel R. Wildcat, "Traditional Knowledge, Culturally-Based Worldviews and Western Science," in *Cultural and Spiritual Values*, p. 195.

6   Ibid.

7   Linda Zagzebski, *Virtues of the Mind: An Inquiry into the Nature of Virtue and Ethical Foundations of Knowledge* (New York: Cambridge University Press, 1989), p. 45.

8   "Kokom" is the Algonquin word of respect for the elderly, which acknowledges and honors their wisdom and longevity.

9   "Migwetch" is the Algonquin word meaning "thank you" in English. It is used to express gratitude and to end prayers.

10 It is believed the hooves provided a source of calcium for individuals with brittle bones, and there is a myth that eating hooves increases the chances for a woman to deliver a baby girl. Hollowed-out hooves were attached together to make rattles, and a pair of hooves could be attached together to make a handle for a stick.

GARRY MARVIN[1]

CHAPTER 9

LIVING WITH DEAD ANIMALS?

Trophies as Souvenirs of the Hunt

In his exploration of trophies in the world of hunting, Ted Kerasote refers to one hunter as "heading to the other side of the world, again to the hunting fields, making memories with his rifle" and to another who, if successful, "will enshrine the trophy in a place of honor."[2] In a recent conversation, a Spanish hunting friend explained to me that each of his mounted heads was *un recuerdo* – a term that refers to reminiscence, to memory, and to a material souvenir. If the hunting trophies displayed in the homes of hunters are treated as shrines to a special memory of a special animal, then they are more complicated than critics of hunting recognize. Trophies may not be simply material celebrations of a hunter's power, domination, and triumph.

My argument here will be twofold. Firstly, for the hunter, hunting trophies are not dead animals but are rather imbued with life. Secondly, although the hunter triumphs over the animal in the sense that the animal is killed, *how* the animal is killed is far more important than the fact that it *is* killed; hunting trophies are indicative of a sense of ethical excellence.

My interest here is in how the material object, in the form of the taxidermied body, relates to memory. This connection is intimately related to the notion of a leftover. The taxidermied animal in a hunter's collection is, at the material level, a vestige of the animal but at a more complex and experiential level, it is also the remainder of a relationship formed during the process of hunting: one that now resides in the home and the memory of the hunter. However, such relationships cannot be immediately discerned in what remains of the body of the animal itself. Without the enlivening presence of the hunter, such objects are mute and can probably only be seen as dead animals. The significance of the trophy, the fact that it is displayed at all, is only revealed when hunters speak about them. Not all are valued equally or in the same manner. Some may be trophies in the original, military sense of spoils of battle and symbols of both victory and defeat. Some may be valued in and of themselves as the biggest, rarest, or the most difficult to hunt. Others, the focus of this piece, are sites of memory that both invoke and evoke the hunter's journey to the animals and the return with them. Not all hunters make the journey in the same manner, for the same purpose, or for the same experiences. My focus here will be on one type of hunter and one set of orientations to hunting.

Cultural Predators

In an early study of types of hunters, Stephen Kellert made the important point that modern leisure or recreational hunters do not form a homogeneous group. He distinguished three categories of hunters: utilitarian/meat hunters, dominionistic/sport hunters, and nature hunters.[3] He suggested that "utilitarian/meat hunters appeared to perceive animals largely from the perspective of their practical usefulness. ... They viewed hunting as a harvesting activity and wild animals as a harvestable crop not unlike other renewable resources."[4] For dominionistic/sport hunters, "the hunted animal was valued largely for the opportunities it provided to engage in a sporting activity involving mastery, competition, shooting skill and expressions of prowess."[5] For nature hunters, "the desire for an active, participatory role in nature was perhaps the most significant aspect of the nature hunter's approach to hunting. The goal was the intense involvement with wild animals in their natural habitats. Participation as a predator was valued for the opportunities it provided to regard oneself as an integral part of nature."[6]

Kellert warns us not to read these as exclusive categories. Although hunters tended "to be orientated toward one *primary* attitudinal relation to hunting," they were "typically characterized by more than one attitude."[7] Hunting is not simply a matter of "attitudinal relation," but also a matter of how attitudes inform and guide hunting practice in relation to different occasions and purposes. Rather than using these types as a classification or categorization of *hunters*, I find them more useful for thinking about modes of *hunting*, or as different *orientations* to hunting in any particular hunting event. Different modes or orientations may come to the fore on different occasions. So, in the context of hunting trophies, a trophy hunter might also espouse the values of a nature hunter and a nature hunter might seek a trophy on a particular occasion, while his or her primary orientation is to achieve an intense involvement with the natural world through hunting. My focus here is on hunters whom Kellert would classify as nature hunters.

The Prize is a Clear Conscience

Such orientations to hunting are connected with what might be termed hunting philosophies. My interest here is not in what philosophers have written about hunting, but rather in the philosophies of hunters that are lived out in practice. My perspective is not that of a philosopher who seeks to interrogate ideas but that of a social anthropologist who seeks to understand how members of social and cultural groups constitute the worlds in which they live and how cultural views relate to cultural practice. Fundamental to this anthropological enterprise is an attempt to understand cultural worlds from within, from the perspectives of those who live in these worlds. In terms of understanding and interpreting the practices, processes, and orientations of nature hunters with regard to trophies, it is essential to pay attention to the philosophies that are generated from within, by and for hunters themselves, as they reflect on what they do and how they are as hunters. Such philosophies are rather different from those that seek to explain or justify their practices to outsiders.

Underpinning the practice of nature hunters is a fundamental belief in, and adherence to, what has been termed the ethics of "fair chase." This ethical approach to hunting is constructed from a set of beliefs about the appropriate and essential relationships that should obtain between the hunter and the prey. Key elements of this relationship are that the hunted animal should be a naturally wild animal; that it is not restricted in any way such that it cannot escape the hunter; that it should not be pursued and killed from a vehicle; that hunters should voluntarily restrict their ability (particularly in terms of the use of technology) to hunt an animal; and that at the moment of taking a shot the hunter must be confident that the shot will be a lethal one. Ethical hunting is summarized in Jim Posewitz's declaration: "Fundamental to ethical hunting is the idea of fair chase. This concept addresses the balance between the hunter and the hunted. It is a balance that allows hunters to occasionally succeed while animals generally avoid being taken."[8]

For nature hunters, this is authentic hunting. For them, the hunted animal should only be converted into a trophy if it has been hunted in an authentic manner; without that process, the trophy has no value. As Arjun Appadurai comments, "Value ... is never an inherent property of objects, but it is a judgment made about them by subjects," and "the difficulty of acquisition, the sacrifice offered in exchange, is the unique constitutive element of value."[9] The "difficulty of acquisition" is of crucial importance here. If the opportunity to kill an animal has been made artificially easy, then there is no challenge for the hunter and, for the hunters I know, this is simply not hunting. For such hunters the nature of the process is essential and the trophy produced as a result comes to represent the experience of that particular hunt. Ethics and authenticity, how one ought to hunt, and how that has informed how one actually hunts, are the personal responsibility of the hunter. The trophy is something that the hunter personally awards himself or herself in recognition of that process. In this sense a hunting trophy is very different from a trophy acquired in a sporting event. Such a trophy is awarded by others as a result of an achievement that is witnessed by others. The process of hunting rarely has witnesses, other than perhaps by guides, and the only judgment of achievement is made by the hunter.[10] The creation of a hunting trophy begins with experience, passes through stages of re-creation, and achieves its full power when it begins its life in the home of the hunter.

Souvenir Parts, Remembered Wholes

In her essay "Objects of Desire," Susan Stewart suggests that the "capacity of objects to serve as traces of authentic experience is ... exemplified by the souvenir."[11] It is in the manner of acquisition and in its relationship to the hunter that the hunting trophy might be interpreted as a souvenir – a material object from elsewhere, and from another time, that is imbued with meaning and memory when brought home. Objects can become souvenirs in a variety of ways. Apparently insignificant objects – such as a ticket stub from a favorite concert, a wine bottle from a memorable occasion, or a child's first clothes – might be kept as souvenirs, as "tokens of heightened moments."[12] Souvenirs also come in the form of specifically manufactured souvenir objects, sold at key tourist sites, that represent those sites through a reproduction of signs and images – models of the Eiffel Tower in Paris, copies of the Statue of Liberty in New York – or, of a slightly different order, rugs from Istanbul, masks from Venice, bottles of maple syrup from Canada, or spices from an Indian market. For a souvenir to be authentic it must be obtained in the place that it represents, by the visitor who has been there. While in the place they represent, souvenir objects are not yet, not fully souvenirs. There they only have the potential for evocation of the experience of that place because the purchasers are still within that experience. The work of the souvenir only begins when it is removed from that place and when immediate experience is replaced by memory. When it is brought home the unindividuated object of the souvenir shop becomes a personal memento of the person who obtained it. But such objects do not speak for themselves; they must be activated, brought to life, either through the thoughts and reminiscences of the owner or when the owner explains their significance to others. As Susan Stewart argues, "We do not need or desire souvenirs of events that are repeatable. Rather we need and desire souvenirs of events that are reportable, events whose materiality has escaped us, events that thereby exist only through the invention of narrative."[13] Hunting trophies come alive through the reveries or narratives of the hunter, but before that, the animal that the mount relates to must be converted into a stable cultural object that can function as a souvenir.

Hunting trophies have "souvenir qualities" in that they are tokens of heightened moments, sometimes emblematic of the place where the animal was hunted, and are objects that are brought back from elsewhere to be displayed as mementos of experience in that other place. However, where they differ from other souvenirs is that authentic trophies cannot be purchased; they must be created by the hunter. There is no such thing as a generic hunting trophy as there are generic souvenirs, and no hunter would display as a hunting trophy an animal that he or she had not personally hunted and killed; a trophy shot by someone else would have no significance for a hunter.[14] The act of their creation begins in the process of hunting itself and continues through the stages of converting a dead animal into a mount: a process that converts an impersonal, living animal into a representation or a re-creation of one that has a unique and personal relationship with the hunter.

As Stewart notes, "The souvenir is by definition always incomplete."[15] The wine bottle no longer contains wine, the child's clothes are no longer worn by the child who made them significant, and the model of the Eiffel Tower bears no relationship to the size and grandeur of the object to which it refers. Stewart also refers to the "incompleteness of the souvenir object" which "stands in a part/whole relationship" to the "scene of its original appropriation."[16] The hunting trophy signifies a part-to-whole relationship in two ways. At one level it is an object that stands for, or represents, the whole of a particular hunting event, but it is also only ever a part of the specific animal to which it refers. Hunters do not seek to convert the entirety of the hunted animal – flesh, organs, bones – into a trophy.[17] In order to represent any animal, most of it must be discarded and only those parts that can be preserved from biological deterioration – skin, skull, hooves, claws, and teeth – are kept to replicate the whole. However, it is the entire body that is first subject to conversion into a souvenir.

The lethal shot and the movement of the hunter towards the dead animal mark the beginning of two kinds of reliving that take that particular hunt into the past and into the future. The hunter begins to relive the hunt as s/he speaks about it with colleagues and guides who might be present. In my experience, once a hunt has moved from an unfocused movement across, and an unfocused scanning of, a landscape to a focused movement towards a huntable animal, the hunter is so enveloped in the immediacy of the process that words and reflection are impossible. With the death of the animal the hunter begins to re-create the experience for himself or herself and for others. The hunter also begins the process of converting the hunted animal into a souvenir, and the first stage of this conversion is the photograph.

Snapshots from the Other Side

The photograph of the hunter posing with the dead animal shares many elements with a tourist's souvenir photographs, created at a place of significance in order to record being there for future display and reflection. A significant feature of touristic photographs, in which the tourist is present, is the relationship between the person and the site. In the act of sightseeing the tourist looks towards the sight of interest. But tourists do not usually ask to be photographed with their backs towards the camera

GARRY MARVIN

in the act of looking at a work of art in a gallery or when walking around a church. The act of recording a person at a place of significance involves a pause and a reversal of angle. In such photographs the site becomes the background, the tourist faces away from it, towards the camera and outwards to the future. Something similar occurs in hunting photographs. Most hunting photographs do not record the hunter in the act of hunting, they record the end of hunting. While hunting, the hunter is absorbed in looking outwards towards the animal (a parallel with the tourist who looks outwards to a site/sight of interest), and this is not usually recorded. Photographs recording the hunter with the dead animal reverse the angle of view: the hunter poses behind the animal, looks towards the camera, and not towards the animal. As with tourist photographs, trophy photographs involve a pause and a concern with pose.

In all hunting events I have witnessed, the posing of the hunter with the dead animal is very carefully managed because, as the hunters have commented, this is a moment that is unique and unrepeatable: it captures being there. In my experience, the posing of the animal is not, as others have argued, to pose the animal in the most lifelike position; hunters are not ashamed of their actions and do not seek to simulate life out of the death they have brought about.[18] Rather, they pose the animal to reveal the physical qualities that the hunter most admires, for example, its size, the quality of its horns or antlers, the size of teeth or paws, or its general beauty. What is also of great significance is creating the connection between the hunter and the hunted animal, for this animal is now a particular and a personal animal: it is the animal of the hunter. Such a photograph is very different from a tourist safari photograph featuring a wild animal. Here images of a lion or an elephant are of specific animals but they are also of an animal in general, an animal with which the tourist has only a fleeting encounter. A tourist might display such a photograph at home, but there is little that can be said about that specific animal because there has been little engagement with it. The hunting photograph is a record of a different order, for it is the record of a relationship that will be recounted in great detail later. The narrative of a hunting photograph involves accounts of how it was to be there, the difficulty or ease of approaching the animal, how and why that particular animal was selected, and how it was to take the shot.

The photograph marks the end of the fleshy, hunted animal and the beginning of the process of re-creating and re-enlivening it in a cultural form. In my experience, and from my reading of the literature of hunters, nature hunters have a highly developed aesthetic appreciation of the animals they choose to hunt. Their accounts of hunting involve descriptions of the pleasures of seeing the beauty of these animals and their ways of being in their natural environments. It is also a series of aesthetic appreciations, considerations, and judgments that draws the hunters' attention to an individual huntable animal on which to focus their sights, in order to make that animal theirs. With the death of the animal a new aesthetic enters, a personal aesthetic that guides the process of recapturing and fixing a sense of what that animal once was and how that animal was seen and experienced by the hunter.

Still Lives

At the point of preparing the hunting trophy most hunters seem to turn to the services of a professional taxidermist because, although they have a vision of what the mounted trophy should look like, they do not have the craft and artistic skills to realize this vision. Here I return to the comment that the trophy is in a part/whole relationship to the hunted animal for it can never be a complete animal. In an important and significant sense, the taxidermied mount is only a superficial animal; it is, literally, only skin deep, but that surface must be crafted to convey a sense of the whole. In this sense a mount is a simulacrum, "a thing having the appearance but not the substance or proper qualities of something" (*Oxford English Dictionary*). A trophy attempts to convey those proper qualities of the living and original animal, but it can never be more than an appearance. Hunters and taxidermists with whom I have spoken have commented that the ideal hunting trophy should be of the whole body, otherwise the trophy will always be partial and impoverished. However, most hunters do not seem to have the space to display all their trophies as complete bodies and, in the collections I have seen, heads are more common than complete bodies.[19] As with representations of people in paintings, photographs, and sculpture, it would seem that it is the head and face of the hunted animal that best conveys the essence of that animal, or can memorialize that animal; it is the part that is the most expressive and individual.

All hunters have told me that expressiveness is what they seek in a mounted trophy. A fine trophy head should communicate the spirit and essence of the animal. The pose in which it is mounted should also be natural, lifelike, and communicate lifefullness. As one taxidermist put it to me when discussing how he was going to mount a full leopard skin, "If it is not done well it appears that the leopard is not there." He also said that he refused to take on commissions when the client wanted something prepared in what he, the taxidermist, regarded as exaggerated, unnatural, overly aggressive, or demeaning poses. I have frequently heard criticisms of trophy mounts in these terms – or in terms of them being lifeless, or as representing stereotypical cultural images of animals – rather than capturing the essence of how the animal normally is in the wild. I questioned one friend about why he had chosen to have his brown bear mounted on all fours rather than having it rearing on two legs to show its full height and the size of its paws. He responded, "Because that is how they usually are, that is how it was when I saw it. Bears do not go around walking on two legs, snarling aggressively." Another friend, commenting on how poorly the natural wolfness of wolves were captured in two snarling heads, said, "This male is too exaggerated, too big, too wild, and with this female they have given her the teeth of a vampire!"

Memories as Reanimation

At the beginning of this chapter I referred to a hunter enshrining a trophy. From my reading and research I do not think that it would be appropriate to think of an enshrinement in the sense of honoring the dead animal as such, although it perhaps has elements of that. Rather, what is enshrined is the memory of the hunt represented in and by the memorial trophy. Hunters tell me that when they sit and contemplate their collection, each trophy unlocks their memory and they return, in their imagination, to how it was to be there on the hunting journey. They remember the pleasures and discomforts of travel, of being in different places, of the scents, sights, and sounds around them. They remember how their bodies responded to the weather and the terrain and how it was to inch themselves carefully towards their chosen animal. This is also how they narrate the significance of a trophy to those whom they invite to see their collection: "That day it was bitterly cold, we left at dawn and we were soon wet through, it took us five hours climbing to find the herd and then we had to crawl…" The description of being there and the approach is usually rich in detail but the moment of killing, unless it was a particularly skillful shot, is hardly elaborated. The kill is that which ends the hunt; to have hunted is the thing, to have been able to get into a position to take the shot.

The hunting trophy, without the hunter, is nothing more than a lifeless artifact. With its hunter it has a memory within which it can live. I believe that this artifact can best be interpreted as an enshrinement of a process, an engagement and a relationship that connects the hunter, the terrain, and the hunted animal. If the hunter has, in his or her terms, hunted properly and well, then the hunting trophy memorializes that hunting. As the hunter and philosopher Allen Jones comments on his style of hunting:

> Hunting is not an attempt to take possession of the animal ... I cannot possess the elk. It's dead. But I can possess the memory of it in the moment before I killed it, which is enough. It's more than enough. What I have brought away is my relationship to the animal, not the animal itself.[20]

NOTES

1 Material for this chapter has been generated from a range of literature written by hunters, but it is also firmly based on an ongoing anthropological ethnographic project that involves fieldwork with hunters in Europe.

2 Ted Kerasote, *Bloodties: Nature, Culture, and the Hunt* (New York: Kodansha International, 1993), pp. 87, 85.

3 Stephen Kellert, "Attitudes and Characteristics of Hunters and Antihunters," *Transactions of the North American Wildlife Resources* 43 (1978): 412–23.

4 Ibid., p. 414

5 Ibid., p. 417.

6 Ibid., p. 415.

7 Ibid., p. 413.

8 Jim Posewitz, *Beyond Fair Chase: The Ethic and Tradition of Hunting* (Helena: Falcon, 1994), p. 57. See also Garry Marvin, "Challenging Animals: Purpose and Process in Hunting," in Sarah Pilgrim and Jules Pretty (eds.) *Nature and Culture* (London: Earthscan, 2010) for a fuller account of the nature of hunting from the perspectives of nature hunters.

9 Arjun Appadurai, *The Social Life of Things: Commodities in Cultural Perspective* (Cambridge: Cambridge University Press, 1988), pp. 3, 4. Here Appadurai is actually citing Georg Simmel. A fuller account of the nature of trophies would allow me to explore the idea that trophies have no intrinsic value as objects and that value is generated in social and cultural contexts. In this chapter my focus is on issues relating to how a trophy is obtained and how its value is generated through the process of individual engagement. Here I am unable to discuss another class of trophy: the trophy as record. Many hunters hunt primarily to obtain trophies of a particular sort and here value is constituted in

GARRY MARVIN

a different manner. For example, the significance or value of the largeness or otherwise measureable trophy quality (rareness might also be important here) of animals that such hunters seek can only be fully understood in the context of those hunters' social, biographical, and autobiographical relationships with record books compiled by associations such as the Safari Club International or the Boone and Crockett Club.

10 Here I am setting aside issues of judgment of the qualities of trophies and the award for trophies that are made for including trophies in record books. Such judgments relate to the material qualities of the trophy rather than to how that trophy was obtained.

11 Susan Stewart, "Objects of Desire," in *On Longing: Narratives of the Miniature, the Gigantic, the Souvenir, the Collection* (Durham, NC: Duke University Press), p. 135.

12 Dean MacCannell, *The Tourist: A New Theory of the Leisure Class* (New York: Schocken), p. 147.

13 Stewart, "Objects of Desire," p. 135.

14 The exception to this would be cases in which a trophy collector was so keen to have a specimen of a particular quality that he paid someone else to hunt and shoot it for him. Hunting colleagues have claimed to me that such practices, which they despise, do exist, but I have no evidence with which to document them.

15 Stewart, "Objects of Desire," p. 136.

16 Ibid.

17 It might be possible to make the argument that the hunter who takes home the meat of a hunted animal and then butchers and preserves it for later eating is also creating a souvenir object and that the eating of such meat is an event of remembrance.

18 See Linda Kalof and Amy Fitzgerald, "Reading the Hunting Trophy: Exploring the Display of Dead Animals in Hunting Magazines," *Visual Studies* 18, no. 2 (2003): 112–22 for arguments relating to dissimulation in trophy photographs.

19 Hunters I know best also decide to have non-taxidermized mounts prepared. These include highly polished half-skulls of animals with horns or antlers attached, mounted on a wooden shield, and polished tusks of wild boar, again fixed to a wooden mount. Such objects commemorate a hunt and animal but they seem to represent the hunters' lesser concern with the individuality of the animal.

20 Allen Jones, *A Quiet Place of Violence: Hunting and Ethics in the Missouri River Breaks* (Bozeman, MT: Bangtail Press, 1997), p. 104.

PART III

EATING NATURE NATURALLY

CHAPTER 10

THE CARNIVOROUS HERBIVORE

Hunting and Culture in Human Evolution

Who said that humans evolved as hunters? This challenge comes not only from those suggesting moral fulfillment in eating vegetables, but also from those merely questioning the morality of hunting. The answer is that our physiology does, as do some unique characteristics, the archaeological record, and especially the ecology of our Ice Age ancestors. As to morality itself, it arises as a necessary byproduct of very early hunting. This does not mean, of course, that what *is* also *ought* to be, but it forces us into a more honest and realistic debate about nature versus nurture.

Unique human characteristics suggest that we have been hunting since the earliest stages in human evolution. We possess an enzyme to digest elastin, a fiber of animal origins; we require vitamin B_{12}, a molecule made only by animals; and we can change trans-fats produced in the rumen of cows or deer into the health-promoting conjugated linoleic acid.[1] We could only evolve such biochemistry if, from antiquity onwards, the meat and fat of animals were an essential part of our diet.

We also have several curious athletic abilities. For instance, we are the only mammal that can stand balancing on one leg.[2] Many birds can do it, but no mammal can except us. What good might that do? It appears that this ability is crucial when stalking prey. We cannot stalk unless we can freeze in mid-stride, balancing on one leg, whenever the prey raises its head to look about. We must balance without a motion, lest the prey notice us and flee. That must not happen too often to a hunter, lest failure results in want, weakness, loss of status, and eventually, life. After all, we stalked not only prey, but also enemies, the deadliest test of stalking skills.

We alone can hurl projectiles with great precision and speed,[3] a valued ability in hunting, sport, and military activities. Did natural selection punish those less competent at throwing missiles? Dire need drove much of the life of our ancient ancestors. Throwing rocks, sticks, and spears provisioned the skillful, both then and now, with high-quality food for themselves and their families.

Moreover, we are the only mammal that skillfully mimics sound (the biological prerequisite of spoken language and music),[4] and we are the most sophisticated imitator of visual actions (the biological basis of technology, culture, and art). Regardless of the reason why these characteristics evolved, they contributed significantly to hunting success.

Furthermore, human beings can develop supreme self-discipline, bordering on the pathological. We need such fortitude when confronting predators and stalking prey or foe. We may have to endure prolonged discomfort, even pain, lest the prey or enemy detect us, or the predator loses its fear. Again, one cannot say that self-discipline evolved because of hunting, but it would certainly help. Yet the archaeological evidence for hunting in early deposits is scarce and all too often questionable.[5] There is little doubt, however, that we emerged as sophisticated hunters late in our evolution, able to live even in icy landscapes with long winters, surviving entirely off large mammals.

A Living Oxymoron: *Homo*, the Meat-Eating Herbivore

There is, however, a conundrum: the pattern of human evolution resembles that of large herbivores, not omnivores or carnivores. Our ancestors' geographic patterns and the timing of their species-formation – namely, how they adapted to landscapes from equator to pole – mimic those of deer, sheep, goats, and cattle but not of large omnivores (e.g., bears) or of large carnivores.[6] Just like other big herbivores, the hominid family began with primitive species in tropical forests. From there we branched out into the savannah, an open habitat characterized by well-spaced trees amidst a rich lower layer of grasses, herbs, and shrubs. The next advance was into the open, treeless steppe, a more seasonal and drier habitat.

After that we moved into temperate zones and deserts, and from there into the rich periglacial landscapes close to continental glaciers. Finally, modern humans migrated into arctic and alpine landscapes. Within each major biome (tropical forest, savannah, steppe, etc.) herbivore lineages generate two or more eco-species that differ ecologically, while retaining essentially the same body plan. When they colonize predator-free marine islands they shrink into "island dwarfs." Some, including humans, also shrank into "tropical forest dwarfs" (pygmies). In the cold but productive periglacial landscapes, they ballooned along with other herbivores into "Grotesque Ice Age Giants."[7] *Homo* followed this herbivorous pattern, from the so-called "hobbit" (*Homo floresiensis*) on the Indonesian island of Flores, to the Neanderthals and Cro-Magnons of Ice Age Eurasia. Carnivores evolve neither island dwarfs nor grotesque giants. In short, in spite of our meat-eating habits or digestive physiology, humans evolved much like large mammalian herbivores. We are a living oxymoron, a carnivorous, even cannibalistic, herbivore.

Indeed, the ecological fate of herbivores is to be caught and eaten by carnivores, and so the primary goal of herbivores is to escape them! We are no exception.[8] While zoologists[9] and some primatologists[10] recognized the significance of predation in our evolution, this insight is rather recent in orthodox anthropology. Humans eventually thwarted predators, and even hunted them. Still, predators may systematically hunt us to this day.[11]

"Man the hunter" could not evolve before overcoming "man the hunted." Freedom from attention by predators is crucial for hunters, for they cannot stalk their prey if their focus is broken by the threat of predators. Moreover, they cannot keep their kill unless it is uncontested by predators. No vocal imitation of prey would be possible if doing so attracted predators that would make the hunter their prey. Furthermore, hunting could not evolve in humans without an ability to kill quickly and silently, as screaming by the prey would attract predators – and in the case of young prey, a screaming victim would bring on a defending mother or an agitated herd. Also, predators must not follow the hunter's scent trail to camp or clean up the scraps around the hunter's camp, as that would endanger the community. Anti-predator adaptations must even go beyond protecting the hunter. They must allow effective foraging by mothers with children. Let us look at these strategies in more detail.

Our anti-predator adaptations are very demanding. This is illustrated by how quickly lions and hyenas switch to preying on people, as seen currently in areas with large concentrations of essentially defenseless refugees.[12] To large predators, humans are prey. Prior to evolving into humans, our ape ancestors climbed trees to escape being killed and eaten. However, hominids could not have evolved into humans until they survived – consistently – on the ground, away from trees, while surrounded by large predators at night when we are almost blind and defenseless.[13] The miracle of human evolution is that we succeeded in surviving large predators on the ground at night, and did so effectively for decades on end, despite crying babies, snoring sleepers, or lusty lovers. Humans are the only primates that can escape predation in the absence of trees, and can thereby disperse across open terrain safely (and thus out of Africa). In the process humans lost some of their ancient ape-climbing specialization, the only primate to do so.[14] Even infant gorillas need trees for security.

Large herbivores in open savannah landscapes inevitably join others for security in the "selfish herd." In these groups, unrelated individuals cluster together, seeking safety in numbers. Deadly strife, so fixed into the biology of territorial ancestors from the tropical forests, is now intolerable. Individuals not only become tolerant of strangers, but their weapons lose potency, in our case through the reduction of canine teeth. A comparable change in weapons can also be seen in the evolution of deer, horses, rhinos, and various extinct lineages of large herbivores.[15] Other ancestral anti-predator adaptations from the savannah are our upright (periscope) posture, long limbs, large, high-placed eyes, keen vision, and very noisy disposition. Originally such traits were highly adaptive for spotting predators across a barrier of high savannah grasses, prior to alerting the group vocally for flight into trees.[16]

In addition, we exploited the weaknesses of predators. We took advantage of their unwillingness to penetrate a wall, their extreme aversion to thorns,[17] their sensitivity to their own species' threat vocalizations, and their strong aversion to injury. Large predators are hypochondriacs and have to be in order to survive and prosper. At night, we could escape predators by building a thorn-covered, domed enclosure on the ground, imitating species-specific threat sounds from within – aided, if need be, by a sharp jab with a pointed stick through the thorn walls. Crucial here is the refinement of our ancestral savannah-ape vocalization into vocal mimicry, the biological prerequisite for language and music.

However, this is not enough. To succeed in the open steppe away from trees, selection favored large body size, dark skin, and the use of tools as weapons. It also promoted new ways to intimidate large predators in daylight, while intellectual forethought (planning) allowed for the systematic destruction of their helpless young. Only consistent intimidation and reduction of predators would allow foraging by women and children, or for the hunters to retain their prey after a hunt. Large body size increases muscle power to effectively use clubs;[18] dark body color is universal in species that confront predators;[19] "mobbing" of predators is common in large prey species, especially if done assertively by a group together with aggressive vocalizations that target specific predators. Elsewhere I have postulated these as the basic anti-predator adaptations of early humans within Africa,[20] and they work to this day. However, for people trying to enter late Pleistocene North America these were not enough, because mega-carnivores apparently kept people out until they went extinct.[21]

Food Safety, Weapons, and the Birth of Ethics

The great cost of hunting would be pointless, however, if the meat we procured was diseased or heavily parasitized. That is, hunting had to yield safe meat safely. Chimpanzees offer a glimpse into these matters.[22] They hunt communally, then grasp their prey and swing it in an arc to smash its skull against the ground or a tree. That is, the prey is almost instantly dispatched by stunning. There is little time for the prey to defend itself and inflict injury on the hunter. A second way chimps dispatch small prey quickly is to pin it and then bite into the skull, crushing it.[23] "Man the hunter" had to routinely debilitate his prey, but as we lack the chimps' strength and massive canines, clearly we had to do so by other methods – i.e., tools.

Moreover, chimps demonstrate how to select *safe* meat. After dispatching the prey, they quickly tear it to pieces and consume it, with little evidence left behind of what happened. The meat is consumed *fresh*. Basically, chimps do not scavenge. That is very sensible, as meat in the moist tropics deteriorates quickly. It soon contains pathogenic bacteria and their toxins, botulism being the deadliest. The chimp's meat-eating strategy is clever: it focuses on young or arboreal prey, which are the least likely to be infected with parasites and pathogens. Consuming prey weakened by old age, disease, parasites, or injury increases the chances of ingesting pathogens. Chimps thus procure safe meat safely.

Hominids had to achieve the same results, if hunting was to provide sustenance in an ongoing fashion. Consequently, our hunting began most likely by killing small, preferably young animals. Scavenging was possible only during long-term aridity, when small pieces of flesh on a carcass dry quickly, bypassing bacterial fermentation. Scavenging probably yielded little meat, but provided marrow fat. Chimps consuming prey focus first on fat. So do carnivores.

"Man the hunter" faced another problem: hunting could not evolve unless the earliest of humans avoided using deadly hunting weapons on each other. That is, they had to be able to control lethal weapons socially, a unique requirement.[24] Humans differ from other animals in using tools as weapons. Some tools, such as clubs, allow us to stun or outright kill an opponent. That's unique! No other mammal can do that. In all other animal combat, the aggressor faces retaliation by the victim.[25] The more effective the retaliation, the more selection against overt aggression. Natural selection thus limits the use of deadly weapons. But none of this applies when tools become weapons. By stunning or killing an opponent instantly, a human aggressor escapes the corrective effects of retaliation. Therefore, to limit the use of tools as weapons on fellow humans, our human ancestors had to learn to rely on social mechanisms.

Let me illustrate the obverse: human bites are very dangerous, and readily lead to deadly infections. If an aggressor bites, he will be bitten back. The victim thus inflicts severe punishment on the aggressor, retaliating, giving tit for tat. Consequently, we evolved a fairly reliable inhibition against biting fellow humans, because aggressors that bit did not live long. While we thus have an instinctive inhibition against using our teeth in combat, we have no such instinctive inhibition against using clubs or rifles. Against tools as weapons we have at best effective social taboos, differentiating *right* from *wrong* actions.

The first tool used as a hunting weapon was probably the digging stick. Access to hidden plant food in the hard soils of dry grasslands was made possible by a digging stick, as our fingers and nails are virtually useless for that purpose.[26] Such a stick had to be made from tough, hard branches, and the first stone tools were most likely woodworking tools for removing thorns and shaving a point on digging sticks. This was the primary tool of females and youths, which they used when foraging for plant foods in the dry season. However, such a stick is also ideal for stunning small prey, and thus a safe way to augment the diet with animal protein, as tubers, roots, and corns are deficient in proteins and fats.

However, digging sticks can also be used in fighting, and can deliver a severe blow to the head. Consequently, from the outset there had to be selection pressures to limit the use of tools as weapons. There had to be learned – that is, culturally transmitted – rules about the appropriate use of weapons. At the same time there had to be a refinement of empathy for the stricken individuals, as well as a refinement of behaviors eliciting empathy, such as infantile crying and begging. With tools as weapons, non-verbal communication had to be refined,[27] a situation favoring the evolution of language. With weapons, dominant individuals could do terrible things to family or kin. They had to be restrained from doing violence to relatives, yet retain their capacity to defeat enemies.

Such social control and refined empathy took time to evolve, as is suggested by the very thick, helmet-like skullcaps of *Homo erectus*. That is, human skulls arguably evolved initially to take the brunt of being hit with sticks! A mop of thick hair on the skull may have cushioned blows suffered in disputes. Ultimately, however, the choice to limit the aggressive use of weapons had to be made by individuals. Consequently, this form of social control meant the ability to recognize *good from evil* – and pass on those insights. Hunting weapons illustrate how potentially deadly artifacts can generate "morality."[28] This had to be so from the very dawn of tool use.

Thinking and Acting with Spears

We have already seen that hunting in hominids arose and evolved in a different manner than in chimpanzees. The small-bodied savannah apes from which we evolved, *Australopithecus*, did not have the strength to catch and smash prey by hand as male chimps do. Our entry into systematic hunting began most likely with the stunning of small prey, including newborn ungulates, using a digging stick. We mastered that way of hunting in about half a million years. During that time we still lived alongside the large, robust savannah apes. At the end of that period we switched from the clubbing of small and medium-sized prey to the killing of larger, even dangerous prey that could not be readily hunted with clubs. The wooden spear's appearance in mid-Pleistocene times speaks of a quantum leap in our understanding of killing.

Spears are problematic weapons, especially primitive ones that have only fire-hardened tips. They can be used to kill prey safely only under very specific, quite limited circumstances. The presence of butchered giant herbivores in the archaeological record early in the Pleistocene indicates that humans had discovered how to kill such herbivores safely. Large prey had to be stuck, say, in a pit or a bog. Here it can neither escape nor attack but is, nonetheless, difficult to kill and dangerous to approach. The quickest way to kill is to puncture both sides of the thoracic cavity with a hand-held lance, which causes the lungs to collapse, leading promptly to suffocation. It's a fairly fast but above all a safe way to dispatch trapped but dangerous mega-herbivores.

Unfortunately, spears – even modern versions – kill slowly. This suggests that throwing spears were initially used to wound harmless prey, after which it was tracked down and dispatched. This, however, requires tracking skills, the reading of small signs and shaping such information into testable hypotheses. Tracking is difficult. It can be taught, but requires fairly sophisticated communication. It also requires an imaginative, alert mind and the ability to predict the actions of the prey. Hunting with primitive spears required fairly sophisticated communication and cooperation, as well as accurate information about prey, hunting strategies, and tactics. Tracking is "reading"; it's the original thriller or detective story.

In addition to tracking, successfully following wounded prey takes great endurance. Herein lies the origin of our exceptional endurance in running and walking compared to other mammals. We can run down not only wounded but also healthy game, given the right circumstances. The original "marathon" resulted in the collection of precious food, the all-important communal recognition and ego-enhancement for the hunters, as well as the reproductive advantages that go with it. The use of spears was thus instrumental in the evolution of many of our most valued intellectual virtues and athletic capacities.

However, it also gave rise to some of the worst. It starts bio-degradation. The invention of spears would allow *Homo erectus* to hunt down the robust, largely vegetarian australopithecines and spear them to death. The heavy skulls of robust australopithecines would be too resistant to clubbing. That would explain why the extinction of robust australopithecines coincides with the advent of spears. We eliminated a competitor. His food was now our own. The history of "man the exterminator" had begun.

Ride 'em Cowboy?

The emergence of our species, *Homo sapiens*, followed the Riss Glaciation and was accompanied by a profound improvement in the hunting spear: a sharp stone blade was hafted to the tip. Subsequently, two extremely different ways of hunting arose, both using spears with hafted stone points, but of different design. Both were sophisticated weapons taking design to the limits of the materials available. In one case it was the stabbing spear as used by Neanderthal man, in the other it was the thrown spear as crafted by Cro-Magnons, our direct ancestors. Although the two peoples hunted in different ways, for a student of large herbivores it's not too difficult to decipher what they did. Both peoples lived in cold glacial areas year round. The attraction was almost certainly the "fleshpots" of large herbivores in the fertile periglacial landscape. However, despite the differences between Neanderthals and Cro-Magnons, the origins of both ways of life were adaptations to desert conditions. Since mega-herbivores are not habitat specific, one way to survive extreme aridity is to focus on mega-herbivores as prey, the Neanderthals' choice. The second way is to exploit the desert in a micro-fashion as hunter-gatherers, akin to the !Kung (Bushmen) of the Kalahari. This was the path taken by modern humans.

To understand the differences in hunting between Neanderthals and Cro-Magnons, one needs to distinguish two opposite manners of minimizing injury in combat. One either stays beyond the reach of the opponent's weapons, or one gets in so close that the opponent cannot use his weapons. One can either use throwing spears and stay beyond the reach of the prey, or close in and distract the prey while another teammate delivers a fatal thrust with a hand-held spear. Our Upper Paleolithic ancestors chose the former route, Neanderthals the latter. The former is "distant confrontation" hunting, the latter is "close-quarters confrontation" hunting.

The Neanderthal diet was carnivorous.[29] They were superlative hunters.[30] But they did not hunt from a distance with ranged weapons. One hunter drew the attention and attack of the prey onto himself. As the beast rushed in, a second hunter grabbed the animal's hair with his powerful hands[31] while biting into the skin to stabilize himself, leading instantly to a "rodeo" with the enraged beast. He preferred prey with long hair to hang on to. Then the first hunter jumped in and thrust the hand-held spear into the beast's inner organs. However, that spear had to be built so as to retain a cutting edge and maintain deep penetration even if the tip was sheared off when hitting bone; Neanderthals thrust with brutish strength.[32] Consequently, a very stout stone tip is required. Nor must it break inside the beast or come loose from the pole, rendering the spear useless. A thrust with poor penetration would instantly put the hunter in danger. These stone spear points resemble medieval boar spears in size and shape. The hafting material was a plastic of great strength made from birch sap.[33] The "crude" spear points may be chipped discards. A massive hand-held boar spear in experienced hands will kill quickly, unlike the narrow-bladed throwing spear. This "rodeo" hypothesis has been confirmed by the pattern of bone breakages commonly seen in Neanderthal fossils, which resemble those in rodeo cowboys.[34]

By contrast, there are few injuries in the Upper Paleolithic skeletons of Cro-Magnons. Their throwing spears had thin, narrow, but sharp blades. When the stone tip hits a bone in the prey, it is likely to shatter. About half of the spears thrown are likely to hit bone and shatter. The other half may penetrate deeply, leading to hemorrhaging from narrow wound channels. This is not likely to kill a large mega-herbivore quickly and may require of the hunters superlative abilities and coordination with others to evade the wounded beast. One probably needed a hunting party of eight or more to bring down the prey quickly.[35] The throwing spear underwent a further improvement via the atl-atl (spear thrower), a device that extended the hunter's throwing arm. The spear could now be hurled farther and with greater force.

The primary prey of Upper Paleolithic hunters were reindeer, and to hunt them successfully the hunter had to regularly intercept the migratory herds. Since reindeer time their annual migrations precisely, success depended on the hunters' ability to use chronological time. That is, one cannot exploit reindeer for food unless one has a calendar to predict the arrival of the herds. Intercepted reindeer can be killed in excess and their meat and fat stored for the lean months ahead.[36] Upper Paleolithic hunters grew luxurious bodies and exceptionally large brains. They innovated in art and music, diversified their food base, and invented the division of labor.[37] This outpouring of human culture is thus linked to both a luxurious development of people and a luxurious periglacial fauna. Our existence then was based on supplying animal food in great abundance year-round. Food could only come from animals during the long winters in the sight of huge continental glaciers. Hunting and fighting sustained these superlatively developed Ice Age humans who left us vivid images of their infatuation with wildlife deep in European caves.[38]

Human evolution owes much to hunting, even though that relationship is complex. Some of our biochemistry could only have evolved if, for long periods, we fed exclusively on meat. A number of uniquely human characteristics are logical only in the context of hunting. Yet we are a living oxymoron: a carnivorous herbivore. In solving the characteristically herbivorous problem of how to escape predation, we began to become human. The complex tool use and visual/vocal mimicry this success required were the precursors of technology, art, even spoken language and music. The roots of morality reside in our use of tools as hunting weapons, which can only be controlled by social convention and the idea of "good and bad." Furthermore, the spear required us to have great observational and hypothetic-deductive skills in tracking, and its improvement split humanity into at least two branches, one of which was ours: the clever and inventive generalist hunter. Therefore, before discussing the morality of hunting, we need to consider hunting and meat eating in our evolution. It may be that questioning the morality of hunting questions our humanity.

NOTES

1   Anu M. Turpeinen et al., "Bioconversion of Vaccenic Acid to Conjugated Linoleic Acid in Humans," *American Journal of Clinical Nutrition* 76, no. 3 (2002): 504–10.
2   Valerius Geist, *Life Strategies, Human Evolution, Environmental Design* (New York: Springer, 1978).
3   Thorwald Ewe, "Präzisionswunder Mensch: Hochleistungswerfer *Homo sapiens*," *Spiegel Online*, July 21, 2007. Available at www.spiegel.de/wissenschaft/mensch/0,1518,495690,00.html (accessed December 12, 2009).
4   Geist, *Life Strategies*, p. 250.
5   Craig B. Stanford, *The Hunting Apes* (Princeton: Princeton University Press, 1999).
6   Valerius Geist, *Mountain Sheep: A Study in Behaviour and Evolution* (Chicago: University of Chicago Press, 1971); Geist, *Life Strategies*, p. 211; Valerius Geist, "On Speciation in Ice Age Mammals, with Special Reference to Deer and Sheep," *Canadian Journal of Zoology* 65 (1987): 1067–84; Valerius Geist, *The Deer of the World: A Study in Evolution and Behaviour* (Mechanicsburg: Stackpole Books, 1998).
7   Geist, *Life Strategies*, p. 211; Geist, *Deer of the World*.
8   Donna Hart and Robert W. Sussman, *Man the Hunted* (Philadelphia: Westview Press, 2009).
9   Geist, *Life Strategies*; Valerius Geist, "Did Predators Keep Humans Out of North America?" in Julian Clutton-Brock (ed.) *The Walking Larder* (London: Unwin Hyman, 1989), pp. 282–94.
10 Adrian Kortland, "How Might Early Hominids Have Defended Themselves Against Large Predators and Food Competitors?" *Journal of Human Evolution* 9 (1980): 79–112.
11 Jim Corbett, *The Jim Corbett Omnibus* (Delhi: Oxford University Press, 1991); Peter H. Capstick, *Maneaters* (Long Beach: Safari Press, 1981),

pp. 108–14; Mikhail P. Pavlov, *The Wolf* (Moscow: Lesnaya Promyshkennost, 1982); Mikhail P. Pavlov, "The Danger of Wolves to Humans," in Will Graves, *Wolves in Russia* (Calgary: Detselig, 2007), pp. 173–94; Johnny Loe and Elvin Röskraft, "Large Carnivores and Human Safety," *Ambio* 33, no. 6 (2004): 283–88; Antti Lappalainen, *Suden jäljet* (The Tracks of the Wolf) (Hämeenlinna: Karisto Oy, 2005); Robert R. Frump, *The Man-Eaters of Eden: Life and Death in Kruger National Park* (Guilford: Lyons Press, 2006); Will N. Graves, *Wolves in Russia: Anxiety through the Ages* (Calgary: Detselig, 2007); Jean-Marc Moriceau, *Histoire du méchant loup: 3 000 attaques sur l'homme en France* (Paris: Fayard, 2007); Valerius Geist, "Death by Wolves and the Power of Myths: The Kenton Carnegie Tragedy," *Fair Chase* 33 (2008): 29–33; Valerius Geist, "Commentary: The Danger of Wolves," *Wildlife Professional* 2, no. 4 (2008): 34–5.

12 Frump, *The Man-Eaters of Eden*.

13 Geist, *Life Strategies*, p. 250; Geist, "Did Predators Keep Humans Out?"

14 Charles Oxnard, *Uniqueness and Diversity in Human Evolution* (Chicago: University of Chicago Press, 1975).

15 Discussed in detail in Geist, *Deer of the World*; mentioned earlier in Geist, *Life Strategies*.

16 Geist, *Life Strategies*, p. 216.

17 Kortland, "How Might Early Hominids Have Defended Themselves."

18 Geist, *Life Strategies*, p. 226.

19 Geist, *Deer of the World*, pp. 34–5.

20 Geist, *Life Strategies*, p. 250; Geist, "Did Predators Keep Humans Out?"

21 Geist, "Did Predators Keep Humans Out?"

22 Stanford, *The Hunting Apes*.

23 Ibid.

24 Valerius Geist, "The Evolution of Horn-Like Organs," *Behaviour* 27, nos. 3–4 (1966): 175–214.

25 Ibid.; Geist, *Life Strategies*, pp. 62–80.

26 Ibid., pp. 247–51.

27 Ibid,, pp. 333–8.

28 Ibid., p. 76.

29 Michael P. Richards et al., "Stable Isotope Evidence for Increasing Dietary Breadth in the European Mid-Upper Paleolithic," *Proceedings of the National Academy of Sciences* 98 (2001): 6528–32. While Upper Paleolithic sites indicate a broad-spectrum diet including freshwater fish, mollusks, and birds, that of Neanderthal is narrowly confined to meat of large herbivores. Their diet was similar to that of large carnivores.

30 Archaeological evidence reveals that Neanderthal sites contain the bones of mid-aged horses, which means the healthiest, most alert, and able horses, but also the fattest ones and thus the very best to eat. Przewalskie's horses, which Neanderthal hunted, are powerful, fast, agile, and aggressive crea-

tures. Neanderthal hunters were so competent that they could literally pick any healthy horse for food. Philippe Fernandez, Jean-Luc Guadelli, and Philippe Fosse, "Applying Dynamics and Comparing Life Tables for Pleistocene Equidae in Anthropic (Bau de l'Aubesier, Combe-Grenal) and Carnivore (Fouvent) Contexts with Modern Feral Horse Populations (Akagera, Pryor Mountain)," *Journal of Archaeological Science* 33 (2006): 176–84.

31 Geist, *Life Strategies*, pp. 284–300; Valerius Geist, "Neanderthal the Hunter," *Natural History* 90, no. 1 (1981): 26–36.

32 M. T. Black, "The 'Trunk Torsion Hypothesis' and Neandertal Superior Pubic Ramal Morphology," *Abstracts for the Paleoanthropology Society Meetings*, Columbus, Ohio, USA, April 27–8, 1999, p. A2; cited in Glenn Morton, "Neanderthal Origin of Bull Fighting?" March 18, 2000. Available at www.asa3.org/archive/asa/200003/0253.html (accessed December 7, 2009).

33 Johan Koller, Ursula Baumer, and Dietrich Mania, "High-Tech in the Middle Paleolithic: Neanderthal Manufactured Pitch Identified," *European Journal of Archeology* 14 (2001): 385–97.

34 Thomas D. Berger and Erik Trinkaus, "Patterns of Trauma Among the Neanderthals," *Journal of Archeological Science* 22, no. 6 (November 1995): 841–52. Compare with Steven Mithen, *The Prehistory of the Mind* (New York: Thames and Hudson, 1996), p. 126: "A very high proportion of Neanderthals suffered from stress fractures and degenerative diseases. In fact they show a very similar pattern of physical injuries to rodeo riders today."

35 Geist, "Did Predators Keep Humans Out?"

36 Valerius Geist, "Of Reindeer and Man, Modern and Neanderthal: A Creation Story Founded on a Historic Perspective on How to Conserve Wildlife, Woodland Caribou in Particular," *Rangifer* 14, special issue no. 14 (2003): 57–63.

37 Stephen L. Kuhn and Mary C. Stiner, "What's a Mother to Do? The Division of Labor among Neandertals and Modern Humans in Eurasia," *Current Anthropology* 47, no. 6 (December 2006): 953–80.

38 R. Dale Guthrie, *The Nature of Paleolithic Art* (Chicago: University of Chicago Press, 2004). See also Geist, *Life Strategies*, pp. 322–3.

CHAPTER II

THE FEAR OF THE LORD
Hunting as if the Boss is Watching

You see what we object to in this spirit is that one side of him is rotting and putrefying, the other side sound and healthy, and it all depends on which side of him you touch whether you see the dawn again or no.[1]

Nothing Wants to Die

Most people like meat and value hunting, which is almost universally considered a prestigious affair. Yet hunters commonly perceive that animals love to live and do not want to die, as they might scream, express pain, and attempt to escape. At the very least, animals normally do not grant the humans permission to kill them, leaving the hunter in a position of debt. This is reflected in the common belief that "the stealing of a life calls for a life in return."[2] The most straightforward response to this ethical principle would be for the hunter to give his own life – not very tantalizing, and in the end, useful only once – or, alternatively, to give something with a value equivalent to the life of the animal. As this exchange does not always take place, hunting is often understood as unethical, an asymmetric relationship between game and hunter. This dilemma between the drive for killing and the bad feelings associated with it has been termed *Tiertöterskrupulantismus* (the experience of scruples about the killing of animals) by Rudolf Bilz and he identified it as a universal psychological principle.[3] All over the world hunters show scruples when killing animals and are ridden by guilt after the hunt.[4] This is expressed in moral sentiments, hunting habits, and in myths: South African G/wi were certain that antelopes hated them since God had told the antelopes that human fires were used for cooking them.[5] The Chenchu of Southern India told a myth where animals came together to discuss how best they could avoid being caught and slaughtered.[6]

Predation becomes all the more objectionable when animals are considered to be human-like, social beings capable of emotions: a hunter chases game that, in another world, has a family waiting. The Algonquins, for example, believed that animals could talk and think and were only outwardly different from humans.[7] The Huaulu of the Moluccas were convinced that animals lived in subterranean buildings that looked like human houses and had *mattiulu*, a soul or animating principle,[8] just as the Latin word "animal" derives from *anima*, "soul." Iglulik Eskimo[9] felt bad because they had to kill animals which had souls.[10] Such conceptions result in a fear of retaliation: Navaho hunters refused to bring home a deer if the dying animal gave a warning shout.[11] Tapirs passing by a grill could recognize the traces of the slaughter of one of their kind and would try to roast the Aparai hunters in French Guiana in revenge.[12]

An Eye for an Eye, a Tooth for a Tooth

To make matters worse, most wild game is protected by a mythical figure, the Master or Mistress of Animals. This designation derives from the Greek *pótnia therōn*, going back to Minoan times and having Near Eastern origins. This strong ruler over the beasts is often depicted tightly holding two animals in his or her fists. In Greek mythology, the Mistress of Animals was the hunting goddess Artemis, later Diana to the Romans. In other regions of the world, this being is known either as the Master or by similar appellations like Mother or Father of Animals, Lord, Ruler, Guardian, or Owner of Animals. This concept is a common worldwide phenomenon and not restricted to specific forms of subsistence or social organization. Foragers (like the Chenchu, Huaulu, San, Pygmies, Cree, Eskimo, Warrau, Selknam, Yamana) from different continents know such a figure. Even in peasant or industrial societies (e.g., in Europe or India), some well-known saints or fairytale characters are really Animal Masters: The Wild Men, Rübezahl (the Silesian Ruler of the Mountains), or Saint Hubertus and Saint Eustace, who, in Christian mythology, protect does from the hunters,[13] as does a Hermit in India, who admonishes the hunting king:

> Why should his tender form expire,
> As blossoms perish in the fire?
> How could that gentle life endure
> The deadly arrow, sharp and sure?
>
> Restore your arrow to the quiver;
> To you were weapons lent
> The broken-hearted to deliver,
> Not strike the innocent.[14]

The Masters of the Animals are often imagined as being akin to the animals, as in Lakandon myths from Mexico where animals are the Animal Master's children.[15] The Taulipang from Brazil likewise held Keyeme to be Father of all Animals, the birds being his grandchildren.[16]

This protective figure returns like for like: the Huaulu Lord of the Forest hunted humans just as they hunted animals.[17] At the Aztec feast of Quecholli drives were held in which humans were chased as deer of the goddess Mixcoatl.[18]

By and large, the Animal Guardian shows astonishing similarities on a worldwide basis: its outward guise can be that of a human or an animal. Otherwise, it appears half-man, half-beast, riding an animal, living beneath the ground, deep in the forest or in the waters. It exhibits many corporeal anomalies: its feet may point in the wrong direction, putting the hunters off the scent, as in the case of the Corupira of South American Indians.[19] Such feet also mark the misanthropic Sasabonsum of the Ashanti and other peoples from the Gold Coast, who was furthermore characterized by a sound front and a putrefying back (cf. the epigraph). This two-sided nature is typical for the Owners of the Animals. It points to their ambivalent nature and affiliation to the realm of the animals. The long-haired Forest Woman of the Mesoamerican Maya reveals her nature by her bony back, as does the Nordic Mistress of Animals, the *skogsfru*.[20] The Estonian forest-spirit appears as a man on his front and as a moss-grown tree trunk from behind.[21] The Lords of the Forest of the Huaulu, the *kaitahu upuam*, were envisaged to look like animals or else like humans with animal feet.[22] Goat-feet betray the animal side of the Russian forest-spirit Ljeschi or of Rübezahl, who was described as half-man, half-billy goat in the seventeenth century.[23] The Keeper of the Buffaloes of the West African Hausa is half-man, half-buffalo.[24] Even though human figures are rare in Upper Paleolithic cave paintings, those pictured are often half-man, half-animal: for example, the famous sorcerers of the Trois Frères cave,[25] or the engraving of a man with a horse's tail on a small stone plate from Lourdes, both in France. These Paleolithic therio-anthropomorphic beings might hint at the fact that even 20,000 years ago there already existed a figure like the Master of Animals.

The ambivalence of this being shown in its outer form symbolizes the tightrope walk between the human drive for hunting and the subliminal imperative to let the animals live. It also mirrors their character: the Shoshone and Gosiute believed that the Keeper of Game could help hunters as well as punish them.[26] Among the South African Bushmen, /Kaggen was reckoned unpredictable and was feared as well as revered, for he could be both evil and good, bring health or sickness.[27] If hunters leave the Animal Masters and their protégés undisturbed, the Guardians can also be friendly or even avert bad luck.

In many cultures, however, taking sentient animal-children away from their protectors and their animal families by killing them puts hunters in a position of debt and lays on them a feeling of guilt.[28] Hunters feel guilty after a kill since animals are considered sentient, human-like beings and the taking of ensouled life is morally problematic. A girl in a Siberian Yukaghir myth thus pities the animals: "When my older brother began to overtake the elk, the latter must have felt sick at heart, so that it began to cry."[29] A Plains-Ojibwa Indian expressed his sympathy and pity to the bear he was hunting: "I am thankful that I found you and sorry that I am obliged to kill you."[30]

Ethnographic, historic, and archaeological sources suggest that hunters worldwide use similar concepts to reduce such guilt: denial, reanimation, or limitation. Philosophically, these methods can be explained in a utilitarian way, but only for non-self-conscious animals:

> in some circumstances – when animals lead pleasant lives, are killed painlessly, their deaths do not cause suffering to other animals, and the killing of one animal makes possible its replacement by another who would not otherwise have lived – the killing of non-self-conscious animals may not be wrong.[31]

This shows that not all killing is immoral to the same extent: to take an animal for your own or your family's survival is less discreditable than hunting for profit. To take only what you need and to give something in exchange relieves the Animal Masters as well as your own moral conscience. Most Game Rulers allow a hunter to take certain animals for his survival, if he guarantees to limit his bag, helps create new animals, or gives other favors in exchange for the game, since this is a way of balancing the reciprocal relationship between hunters and the Animal Masters and their game.

In what follows, I present some "solutions" to the problem of coping with the guilt involved in hunting adopted by hunters from all over the world and from different time periods. Some of these "solutions" are only used to satisfy the Animal Master and escape revenge. Others are used to accomplish a morally acceptable killing.

Solution 1: Keep Your Powder Dry

To avert revenge, you may thank the animals, beg them not to be offended, apologize for depriving them of life, and appease their spirits: the Ostyak west of the Ural Mountains held a dance of propitiation and asked a bear for mercy, pleading with him not to take revenge.[32] The Kamchadal always begged an animal's pardon and paid it compliments to induce it not to take vengeance on them.[33]

In order to ward off the revenge of the animal or its Master, hunters in many cultures render the animal defenseless by putting out the animal's eyes or pulling out its teeth and claws. The guilty hunter has difficulties looking at the eye, which seems to stare at him in rancor. Reports from Dièreville from the beginning of the eighteenth century mention that the Micmac tore out the eyes of all slain animals.[34] In Cameroon a dead leopard's eyes were sealed with leaves.[35] To make the retaliation of a slain bear impossible, Komi hunters of Siberia tore out its eyes, cut off its paws, or pulled out its claws and cut the foot's sinews so the animal, blind, lame, and defenseless as it were, would not be able to follow the hunters.[36]

Solution 2: Pretend It Wasn't You

With the denial of the responsibility for the kill, you are – at least in the eyes of the animal and its Master – no longer accountable for the deed. By telling the animal that it was not you who killed it, you can try to escape the consequences of immoral bloodshed. Jonathan Smith argues that hunters are very well aware of this self-deception: they shift the blame and lay it on someone else.[37] This is done either by the use of euphemisms and code names for the actions involved in hunting and butchering or by directly blaming another person or the animal itself.

The use of taboo names or special hunting languages rests on the aforementioned belief that animals understand human speech. When destroying a bear's den, Sámi hunters took care not to speak to each other, so the bear would not realize their ethnic affiliation.[38] Arriving with their bag in the village, they indicated to the bear whom it should hold responsible instead: "Here come the men out of Sweden, Poland, England, and France."[39] Similarly, the Yakut blamed the Russians for the killing of a bear: "No, don't believe us capable of having perpetrated such a murder ... They are either some Russians or Tungouses who have done the evil deed."[40]

Next to this concealment by words comes the "real" concealment: immediately after killing a jaguar a Guaraio hunter would throw away his bow and arrows so as not to disclose his identity.[41] To protect the Warrau hunter from the Orinoco and his family from any harm inflicted by the spirit of the animal he had destroyed, arrows were stuck into the ground in the middle of the pathway leading from the place of the kill towards the house.[42] The Sámi equally placed sticks on their path home so that the spirits of the dead animals could not find their trails in the snow and follow them.[43]

Often, hunters are not allowed to transport or eat the meat of the animal they have taken (as was the case for a Kwakiutl hunting novice from the Pacific Northwest, a young Chickasaw hunter from the Southwest, a Hopi rabbit hunter, a Huaulu, as well as a Seltaman in New Guinea).[44] By exchanging kills, it becomes more difficult for the animals or their Masters to rightly address their revenge: the guilt is shared and diluted. James Serpell points out that even in modern meat industries the burden of responsibility is split up amongst as many people involved as possible, thus reducing the guilt for each participant.[45]

Frequently, the animal is told that the killing was accidental. Pygmies of Gabon placated a dead elephant by singing to him: "Our spear has gone astray, O Father Elephant. We did not wish to kill you ... It is not the warrior who has taken away your life – Your hour had come."[46] Finnish hunters tried to convince a bear that its death was due to its own fault and the bad weather conditions, not to the hunters' intentions or weapons:

> Otso, thou my well beloved,
> Honey-eater of the woodlands,
> Let not anger swell thy bosom;
> I have not the force to slay thee,
> Willingly thy life thou givest
> As a sacrifice to Northland.
> Thou hast from the tree descended,
> Glided from the aspen branches,
> Slippery the trunks in autumn,
> In the fog-days, smooth the branches.[47]

At the same time, this is an example of the ambivalence and fear felt even at the suggestion of the animal giving itself freely and as a gift.

Solution 3: Give, and Ye Shall Receive

The idea that the animal rendered itself voluntarily or is given to the hunter by its Master makes it easier for the hunters to kill it and take the meat offered: some North and South American Indians believed that the animal gave its life as a "gift" to the hunter, the refusal of which would be an offense. The African Lele held that the Game Ruler sent an animal to hunters to punish it for some transgression.[48] The Master of Animals from the South American Chibcha was believed to mark the animals the hunter was allowed to pursue.[49] For the Brazilian Tucano, the Game Owner equally dictated which animals had to surrender themselves to the hunters.[50] The voluntary nature by which the animals give up their lives is, however, circumscribed, as becomes clear in a Kuna song from Panama about a shell woman: "God has created us as food for the people. How sad! There is no salvation."[51] Some Cree likewise said that it was *itatisiwak*, or "natural" for animals to avoid hunters.[52] Kwakiutl hunters considered killing an aggressive act even though they thought the animals would render themselves freely.[53]

This problem is solved by reacting to the animal's donation in a proper, compensating way, thus balancing the reciprocity in which you are engaged with the Animal Master: in many myths covenants are established with the Forest Beings to obtain some of their animals. When the Chorti hunters of

Guatemala asked him for permission and burnt copal, information on the location of the deer was granted by the Master of Deer, Ah wink-ir masa.[54] Lord Buffalo Usse, who was perceived of as father of animals by the Tim and Basari in Togo, bestowed on the hunter the right to kill animals from specific herds. He had, however, to drop some blood from every animal killed into the "horn of blood."[55] The Norwegian Lady of the Forest, Huldra, who advanced the interests of the wild animals, would grant game to the generous hunter who gave something in exchange.[56]

Solution 4: Take Only What You Need

All Animal Masters try to protect wild game and keep the number of animals killed by hunters as small as possible. Many societies, as well as many Game Guardians, do, however, hold the belief that when you have to kill to survive you may do so, but when you kill for other reasons, it is morally wrong. A waste of meat is discredited because it implies killing beyond necessities. As a hunter, you may go hunting if you take little, ideally only that which is given freely, and do not hurt the game more than necessary. Observing these rules, you will be able to catch animals despite the Game Rulers' general disapproval of hunting. The Mizaclic of the Chuh Indians from Guatemala warned a hunter who had only injured a deer: "Kill it and take your dog with you; but another time shoot better, and do not torture my creatures."[57] The Pinga of the Caribou Eskimo watched over the herds and disapprovingly drove them away if people took too many heads of game.[58] The Warrau were punished by the Hebu if they took more than was absolutely necessary.[59] The Yukaghir *péjul* likewise permitted only a certain amount of game to be taken.[60] They tell a story of a Russian hunter who was murdered for having snared too many fur animals:

This was long ago. There lived here a Russian, Petko'v by name, with three sons and one daughter. They secured fur animals by means of Russian magic. As soon as the snow fell in the autumn they would place around their house and on the roof various traps and snares. ... Along these footpaths the sables, foxes, squirrels, and other animals would run right into the snares. ... But an end came to their well-being and their abuse of the animals. Once the youngest son ... approaching ... their house ... was much surprised to see that the windows were dark ... he felt that a misfortune had occurred. ... He lit the lamp and looked: on the beds corpses were lying. Suddenly he noticed standing in the corner something terrible and hairy.

As he saw it, he ran out of the house, jumped down to the sledge and drove the dogs back. ... But the hairy being, who was Yo'bin-po'gil', the Owner of the Forest, ran after him, soon he overtook him. ... "Now, you cannot escape me," he said, "you have exterminated enough of my animals."[61]

To catch too many shrimps was a risky affair for Huaulu women: "When we hear the voice of the lord of the land it means that he is angry at us ... because we have taken his meat ... Then the lord of the land may kill us."[62] In sixteenth-century Switzerland, the *Herdmännlin* appointed the number of animals hunters were allowed to kill. If the hunters did not adhere to this number, they were bound to die.[63]

Solution 5: Cheat Death

In the strict sense, only the divinity who gives life is allowed to take it away.[64] It is the Animal Master or Mistress who tries to keep the number of animals as high as possible, reproducing them by raping the hunters' wives or having sexual intercourse with the hunters. This shows in their marked sexual organs and irrepressible sex drive: many Animal Masters are depicted with big phalli, like the Warrau Hebu or the Yoši of the Ona of South America.[65] This feature can also be found on prehistoric European cave paintings: the previously described "sorcerers" as well as others, such as an engraving from Le Portel, are shown with erect penises. The Animal Masters of the African Amhara and Galla or the Huaulu were said to abduct women and rape them, enhancing nature and the animal life.[66] The lustful Animal Mistress *skogsfru* in Scandinavia, the beautiful Forest Mother in the Caucasus Mountains, the female Ruler of the Altai Mountains, or the libidinous *vörys-mort* as well as the predatory Rübezahl all became involved in erotic affairs with hunters or their wives.[67] The Animal Guardians have an interest in the procreation of their protégés. A hunter who only kills and does not recreate must therefore fear being punished. At the same time, he might himself feel guilty for his engagement in an unequivocal relationship with the game animals or their Rulers. As was argued above, there is a moral dilemma associated with the killing of animals without replacing them, as the killing of an animal normally ends a life without starting another, even though something might be given in return or the kill might be strictly limited to the necessities. A solution to this problem is to participate in the replacement of the dead animal.

This can be done by having sexual intercourse with the Guardians of the Game, as was practiced by many North and South American shamans. Another possibility is to restore all or some of the animal's bones or organs to its Master, who can create new animals from the offerings. Early sources from the seventeenth century recount that Enets, Nganasan, Yukaghir, and Tungus used to hang the remains of slain animals high up on trees, because they believed new animals would grow out of them.[68] The Orochi told a dead bear to be renewed by the Animal Master: "Go fast; go to your master; put a new fur on, and come again next year that I may look at you."[69] The Eskimo had to return the bladders, eyes, or other organs of sea animals to the sea to allow for new life.[70] Peruvian Aymara placed fishbones in the water for the Animal Master to revitalize them.[71] The Ila of Zambia used to bury an elephant's tusk to ensure the species' persistence.[72] Philippine Negritos attached wild animals' skulls to trees, as did the Huaulu, for the Lord of the Land to "make [new game] descend."[73] Similar beliefs can be found in European rituals, myths, and folk-stories: the Greek offering of Prometheus, which included skin, fat, intestines, and bones, can be traced back to the idea of regeneration out of bone and organ substance.[74] The *Salige Frauen* of the Alps were capable of reviving animals out of bones,[75] as was Thor in old Norse mythology.[76] This tradition can possibly be traced back to Upper Paleolithic times:[77] in Eliseeviči (Ukraine), Bouret' (Siberia), and Willendorf (Austria), small ivory figurines were deposited together with animal bones.[78] The Sámi people similarly used to bury animal bones beneath the figure of the Mistress of Animals, *possjoakka*.[79] The Samoyed and other Siberian peoples put up representations of the Master of the Animals in the taiga, under which they deposited the bones or skulls of slain animals.[80] Archaeological finds, like the deposition of bones of mammoth and wolves in the Epiaurignacian in Langmannersdorf in Lower Austria,[81] the disposal of unbroken boar skulls and mandibles in Mesolithic bogs of Löberöd and Vissmarlöv in Scania, South Sweden,[82] or the Early Bronze Age burial of an aurochs in Heathrow, London, UK,[83] may have had similar motivations of revitalizing the animals.

The Keepers of the Game as a Moral Authority

Many different cultures worldwide and in different time periods believe in a Master or Mistress of the Animals. This figure shows striking similarities concerning appearance, habits, and the intention to protect game animals and to punish hunters who transgress his or her rules. The belief in this figure can be traced back to the hunters' psychological dilemma of killing human-like, sentient animals. The universal fear of punishment by this being shows that hunting is often considered as morally wrong. Different "solutions" offer ways to evade this difficulty: one can persuade the Animal Masters or the prey that it was not the hunter himself who committed the deed or that the animal did not really die but offered itself freely, or else one can render the animal incapable of revenge by destroying its claws and teeth. The hunters, however, are more easily relieved morally when using other "solutions": those that shield them from the animals' revenge and blood guilt and that ensure future game supply and anticipate over-hunting. This is achieved by not taking more than is needed for survival, by hunting expertly without causing unnecessary pain, by giving something in exchange for the kill, and by trying to revive the animals taken. These combined "solutions" amount to a "hunting code of ethics" *Weidgerechtigkeit*, embodied in the sanctioning figure of the Animal Master, who holds dominion over the game of the forest and defends it against immoral over-hunting.

NOTES

1 The Ashanti of the Gold Coast, on the forest spirit, in Robert Sutherland Rattray, *Religion and Art in Ashanti* (Oxford: Clarendon Press, 1927), p. 27.

2 Valerio Valeri, *The Forest of Taboos: Morality, Hunting and Identity among the Huaulu of the Moluccas* (Madison, WI: University of Wisconsin Press, 2000), p. 309.

3 Rudolf Bilz, "Tiertöter-Skrupulantismus," *Jahrbuch für Psychologie und Psychotherapie* 3 (1955): 226.

4 Ivar Paulson, *Schutzgeister und Gottheiten des Wildes (der Jagdtiere und Fische) in Nordeurasien: Eine religionsethnographische und religionsphänomenologische Untersuchung jägerischer Glaubensvorstellungen* (Stockholm: Almquist and Wiksell, 1961), p. 228; Karl Meuli, "Griechische Opferbräuche," in Olof Gigon et al. (eds.) *Phyllobolia für Peter von der Mühll* (Basel: Benno Schwabe, 1946), pp. 185, 249; James Serpell, *In the Company of Animals: A Study of Human–Animal Relationships* (Cambridge: Cambridge University Press, 1996), p. 181.

5 George B. Silberbauer, *Hunter and Habitat in the Central Kalahari Desert* (Cambridge: Cambridge University Press, 1981), p. 63.

6 Christoph von Fürer-Haimendorf, *The Chenchus: Jungle Folk of the Deccan* (London: Macmillan, 1943), p. 228f.

7   Robert A. Brightman, *Grateful Prey: Rock Cree Human–Animal Relationships* (Berkeley: University of California Press, 1993), p. 159.

8   Valeri, *The Forest of Taboos*, pp. 183ff., 306.

9   While the preferred term is "Inuit," the author prefers to use the term "Eskimo" instead [Ed.].

10 Paulson, *Schutzgeister und Gottheiten*, p. 228.

11 Willard Williams Hill, *The Agricultural and Hunting Methods of the Navaho Indians* (New Haven, CT: Yale University Press, 1938), p. 143.

12 Walter Edmund Roth, *An Inquiry into the Animism and Folklore of the Guiana Indians* (Washington, DC: United States Government Printing Office, 1908–9), p. 294.

13 Lutz Röhrich, "Die Sagen vom Herrn der Tiere," in *Internationaler Kongress der Volkserzählungsforscher in Kiel und Kopenhagen 1959* (Berlin: Walter de Gruyter, 1961), p. 343.

14 Arthur W. Ryder, *Kalidasa: Translations of Shakuntala, and Other Works* (London: J. M. Dent and Sons, 1914), p. 5.

15 Christian Rätsch and K'ayum Ma'ax, *Ein Kosmos im Regenwald: Mythen und Visionen der Lakandonen-Indianer* (Cologne: Eugen Diederichs, 1984).

16 Adolf E. Jensen, *Mythos und Kult bei Naturvölkern: Religionswissenschaftliche Betrachtungen*, 2nd ed. (Wiesbaden: Franz Steiner, 1951), p. 169.

17 Valerio Valeri, "Wild Victims: Hunting as Sacrifice and Sacrifice as Hunting in Huaulu," *History of Religions* 34 (1994): 117.

18 Josef Haekel, "Der 'Herr der Tiere' im Glauben der Indianer Mesoamerikas," *Mitteilungen aus dem Museum für Völkerkunde in Hamburg* 25 (1959): 67.

19 Otto Zerries, *Wild- und Buschgeister in Südamerika: eine Untersuchung jägerzeitlicher Phänomene im Kulturbild südamerikanischer Indianer* (Wiesbaden: Franz Steiner, 1954), p. 9.

20 Erland Nordenskiöld, *Forschungen und Abenteuer in Südamerika* (Stuttgart: Strecker und Schröder, 1924), p. 278; Hans Peter Duerr, *Sedna: oder Die Liebe zum Leben* (Frankfurt am Main: Suhrkamp, 1984), p. 278.

21 Paulson, *Schutzgeister und Gottheiten*, p. 144.

22 Valeri, *The Forest of Taboos*, pp. 28, 318.

23 Lutz Röhrich, "Europäische Wildgeistersagen," *Rheinisches Jahrbuch für Volkskunde* 10 (1959): 108; Johannes Praetorius, *Bekannte und unbekannte Historien von dem abenteuerlichen und weltberufenen Gespenste Rübezahl* (Leipzig: Insel-Verlag, 1920), pp. 10ff.

24 Hermann Baumann, "Afrikanische Wild- und Buschgeister," *Zeitschrift für Ethnologie* 70 (1938): 224.

25 Duerr, *Sedna*, p. 305; Johannes Maringer, "Priests and Priestesses in Prehistoric Europe," *History of Religions* 17 (1977): 104.

26 Haekel, "Der 'Herr der Tiere' im Glauben der Indianer Mesoamerikas," p. 68.

27 Mathias Georg Guenther, *Bushman Folktales: Oral Traditions of the Nharo of Botswana and the /Xam of the Cape* (Stuttgart: Franz Steiner, 1989), p. 117.

28 James A. Serpell, "Animals and Religion: Towards a Unifying Theory," in Francien Henriëtte de Jonge and Ruud van den Bos (eds.) *The Human–Animal Relationship: Forever and a Day* (Assen: Van Gorcum, 2005), p. 13.

29 Waldemar Jochelson, *The Yukaghir and the Yukaghirized Tungus* (New York: E. J. Brill/G. E. Stechert, 1926), p. 147.

30 A. Irving Hallowell, "Bear Ceremonialism in the Northern Hemisphere," *American Anthropologist* 28 (1926): 56.

31 Peter Singer, "Practical Ethics," in Susan Jean Armstrong and Richard George Botzler (eds.) *The Animal Ethics Reader* (London: Routledge, 2003), p. 43.

32 Hallowell, "Bear Ceremonialism," p. 56; Gustav Klemm, *Allgemeine Cultur-Geschichte der Menschheit. Die Hirtenvölker der passiven Menschheit* (Leipzig: B. G. Teubner, 1844), p. 125.

33 Hallowell, "Bear Ceremonialism," p. 56.

34 Calvin Martin, "The European Impact on the Culture of a Northeastern Algonquian Tribe: An Ecological Interpretation," *William and Mary Quarterly* 31 (1974): 24.

35 Hermann Baumann, "Nyama, die Rachemacht," *Paideuma* 4 (1950): 220.

36 Meuli, "Griechische Opferbräuche," p. 245.

37 Jonathan Z. Smith, "The Bare Facts of Ritual," *History of Religions* 20 (1980): 125.

38 Neil S. Price, "The Viking Way: Religion and War in Late Iron Age Scandinavia" (PhD diss., Uppsala University, 2002), p. 247.

39 Klemm, *Allgemeine Cultur-Geschichte der Menschheit*, p. 14.

40 Hallowell, "Bear Ceremonialism," p. 58.

41 Zerries, *Wild- und Buschgeister*, p. 139.

42 Roth, *Inquiry*, p. 293.

43 Meuli, "Griechische Opferbräuche," p. 230.

44 Franz Boas, "Current Beliefs of the Kwakiutl Indians," *Journal of American Folklore* 45 (1932): 233; Frank G. Speck, "Notes on Chickasaw Ethnology and Folk-Lore," *Journal of American Folklore* 20 (1907): 54; Georges Devereux, "La chasse collective au lapin chez les Hopi, Oraibi, Arizona," *Journal de la Société des Américanistes* 33 (1946): 77; Valeri, *The Forest of Taboos*, p. 49; Harriet Whitehead, *Food Rules: Hunting, Sharing, and Tabooing Game in Papua New Guinea* (Ann Arbor: University of Michigan Press, 2000), p. 98.

45 Serpell, *In the Company of Animals*, p. 204.

46 Baumann, "Afrikanische Wild- und Buschgeister," p. 220.

47 Elias Lönnrot, *The Kalevala: The Epic Poem of Finland*, trans. John Martin Crawford (Cincinnati: Robert Blake, 1910), p. xlvi.

48 Brightman, *Grateful Prey*, p. 91.

49 Otto Zerries, "Wildgeister und Jagdritual in Zentralamerika," *Mitteilungen aus dem Museum für Völkerkunde in Hamburg* 25 (1959): 144.

50 J. Baird Callicott, *Earth's Insights: A Multicultural Survey of Ecological Ethics from the Mediterranean Basin to the Australian Outback* (Berkeley: University of California Press, 1994), p. 139.

51 Erland Nordenskiöld, *An Historical and Ethnological Survey of the Cuna Indians* (Gothenburg: Göteborgs Museum, 1938), pp. 651, 343.

52 Brightman, *Grateful Prey*, p. 188.

53 Johnson Donald Hughes, *American Indian Ecology* (El Paso: Texas Western Press, 1983), p. 26.

54 Haekel, "Der 'Herr der Tiere' im Glauben der Indianer Mesoamerikas," p. 61.

55 Eike Haberland (ed.) *Leo Frobenius 1873–1973: eine Anthologie* (Wiesbaden: Franz Steiner, 1973), p. 65.

56 Ronald Grambo, "The Lord of Forest and Mountain Game in the More Recent Folk Traditions of Norway," *Fabula* 7 (1964): 36.

57 J. Kunst, "Some Animal Fables of the Chuh Indians," *Journal of American Folklore* 28 (1915): 354ff.

58 Alexander Gahs, "Kopf-, Schädel- und Langknochenopfer bei Rentiervölkern," in Wilhelm Koppers (ed.) *Festschrift P.W. Schmidt: 76 sprachwissenschaftliche, ethnologische, religionswissenschaftliche, prähistorische und andere Studien* (Vienna: Mechitharisten-Congregation-Buchdruckerei, 1928), p. 255f.

59 Zerries, *Wild- und Buschgeister*, p. 125.

60 Jochelson, *The Yukaghir*, p. 212.

61 Ibid., p. 149ff.

62 Valeri, *The Forest of Taboos*, p. 306.

63 Röhrich, "Europäische Wildgeistersagen," p. 98.

64 Jean Soler, "Les raisons de la Bible: règles alimentaires hébraïques," in Jean-Louis Flandrin and Massimo Montanari (eds.) *Histoire de l'Alimentation* (Paris: Fayard, 1996), p. 83.

65 Zerries, *Wild- und Buschgeister*, p. 379.

66 Baumann, "Afrikanische Wild- und Buschgeister," p. 238; Valeri, *The Forest of Taboos*, pp. 317, 28, 305.

67 Adolf Dirr, "Der kaukasische Wild- und Jagdgott," *Anthropos* 20 (1925): 144ff.; Duerr, *Sedna*, p. 278; Otakar Nahodil, "Mutterkult in Sibirien," in V. Diószegi (ed.) *Glaubenswelt und Folklore der sibirischen Völker* (Budapest: Akad. Kiadó, 1963), pp. 496, 114; Praetorius, *Bekannte und unbekannte Historien*, p. 114.

68 Paulson, *Schutzgeister und Gottheiten*, pp. 200, 184.

69 Alexander M. Zolotarev, "The Bear Festival of the Olcha," *American Anthropologist* 39 (1937): 123.

70 Edward William Nelson, *The Eskimo about Bering Strait* (Washington, DC: United States Government Printing Office, 1896–7), p. 437.

71 Zerries, *Wild- und Buschgeister*, p. 320.

72   Baumann, "Afrikanische Wild- und Buschgeister," p. 232.

73   Duerr, *Sedna*, p. 314; Valeri, *The Forest of Taboos*, p. 305.

74   Meuli, "Griechische Opferbräuche," p. 261; Walter Burkert, *Homo Necans: The Anthropology of Ancient Greek Sacrificial Ritual and Myth* (New York: Walter de Gruyter, 1972), p. 21.

75   Georg Graber (ed.) *Sagen aus Kärnten* (Leipzig: Dieterich'sche Verlagsbuchhandlung, Theodor Weicher, 1914), p. 65.

76   Snorri Sturluson, "Gylfaginning," xliv, in Karl Simrock (ed.) *Die Edda: die ältere und jüngere, nebst den mythischen Erzählungen der Skalda* (Stuttgart: J. G. Cotta'sche Buchhandlung, 1876), p. 277ff.

77   Walter Burkert, *Griechische Religion der archaischen und klassischen Epoche* (Stuttgart: W. Kohlhammer, 1985), p. 234; Åke Hultkrantz, "The Owner of the Animals in the Religion of the North American Indians: Some General Remarks," in Åke Hultkrantz (ed.) *The Supernatural Owners of Nature: Nordic Symposium on the Religious Conceptions of the Ruling Spirits Genii Loci, Genii Speciei and Allied Concepts* (Stockholm: Almqvist and Wiksell, 1961), pp. 55, 58.

78   Josef Bayer, "Die Venus II von Willendorf," in Josef Bayer (ed.) *Eiszeit und Urgeschichte: Jahrbuch für Erforschung des vorgeschichtlichen Menschen und seines Zeitalters* (Leipzig: Hiersemann, 1930), p. 51ff.; Henri Delporte, *L'image de la femme dans l'art préhistorique* (Paris: Picard, 1993), p. 202; Franz Hancar, "Die Venusstatuette von Jelisejevici (Kreis Brjansk)," *Ipek* 18 (1949): 1ff.

79   Duerr, *Sedna*, p. 312.

80   Gahs, "Kopf-, Schädel- und Langknochenopfer bei Rentiervölkern," p. 232.

81   Wilhelm Angeli, *Der Mammutjägerhalt von Langmannersdorf an der Perschling* (Vienna: Akademie der Wissenschaften, 1953), p. 28ff.

82   Ola Magnell, *Tracking Wild Boar and Hunters: Osteology of Wild Boar in Mesolithic South Scandinavia* (Stockholm: Almqvist and Wiksell International, 2005), p. 50.

83   Jonathan Cotton et al., "Taming the Wild: A Final Neolithic/Earlier Bronze Age Aurochs Deposit from West London," in Dale Serjeantson and David Field (eds.) *Animals in the Neolithic of Britain and Europe* (Oxford: Oxbow, 2006), p. 152.

CHAPTER 12

HUNTING

A Return to Nature?

 There is something about the idea of a "return to nature" that resonates in a time of environmental crisis and political anxiety. Perhaps our problems can be traced to the fact that human beings have separated themselves too far from nature, that we have lost touch with our natural origins, that we are no longer grounded in natural realities and constraints. It is not unusual to hear calls for living closer to nature, or more in harmony with nature's way. In this essay, I shall explore the notion that hunting is a practice that could return us to nature. To do this, we must understand what it might mean to "return to nature" and whether hunting is the only or the best way to accomplish this goal. While I do not rule out the possibility that some forms of hunting might succeed in returning the hunter to a way of life closer to nature, I shall argue that it may not be the practice that most fully solves the problems that lead people to seek such a return. To show this, we must consider what it means to be alienated from nature and what is to be gained by returning to nature.

There are, of course, many kinds of hunting and different defenses of its morality. Not all hunters seek a return to nature or deeper philosophical justifications of hunting's significance. For some, game management or economic duress represent sufficient explanations of what matters. My reflections here, however, relate to those hunters who seek a deeper account of hunting and its meaning. Can hunting return us to nature? What would that mean?

The metaphor of a return to nature is not merely a literary ornament that writers on hunting use to enhance the appeal of their account of the hunter's way of life. Metaphors, as Lakoff and Johnson have argued, are conceptual structures that we live by.[1] Metaphors influence what questions we ask, what inferences we draw, and what actions we take. To say that hunting returns the hunter to nature points to a deeper defense of sport hunting than arguments that appeal to management of overpopulated deer, or to the economic benefits hunters bring to rural communities. This metaphor also structures the questions we need to ask.

In order to return to nature, it must be the case that before we hunt we exist somewhere else that is separated from nature. How should we characterize that space? What are the benefits of returning to nature and the problems with the alienated state we wish to escape? Is a return possible? What do we bring back to nature and will nature welcome our return? What does a way of life closer to nature look like and how is it to be contrasted with the life we currently lead?

We can use these questions to investigate what it means to say that hunting is a return to nature and to assess the value of such a return. These questions also permit comparisons between hunting and other possible ways of returning. For example, could an agrarian way of life constitute a return to nature? Writers on hunting tend to discount the possibility that farming could return a person to nature. As José Ortega y Gasset writes in his classic *Meditations on Hunting*, only the hunter acts within the countryside; the tourist and the farmer can only remain outside or on top of the countryside.[2]

If hunting returns us to nature, what nature does it return us to? For some, nature is what is completely outside human culture, untouched by human artifacts and purposes. Nature is what is not made, what has not been interfered with or altered by human hands.[3] But try as we might, we cannot return to such a nature. Nature untouched cannot be restored or reentered without negating what makes it nature. Even the hunter's return is human interference. So, if hunters return to nature, it cannot be this concept of nature that is intended.

Writers such as Ortega and James Swan see hunting as an essential bridge to a more natural existence that civilized human beings have abandoned.[4] By hunting, a person reconnects with his or her animal nature, a primal nature that has remained constant since Paleolithic human beings emerged from nature into history. For Ortega, this Paleolithic essence remains a "permanent availability" to which we can turn at any time to escape the constraints of modern existence. Hunting returns us to a way

ROGER J. H. KING

of seeing the world that imitates that of other animals. Indeed, for him, hunting is the only way to reenter nature because it is the only way to be with and interact with wild animals.[5] Human beings are essentially predatory, in his view, and thus naturally respond to wild animals by pursuing them. However, for Ortega, this return to nature is not permanent. It takes the form of a "vacation" or a diversion from the hunter's predicament as a civilized being subject to the constraints of history, culture, and community. We hunt in order to distract ourselves from our humanity.

For James Swan, the return to nature is also a return to the acknowledgment of our animal nature. Taking his cue from indigenous peoples such as the Inuit, Swan emphasizes the importance of feeling the continuity between human and non-human life.[6] All animal life is interconnected, in this view, and communication is possible between wild animals and human beings if one's spirit is properly attuned. Hunting becomes a kind of healing, a making whole, that enables a deep kinship with nature by integrating aspects of the human being that civilized life keeps apart. Swan's view comes out in a quotation from Eric Fromm: "In the act of hunting, a man becomes, however briefly, part of nature again. He returns to the natural state, becomes one with the animal, and is freed of the existential split: to be part of nature and to transcend it by virtue of his consciousness."[7] Thus, for Swan, in returning us to our animal nature, hunting also opens up the potential for greater spiritual communication with nature as a whole.

But what is it that the hunter seeks to return from? A return implies a departure from an alienated condition or a space of exile. At its most basic, the alienated condition is civilization. But what is it about civilization that is to be rejected? Aldo Leopold offers one characteristic description:

> Your true modern is separated from the land by many middlemen, and by innumerable physical gadgets. He has no vital relation to it; to him it is the space between cities ... Turn him loose for a day on the land, and if the spot does not happen to be a golf links or a "scenic" area, he is bored stiff ... Synthetic substitutes for wood, leather, wool and other natural land products suit him better than the originals. In short, land is something he has "outgrown."[8]

In this account, to live far from nature is to be surrounded by human artifacts and technology, to live in urban environments, and to have no direct work-related interaction with nature.

Swan emphasizes the passivity of the civilized way of life.

> Life for modern man has become a spectator sport. Television, movies, concerts, magazines, newspapers, books, CD ROM, and video games all provide information about reality. We live our lives at a safe distance from so many things, overwhelmed by information.[9]

Hunting provides a counter-force to this passivity. It forces the hunter to face mortality and to realize that violence and death are not abstractions, but conditions of life. According to Swan, urban life separates people from wild places, from contact with death, and from understanding the sources of the food they eat. This detachment from reality, whether through televised violence or supermarket food, means that urban residents never develop "an emotional awareness of the consequences of their actions (like eating meat) that support death."[10] A life alienated from nature impairs our imagination, therefore, as well as our cognitive understanding of the world.

For Ortega, the problem with civilization is that it humanizes the planet and destroys its spontaneity.[11] Even conservation is a threat to hunting because it removes wildness and subjects it to "civilization – that is to say, other men, the civitas, the law, the state."[12] This civilization produces an ennui that can only be overcome by the "pleasure in the artificial return to [nature], the only occupation that permits him something like a vacation from his human condition."[13]

One of the hunter's central critiques of civilized life is that it dulls human perception and imagination. As Leopold suggests, the modern urban citizen is bored by nature unless it can be put to some recreational or aesthetic use. Hunters and others level this charge against the backpacker and urban environmentalist, often unfairly. But more important than mere boredom is the charge that civilized human beings have lost contact with their bodies and with the spiritual, both of which Swan sees as rejuvenated by hunting and the return to nature:

> A good hunter must learn to link personal thoughts, actions, and moods with the larger forces of nature to increase his chances for success. Being at the right place at the right time is at the core of hunting success. A hunter seeks to blend with the overall field of mind within which we live, putting aside personal ego to increase the intuitive sensing needed to pull out harmonies from the collective consciousness.[14]

🦌   ROGER J. H. KING

Similarly, Ortega emphasizes the alertness of the hunter, the way in which the hunter's attention is heightened as he or she scans the countryside in wait for his or her prey:

> But this itself – life as complete alertness – is the attitude in which the animal exists in the jungle. Because of it he lives from within his environment. … Only the hunter, imitating the perpetual alertness of the wild animal, for whom everything is danger, sees everything and sees each thing functioning as facility or difficulty, as risk or protection.[15]

Achieving this alertness, for Ortega, is also a matter of setting aside our intellect and reason in favor of our senses and instincts. Human reason is the source, for Ortega, of human superiority over the animal, but also the source of our alienation from animals and nature. Hunting is the solution to this problem of a life based too completely on reason.

From this discussion, we begin to see what it means for the hunter to return to nature. Hunting is intended to be a solution to the degradations of civilization: the physical detachment from the wild, the flight from mortality, the irresponsibility of depending on a nature that is invisible to us, the imbalance of reason over the senses, the blindness to everything that is not managed and controlled for human purposes. Escaping this alienated and alienating state of affairs is imperative if we are to achieve a sustainable and environmentally responsible presence on the planet. But is hunting capable of dealing with all this? And if so, is it uniquely qualified to end this alienation from nature?

It is interesting to see the extent to which agrarian writers share some of the concerns about civilization that the hunting arguments identify. Wendell Berry, for example, notes how industrial civilization contributes to the invisibility of nature and thus to our alienation from it.

> One of the primary results – and one of the primary needs – of industrialization is the separation of people and places and products from their histories. To the extent that we participate in the industrial economy, we do not know the histories of our families or of our habitats or of our meals. This is an economy, and in fact a culture, of the one-night stand.[16]

Sharing Swan's concerns about the fragmentation of the individual in civilized cultures, Berry also calls for a reconciliation of nature and culture, the senses and intellect. This reconciliation, he thinks, will be the work not just of artists and scholars, but of "farmers, foresters, scientists, and others."[17]

Norman Wirzba also attacks the denigration of the body in modern industrial society. Like Swan, Wirzba is concerned with the passivity and alienation that he sees in modern consumerism. Consumerism is

> an approach to reality that fundamentally alters the ways we engage and relate to the world around us. ... Our engagement with the external world, now increasingly characterized in terms of commodity exchange, has less to do with reality itself than with marketable images that determine production and spending. Our perception and reception of the world are thus made oblique. We do not encounter reality on its terms. ... A consumer mentality, in other words, contributes to our overall ignorance about the truth of reality.[18]

Agrarian writers share the hunter's dismay at the extent to which civilized life blocks our perception of nature, undermines a sense of relatedness and responsibility for how we affect natural environments, and turns civilized individuals into passive, deluded consumers. To combat this separation and return to nature means to return to an agricultural way of life that is attentive to human dependence on the land.

While it is true that some of the concerns about civilization that preoccupy proponents of hunting map onto those that worry agrarians, the solutions proposed have little in common. As we have seen, the case for hunting is that it can return us to our animal selves, a prehistorical nature that reenters the landscape and participates by mimicking animal ways. The agrarian emphasis, however, lies in the reconciliation of culture with nature, the integration of cultural ways and the ways of nature so that they harmonize. While the hunter returns to nature by reviving internal capacities latent in the individual, agrarians focus on reconstructing communities and community practices on the land.[19]

Can hunting and a certain kind of agrarian culture both return us to nature? To answer this, we need to go back to the question whether hunting can solve the problems of alienated life. I suggest that it cannot.

Let me indicate two difficulties. First, as Ortega makes clear, the return to nature that hunting might bring about is, at best, a temporary escape, a vacation from the civilized condition. Even supposing that modern humans could reenact a Paleolithic or animal mode of experience by means of the hunt, this mindset cannot be sustained. Ortega does not propose, for example, that we extend our Paleolithic worldview beyond the hunting grounds, reenacting our animal nature in social relations or reproduction. But the inadequacies of civilization that Ortega and Swan

ROGER J. H. KING

identify are far-reaching and intransient. They require enduring and systematic responses, not the "one-night stands" that Ortega seems to offer.

Second, the transformation of perception that Ortega describes as one of the core accomplishments of the successful hunter is not as far-reaching as it seems. The alertness of the attentive hunter spreads itself over the landscape in an active way, imitating the sensitivities of the animal, but it is, like all perception, a selective attention. While attending to the landscape in search of signs of the prey, the hunter, like the predatory animal, is inevitably oblivious to a good deal of the landscape. What is the past ecological and human-use history of the forest hunting grounds? Are all the plants and animals native or have some been introduced from elsewhere? Is there evidence of pollution, climate change, or species extirpations in the forest? Barry Lopez writes:

> I think of two landscapes – one outside the self, the other within. The external landscape is the one we see – not only the line and color of the land ... but also its plants and animals in season, its weather, its geology, the record of its climate and evolution. ... These are all elements of the land, and what makes the landscape comprehensible are the relationships between them. One learns a landscape ... by perceiving the relationships in it.[20]

The hunter's interest in the landscape as hunting grounds does not exhaust what must be known about that landscape if we are to confront and control the ravages of industrial civilization. We must learn to perceive much more than the animal sees and we must learn to see it in ways that cannot be part of the animal's repertoire. To fail to develop this enhanced perception, indeed, an enhanced ecological literacy, is to fail to escape the dismal prospects current civilization presents.[21]

It might be objected here that perhaps the problem the hunter seeks to solve by returning to nature is not the problem that the agrarian seeks to solve, despite some significant overlap in their characterizations of what it means to be alienated from nature. Hunters looking for a return to nature seek to resolve a problematic alienation within themselves; they seek to make themselves whole again by a practice that enables the individual to achieve a closer relationship with wild nature. Their goal is not social transformation, nor a resolution to the social problems arising from our separation from nature, only an individual self-transformation. Learning to perceive like an animal, learning to develop a sense of kinship with other animals, and developing the full range of sensory capacities over and beyond the intellect are all individual goals the hunter might achieve regardless of the continuing attractions of civilized life.

At the heart of this defense is Ortega's notion, shared by others, that Paleolithic human nature remains intact within each individual. By tapping into this inner self, individuals might escape their civilized personas and reenergize the predatory animal nature remaining at the foundation of the self. The hunter's return to nature is, really, a return to himself or herself, an inner, personal journey rather than a social one.

Let me suggest two reasons why I do not think this is satisfactory. First, every aspect of actual sport hunters' activities is cultural through and through. From the legal regulation of hunting seasons, hunting licenses, bag limits, target species, permissible weaponry and tactics, and the rights of private property owners, to the justifications of hunting that appeal to game management, family tradition, rural economic benefits, conservation dollars for habitat protection, and personal pleasure in the outdoors, the practice of hunting is saturated with cultural values and culturally specific technology. The similarity between this and hunting by Paleolithic man or by other animal predators is superficial at best.

A second related point is the objection that hunters depend upon and draw knowledge from a hunting community. While animals learn quickly and by instinct how to hunt and how to evade predators, the human hunter must learn from other hunters as well as from the memories and experience of the hunting community through time. The nature that hunters return to is not an animal nature, devoid of the distortions of human civilization and intellectual achievement, but a culturally interpreted nature, and they return bearing all that human culture makes available to them. Sport hunting is an activity within civilization, not an evasion of it, just as a vacation from work is part of being an employee, not an escape from it. The passion that Ortega and Swan evidence in their writing about hunting is as much a sign of their dissatisfaction with a particular form of civilization as it is of the pull of nature.

My conclusion here is not that hunting could not contribute in some way to a return to nature, but that the idea that single individuals could flee civilization on their own without addressing either the problems of civilization they leave behind or the alternative way of life that might resolve those problems is a dead end. Wendell Berry has argued that one of the central failures of the contemporary conservation movement is that it has not articulated an alternative economic system that could compete with the prevailing, and environmentally unsustainable, industrial capitalist model.[22] It is irresponsible to suppose that hunting has

ROGER J. H. KING

returned us to nature "while in virtually every act of our private lives, we endorse and support an economic system that is by intention, and perhaps by necessity, ecologically irresponsible."[23] Failure to address the problems of civilization at the community or social level will undermine the individual's efforts to achieve wholeness and kinship with nature at the individual level. The division between these two levels needs to be closed.

If we are going to be able to explicate hunting as a return to nature in any substantial and morally constructive sense, then hunting must fit into the broader framework of a way of life that actively opposes and seeks to resolve the problems with civilization that have been identified.

The first step in articulating this return is to acknowledge that nature is an active agent, not a passive vessel waiting to welcome us home. We must ask whether nature will have us back and how we might make ourselves worthy of being allowed to return. At the outset, it is obvious that nature will not have us all back. We cannot all become hunters and return to nature on that path; there are too many of us to make that reentry anything but a disaster for the natural world. It is essential to take seriously this recognition that nature has the option not to tolerate our return. We must not just tell the story of how hunters return to take their prey by skilled and respectful imitation of animal ways, but also the story of the innumerable ways in which nature itself stalks the human and places limits on our intentions. The writer bell hooks recounts that:

> As a child of the hills, I was taught early on in my life the power in nature. I was taught by farmers that wilderness land, the untamed environment, can give life and it can take life. In my girlhood I learned to watch for snakes, wildcat roaming, plants that irritate and poison. I know instinctively … that it is humankind and not nature that is the stranger on these grounds. Humility in relation to nature's power made survival possible.[24]

For bell hooks, the cultivation of attentiveness means not the attentiveness of the predator, but that of the prey. Humility is the virtue she draws from her experience in nature, not Ortega's keenly honed predatory attentiveness. In returning to nature, we must acknowledge our vulnerability to nature's inhospitality.

The second step is to recognize that we never return to "nature" in the abstract, but to some particular nature, a particular place. When we return to nature we return to the Penobscot River watershed in Maine, to the short grass prairie of eastern Kansas, or to the Douglas Fir-Hemlock forests of the Pacific Northwest. We return, therefore, to bioregions and to sub-units of those bioregions. A return to nature in the abstract merely perpetuates the tendency of civilized human beings to see the world in terms of intellectual abstractions rather than in the concrete terms of the world as experienced. To really return to a place in nature requires that we know and feel what nature will permit us to do there, in that place, not in general.

The third step is to realize that a reinhabitation of concrete particular places requires what we may call "thick" relations to nature, not "thin."[25] We have thick relations to those with whom we share aspects of our life. They link us to family, friends, and neighbors and to others with whom we have some shared experience. Memory is an essential element of thick relations, since it ties the present to the past, enhancing intimacy and community. Thin relations, on the other hand, link us to strangers, to others we know only in abstract ways. We do not share a history with these people or things.

Returning to nature means cultivating thick relationships with our bioregions rather than relying on the thin relations appropriate to a stranger; it is about returning to a sense of intimacy with the natural world that is based in acknowledgment of shared history, shared community, and a shared future. Those living close to nature do not just feel a distant respect for nature, they care about individuals, are intimate with the life ways of particular places, share a community of engagement and exchange with non-human beings, and would feel shamed to betray their loyalty to the mixed human/non-human community they inhabit.

Returning to nature means becoming a member of a community of memory, one in which attentiveness to and knowledge of nature are cultivated, built up, sustained, and enacted. Through membership in such a community, animals cease to be abstractions; they become individuals with whom one participates in creating and sustaining a shared, meaningful life. Finding a place in nature means learning how to become neighbors again not only with the wild animals who inhabit the place, but with all the other elements of the land community, biotic and abiotic. To develop thick relations to nature is, in essence, to follow Leopold in seeing the land as a community to which human beings may seek to belong. This belonging takes the form of deep knowledge, experience, engagement, and the confrontation with the realities of life and death in that place.

While isolated individuals might, to a degree, be capable of developing thick relations to nature, agrarians are right that such relations are best sustained by the memories, practices, and cooperation of a community.[26] My argument is that if hunting can return us to nature, it must do so by being part of a community-scale redirection of human aspirations and hopes. It must be part of a reevaluation and dissolution of an unsustainable civilization. To suppose that we might retain our civilized roles as corporate managers or industrial workers yet return to nature during the hunting season ignores the underlying schizophrenia involved. The individual healing that happens there is no deeper than the restless sleep of the exhausted worker. The next day it all begins again. Nothing has changed. To count as returning to nature, however, hunting must be part of an alternative to "civilization" that changes many of the fundamentals of contemporary life.

Unfortunately, achieving a return to nature through a way of life that cultivates thick relations to nature will still not be sufficient to confront the global problems of civilization. Environmental, economic, and political forces are no longer merely local in scope and impact. Sustaining a return to nature requires that our ecologically literate attention be in two places at once: our bioregional home and the abstract landscape of global civilization. Despite the longing of many hunters and agrarians for a pure return to nature, human beings will be condemned to live in two discordant worlds for the foreseeable future.

NOTES

1   George Lakoff and Mark Johnson, *Metaphors We Live By* (Chicago: University of Chicago Press, 1980).
2   José Ortega y Gasset, *Meditations on Hunting*, trans. Howard B. Wescott (New York: Charles Scribner's Sons, 1972), p. 140.
3   Eric Katz, "The Big Lie: Restoration of Nature," in *Nature as Subject: Human Obligation and Natural Community* (Lanham: Rowman and Littlefield, 1997), pp. 93–108.
4   James Swan, *In Defense of Hunting* (San Francisco: HarperSanFrancisco, 1995).
5   Ortega, *Meditations on Hunting*, pp. 139–40.
6   Swan, *In Defense of Hunting*, p. 44.
7   Eric Fromm, *The Anatomy of Human Destructiveness* (New York: Rinehart and Winston, 1973), p. 132; cited in Swan, *In Defense of Hunting*, p. 49.
8   Aldo Leopold, *A Sand County Almanac: With Essays on Conservation from Round River* (New York: Ballantine, 1966), pp. 261–2.
9   Swan, *In Defense of Hunting*, p. 97.
10 Ibid., pp. 134–5.
11 Ortega, *Meditations on Hunting*, p. 79.

12 Ibid.
13 Ibid., p. 29.
14 Swan, *In Defense of Hunting*, pp. 32–3.
15 Ortega, *Meditations on Hunting*, pp. 150–1.
16 Wendell Berry, "The Whole Horse," in Eric T. Freyfogle (ed.) *The New Agrarianism: Land, Culture, and the Community of Life* (Washington, DC: Island Press, 2001), p. 64.
17 Ibid., p. 70.
18 Norman Wirzba, "Placing the Soul: An Agrarian Philosophical Principle," in Norman Wirzba (ed.) *The Essential Agrarian Reader: The Future of Culture, Community, and the Land* (Lexington, KY: University of Kentucky Press, 2003), p. 92.
19 Eric T. Freyfogle, "Introduction: A Durable Scale," in *The New Agrarianism*, pp. xiii–xli.
20 Barry Lopez, "Landscape and Narrative," in *Crossing Open Ground* (New York: Vintage, 1989), p. 64.
21 See Roger J. H. King, "Educational Literacy in the Context of Environmental Ethics," *Proceedings of the 20th World Congress of Philosophy* (1988). Available at www.bu.edu/wcp/Papers/Envi/EnviKing.htm (accessed December 12, 2009).
22 Berry, "The Whole Horse," pp. 71–2.
23 Ibid., p. 65.
24 bell hooks, "Earthbound: On Solid Ground," in Alison H. Deming and Lauret E. Savoy (eds.) *The Colors of Nature: Culture, Identity, and the Natural World* (Minneapolis: Milkweed Editions, 2002), p. 67.
25 Avishai Margalit, *The Ethics of Memory* (Cambridge, MA: Harvard University Press, 2002), pp. 7–8.
26 See Brian Donahue, "Reclaiming the Commons," in *The New Agrarianism*, p. 265.

CHAPTER 13

THE CAMERA OR THE GUN
Hunting through Different Lenses

Generally speaking, the current intellectual climate can be quite hostile towards hunting; in fact, some would take this a step further to contend that anti-hunting attitudes are fairly well entrenched within academia. Recently I told a fellow academic – who is also a hunter – that I was taking on a philosophical analysis of hunting, whereupon he immediately became thoroughly defensive, asking through clenched teeth, "Oh really? And what are you writing on?" He had already concluded that whatever it was, I must be gearing up to lambaste the activity. This is understandable when we look at well-known intellectuals and their positions on hunting.

In his work *Practical Ethics*, the famous animal liberation theorist Peter Singer argues against the use of non-human animals as food and in research. In what amounts to a one-line addendum, he critiques hunting *in all its forms* as a topic that raises issues similar to the ones he has already treated in his book, and so, with the conceptual heavy lifting completed, he hands them off to the reader to "apply the appropriate ethical principles to them."[1] That is, hunting is so clearly unethical that he need not even carry out an analysis to show this to be true! We, the readers, can simply figure this out on our own.

The animal rights theorist Tom Regan is equally dismissive of hunting in his defense of non-human animals. Regan, when defining what it means to be an animal rights advocate, claims he is committed to three goals: "(1) the total abolition of the use of animals in science; (2) the total dissolution of commercial animal agriculture; (3) the total elimination of commercial and sport hunting and trapping."[2] This constitutes another universal call for the cessation of hunting as an activity.

These are just two examples of popular and well-known theories that have inspired organized and calculated attacks on hunting as a practice. The focus of this chapter is not to provide a general philosophical response to these attacks, but to hone in on one specific issue that arises in these debates – that of wildlife photography as an ethically superior replacement for any hunting that attempts to kill a prey animal. Proponents of this so-called "photographic hunting" argue that even if there are benefits to weaponized sport hunting, similar benefits may be achieved through photographic hunting, and thus it is ethically preferable to sport hunting because the latter needlessly entails the death or injury of an animal. This chapter will evaluate such arguments against sport hunting to determine whether photographic hunting is an adequate replacement for weaponized hunting or whether something is lost in the former that is only to be found in the latter. Furthermore, if something is lost, we will look at whether this loss represents a significant reason to protect and maintain the practice of hunting properly speaking.

Must We Shoot to Kill?

Even if you are open to the possibility of there being benefits to the activity of hunting, you may still question whether those same benefits can't be derived from a far less violent and more inconsequential activity – photographic hunting. So I ask, must we shoot to kill? First, we need to look at what some of the alleged benefits of hunting are, and whether or not these benefits can only be derived through killing or attempting to kill an animal. One benefit of hunting is that it requires a rich understanding and knowledge of the environment the hunter acts within, and the animals he or she seeks. It is a simple but significant fact that for a hunter to be successful, he or she must have knowledge of the quarry. If I set as my objective to hunt and kill a beaver, but I know little to nothing about where beavers live, what they eat, and thus where and when I am likely to find one, I am likely to be frustrated in my efforts. To be successful requires intimate experiential knowledge of the prey species – its habitat, its food, its various behaviors, and so on.

Why is this simple fact so significant? It is significant because in recent years, environmental degradation and threats posed to ecosystems on a local and global scale have been blamed not only on humanity's inappropriate understanding of our role within ecosystems, but more fundamentally on a lost connection to environments and a loss of environmental knowledge.

As the majority of the world's citizens now live in urban areas, participation in wild nature beyond urban settings has decreased. Knowledge about natural environments is more often gained through textbooks than through activities which, like hunting, provide what may be called an "immersive learning experience." If most of us live in urban areas and don't venture out into non-urban ecosystems, we may not know the threats that these ecosystems are under. By contrast, the hunter is immersed in these environments and is witness to the animals and their habitats (or lack thereof), and thus has the potential to acquire a rich understanding of the overall health or sickness of animal populations or ecosystems as a whole. Perhaps surprisingly, hunters – who are often accused by environmentalists and others of being environmentally unfriendly in their actions – may have the best knowledge and understanding of environmental threats, and be in a position to remedy them.

A related point, and one made by the thoughtful hunter Aldo Leopold, is that the best way to ensure that people act ethically towards the natural environment is to inculcate in them feelings of love towards the environment. One of the best ways to do this, or perhaps the only way to do this, is to encourage actual experiences in wild, non-urban settings. One of the best ways to do this is by engaging in the hunt.

Let's pause for a second. So far, I don't believe that any of the benefits I've listed here can be attained only through weaponized hunting. I would suggest that they can all be equally derived from photographic hunting; many of the skills and environmental knowledge required of the weaponized hunter will likewise be required of the photographic hunter. He or she will need to know the animal sought, its habitat, its tracks, and its calls if he or she wishes to successfully photograph it. The photographic hunter must be stealthy in order not to frighten away the quarry and miss snapping a photo.

So, photographic hunting appears morally superior to weaponized hunting, because similar skills and knowledge are employed and similar value is derived, all without necessitating any harm to any animal. The act of shooting a photograph may momentarily anger or startle the target animal, but beyond that, little harm is apparently done. Even aspects of the hunters' code of sportsmanship (such as refraining from taking a shot that is not likely to result in the animal's quick death) recognize the obligation to minimize pain and suffering where possible, and thus could be understood to encourage photographic rather than sport hunting.[3] If we agree that hunting and killing an animal cause it pain and suffering, and photographing an animal causes less pain, then we should be morally obligated to arm ourselves with cameras rather than rifles on the hunt.

None of the benefits I've described in this section require that we must hunt to kill. These benefits of sport hunting may just as equally be obtained through photographic hunting. So, we ought to shoot with our cameras ... right? Like an infomercial, I implore: "but wait, there's more!"

I suggest that while the benefits described above are very real (and make photographic hunting a good practice in its own right), there is more to the act of hunting than can be captured by photographic hunting. Indeed, not only can photographic hunting not capture *all* of the benefits of sport hunting; as we shall see, if the photographic hunter conceives of his or her activity as an ethical replacement to sport hunting, this may turn the benefits of that activity upside-down and risk compromising the photographic hunter's position relative to the environment.

But what other important difference is there between photographic hunting and sport hunting? The difference may lie only in the final moment of the pursuit: the kill. However, this final moment is what many anti-hunters object to in sport hunting. So if I'm suggesting there is extra value in sport hunting that is not found in photographic hunting, then it must be in this contentious final moment. What benefit could there be in this? Why is an action that flies in the face of many people's ethical sensibilities worth preserving?

Hunting in the Real World

To speak merely of "hunting" is perhaps misleading, however, because it can take so many different forms, and not all are equally defendable. Some forms of hunting lack the redeeming qualities needed to justify their continuation. For example, while I was preparing this chapter a colleague alerted me to a news article entitled "Internet Hunting: Click & Kill," which documents an alarming modification of what is called a "canned hunt." A canned hunt is when an animal is confined within an enclosed space and the "hunter" kills the animal, which has no opportunity for escape. Canned hunts go against many hunters' understanding of sportsmanship. In Internet hunting, a tripod is set up within the enclosed space and equipped with a gun, such that from their home computer anyone can manipulate the tripod, take aim, and shoot an animal within the enclosure. I have no problem admitting that this is reprehensible! Indeed, one hunter in the article was quoted as saying, "It makes the people that hunt the right way look bad."[4] It is these aberrations that often make generic attacks on the practice of hunting so easy.

The question is, if this is one example of hunting the wrong way, then what is hunting the right way? What are the redeeming elements of the *true* hunt (if that can be identified) that make it an activity worth maintaining in the face of criticism and calls for its cessation? What remains is the role in which the hunter finds him or herself when engaged in the hunt relative to the surrounding environment.

Sport hunting connects us with wild nature in a way that many other "outdoor activities" do not. It opens our eyes to realities of the world from which we are often shielded, for example, the reality and necessity of death.[5] While the death dealing inherent to the hunt is criticized and hunters themselves are often portrayed as violent, in fact most of the meat we consume comes from animals that are dealt mechanical and impersonal deaths.[6] I have many friends and students who are meat eaters but who become offended and sickened if the animality of the food they eat is specifically called to attention; many of us prefer simply not to know where our food comes from.

This, however, can have devastating consequences. A discernible result of being shielded from ecological realities is a tendency to highlight natural processes of symbiosis or harmony while negating processes like predation. Rather than being recognized as an essential process of ecosystems without which the natural world as we know and love it could not have come into existence, predation comes to be seen as an undesirable process of wild ecosystems, and one that should be eliminated to the extent that it is possible.[7] Thus individuals may define themselves as environmentalists while rejecting parts of nature that are essential to its functioning.

Participating in weaponized hunting confronts the hunter with the seeming contradictions and mysteries of the natural world, and forces him or her to enter into them rather than be shielded from them. Photographic hunting fails to root the participant within an environment and connect him or her to the animals in the same way that sport hunting does. At best, photographic hunting can be considered a different sort of activity with its own merits; at worst, it is an unsatisfactory replacement for sport hunting with potentially destructive human and environmental impacts.

The Mastery of the Spectator and the Humility of the Hunter

Wildlife photography as environmentally unfriendly? Surely this is an exaggeration! But let us look more closely at the point at which these two activities fundamentally diverge: the moment of the kill. José Ortega y Gasset defines the hunter as a killer: "The hunter does not just come and go, working hard in valleys and on cliffs urging on his dogs; rather, in the last analysis, he kills. The hunter is a death dealer."[8] This fact is precisely what many anti-hunters lament and why photographic hunting is seen as infinitely more desirable. But while this death dealing can be summarily dismissed as brutality, authors like Ortega and Paul Shepard enter into this mysterious event, elegantly describing how the kill is something all good hunters confront with a sense of unease and internal conflict – yet not to such a degree as to convince them that refraining from killing is in fact morally preferable.

It is clear what prey animals stand to lose in the hunt, but what does the hunter stand to gain from the kill? Why is it important that the hunter kill and not photograph at the ultimate moment? Paul Shepard poses a similar question and provides a response: "What do the hunt and kill actually do for the hunter? They confirm his continuity with the dynamic life of animal populations, his role in the complicated cycles of elements, in the sweep of evolution, and in the patterns of the flow of energy."[9]

This is the aspect of rooting the hunter within an ecosystem that I described above. While photographic hunters may require similar knowledge leading up to the final moment, their activity does not allow them to enter into the mysteries of the kill in the same way and thus they are denied the knowledge gained from that activity. This knowledge of our role within ecosystems and continuity with other animals is what we lose when favoring photographic hunting over and against sport hunting.

This fact is enough in itself to challenge whether the two activities are similar at all, even in all the moments leading up to the kill. The sense of purpose and the way the two activities and objectives root the hunter in the environment color them in very different ways, such that even if both

🦌 JONATHAN PARKER

types of hunter fail in their ultimate objective, what they did, how they felt and conducted themselves – in short, how they existed in the environment – was fundamentally different.

The literature in environmental ethics has often placed the blame for our current ecological crisis on a false understanding of our role within the environment. Either our (Western) religions or our conceptual frameworks more broadly understood have led us to falsely perceive ourselves at an elevated position in comparison to the rest of nature and the animal kingdom. This falsely conceived role has led to a posture of mastery, which has led to environmental degradation and destruction.

Of course, it is *hunting* that is often described as an act of mastery and oppressive possession. Alternatively, I suggest that photographic hunting employs a false and dangerous understanding of our human role within ecosystems. Consider the following from Ortega:

> We fall, therefore, into a new immorality, into the worst of all, which is a matter of not knowing those very conditions without which things cannot be. This is man's supreme and devastating pride, which tends not to accept limits on his desires and supposes that reality lacks any structure of its own which may be opposed to his will. This sin is the worst of all, so much so that the question of whether the content of that will is good or bad completely loses importance in the face of it. If you believe that you can do whatever you like – even, for example, the supreme good – then you are, irretrievably, a villain. . . . One can refuse to hunt, but if one hunts one has to accept certain ultimate requirements without which the reality of "hunting" evaporates.[10]

By not hunting, then, we are cut off from these ultimate realities that cannot be accessed through photographic hunting. Worse than that, Ortega suggests anti-hunters are hubristic in the sense that they believe it is possible to remake themselves and the world according to their own ethical sensibilities, regardless of any limits or requirements imposed by nature. This suggests that there is nothing ultimate in the natural world that could rightly oppose our thoughts and desires. This is where Ortega is most critical of photographic hunting – he thinks it disconnects us from the ultimate realities that exist in the natural world, and by being so distanced we are put in a false position of mastery that supposes we can do as we please.

The irony here is that whereas anti-hunters point to hunting as demonstrating an elevated understanding of human mastery over nature and other animals, true hunters see the act of hunting as humbling the human and affirming the continuity of humans with non-human animals. Sportsmanship as a limitation on the hunter's ability to use technology to easily capture or kill prey animals is often spoken of as humbling the hunter. That is, the objective is not to demonstrate our mastery by killing as many animals as quickly as possible, but the opposite: hunters voluntarily impose rules and limitations on their actions and their accouterments.

However, anti-hunters could easily discount this self-limitation by seeing it as a means to increase the pleasure and ultimate satisfaction of the hunter, and thus not authentically humbling. But there is a deeper dimension to this yet. Ortega talks about the lives of prey species as being fundamentally centered around the avoidance of capture, and by following our instincts to capture or kill prey species, we participate in something original and true, often spoken of in terms of its sacredness. By doing so, the hunter affirms the natural processes that make this world we love what it is.

I mentioned earlier that it is not unusual for people who self-identify as environmentalists and/or animal lovers to oppose hunting, and more generally to be upset by the fact of predation in wild ecosystems. By extending their human ethics and sympathies, such people often see hunting as ethically wrong and analogous to murder. Taking this extensionist logic a step further, the very existence of predation can be, and is, called into question and lamented.[11] If predator eradication is deemed too cruel and violent, then proposals such as genetically modifying predatory species to prefer plant material rather than animal flesh are put forward. This is the kind of thinking that really demonstrates a profound sense of mastery and an elevated and alienated understanding of the human role within the environment. To think that we may stamp our sensibilities and sympathies onto the natural world and thereby radically alter its functionality demonstrates a profound sense of mastery and elevated understanding of who we are as a species and what we may do.

Predation is one of the conditions without which the world as we know it could not be.[12] Herein lies the irony. Anti-hunter environmentalists and anti-hunting animal lovers love a world and creatures that are only possible due to the fact of predation. Remove this one element from our ecosystems and we would have a radically different world, wherein the majestic creatures we appreciate would never come to be. So rather than hunters being the masters and oppressors of wild nature, the reverse is true. Hunting is an activity that puts the participant in touch with those ecosystemic truths that are obscured to the non-hunter and the photographic hunter.

🦌 JONATHAN PARKER

What Photography Cannot Capture

I am suggesting, therefore, that insofar as we conceive *wildlife photography as ethically superior* to weaponized hunting, we actually end up with a misconceived and potentially dangerous perspective that loses touch with fundamental knowledge of the environment and, by doing so, risks assuming a stance of mastery that is environmentally destructive. That is, rather than connecting and rooting the participant *in* the environment, photographic hunting situates a person *over* and *outside of* the environment – more akin to a spectator than a participant. This mode of thinking can lead to the desire to remake the natural world into one that pleases our human moral sensitivities.

Even though sport hunters are often conceived of as ignorant and morally reprehensible individuals who unnecessarily destroy or inflict pain upon animals and the environment, I have suggested here that the sport hunter is actually primordially rooted in an environment. Hunting facilitates access to ecosystemic truths and realities, a realization and closer feeling of continuity with non-human animals and nature, and is thus morally and environmentally praiseworthy. Hunting represents true or authentic participation in wild nature, the sort of participation that is normally inaccessible to contemporary human beings.[13]

Photographic hunting need not be seen as a morally reprehensible activity, as Ortega suggested earlier. It can be a great activity and hobby that brings people into contact with the natural world around them and has the potential to foster in them feelings of love and responsibility to the natural world. The danger lies in suggesting that all the benefits of sport hunting can be found within the activity of photographic hunting, and thus there is no justifiable reason for the continuance of sport hunting as a practice.

What I have argued for in this essay is that photographic hunting *cannot* be conceived of universally as a wholesale ethical *replacement* for sport hunting. The two activities root the participant in the environment in different ways and there is much that is lost in photographic hunting that doesn't translate over from the benefits of sport hunting. There surely are contexts and scenarios where sport hunting should be limited or restricted, and ethical sport hunters are often the first to agree or suggest that. However, in our current worldwide situation, we need the insights of those who have this profound and deep access to environmental truths and mysteries obscured from so many of us in contemporary society; these are the sport hunters, our "agents of awareness,"[14] and photographic hunters cannot replace them.[15]

NOTES

1   Peter Singer, *Practical Ethics*, 2nd ed. (Cambridge: Cambridge University Press, 1993), p. 68.
2   Tom Regan, "The Case For Animal Rights," in Peter Singer (ed.) *In Defence of Animals* (Oxford: Blackwell, 1985), p. 13.
3   See Brian Luke, "A Critical Analysis of Hunters' Ethics," *Environmental Ethics* 19, no. 1 (Spring 1997): 25–44.
4   Drew Sandholm, "Internet Hunting: Click & Kill," *KSFY.com Action News*. Available at www.ksfy.com/news/15148431.html (accessed October 5, 2009).
5   For more on this see T. R. Kover's essay, "Flesh, Death, and Tofu: Hunters, Vegetarians, and Carnal Knowledge," in this volume.
6   Paul Shepard, *The Others* (Washington, DC: Island Press, 1996), pp. 305–6.
7   See, for example, Tyler Cowen, "Policing Nature," *Environmental Ethics* 25, no. 2 (Summer 2003): 169–82.
8   José Ortega y Gassett, *Meditations on Hunting*, trans. Howard B. Wescott (Belgrade, MT: Wilderness Adventures Press), p. 97.
9   Paul Shepard, *Encounters with Nature*, ed. Florence R. Shepard (Washington, DC: Island Press, 1999), p. 74.
10 Ortega, *Meditations on Hunting*, p. 103.
11 See, for example, Ty Raterman, "An Environmentalist's Lament on Predation," *Environmental Ethics* 30, no. 4 (Winter 2008): 417–34.
12 Holmes Rolston, III, "Disvalues in Nature," *Monist* 75, no. 2 (April 1992): 250–78.
13 Cf. Ortega, *Meditations on Hunting*, p. 130.
14 Shepard, *Encounters with Nature*, p. 76.
15 I would like to thank Nathan Kowalsky and Richard Kover for their helpful comments and editorial contributions to this essay.

CHAPTER 14

FLESH, DEATH, AND TOFU

Hunters, Vegetarians, and Carnal Knowledge

We could have planned things more mercifully, perhaps, but our plans would never get off the drawing board until we agreed to the very compromising terms that are the only one that being offers. The world has signed a pact with the devil; it had to. It is a covenant to which every thing, every hydrogen atom is bound. The terms are clear: If you want to live, you have to die; you cannot have mountains and creeks without space, and space is a beauty married to a blind man. The blind man is called Freedom and he does not go anywhere without his great dog Death. The world came into being with the signing of a contract. ... This is what we know. The rest is gravy.
Annie Dillard, *Pilgrim at Tinker Creek*[1]

Who does not love life? Surely, the love of life is the ultimate truism, a statement to which all would assent, the foundation of our various religious traditions, philosophical systems, and all that we value. It also lies at the very heart of the hunting debate, with both sides appealing to this love of the natural world and ultimately life itself.

For many hunters, the hunt is a vital, visceral activity that throws one both physically and mentally into the heart of the natural world and confronts one with the fundamental issues of existence. The hunt, for them, is no simple recreational activity but a fundamental celebration of the natural world and life itself. In fact many hunters claim to love and respect the prey, and to feel a strong empathetic bond that borders on identification between themselves and the prey during the hunt.

However, for many opponents of hunting, such talk of love and the celebration of nature and wild animals by hunters is simply self-serving deceit to disguise their own dark, murderous bloodlust and hatred of nature. Quite simply, they ask, how can one love and identify with wild animals and then deliberately go out and take their lives? The answer to this question lies at the heart of the human condition, our relationship with and connection to the natural world: a tie that connects us not only to all life, but also to the inevitability of death itself.

Historically, much of the Western philosophical tradition has been committed to strenuously denying humanity's connection to nature and particularly our similarity to other animals, seeking to define the value and importance of human life precisely in terms of those features (such as language, rationality, conscious awareness, and culture) that were seen to distinguish us from other animals. In recent years, however, animal rights/liberation philosophers, such as Peter Singer and Tom Regan, have sought to challenge this absolute division between humanity and all other animals. Arguing that this division is motivated solely by the human need to justify its domination and exploitation of non-human animals, animal advocates point out that empirical evidence indicates that not only are humans animals, but also that other non-human animals share certain capacities with us, such as the ability to experience pain and pleasure, and perhaps in certain cases a limited degree of proto-conscious emotional awareness and forethought. On the basis of this, animal rights/ liberation theorists call on us to see our affinities with other animals and extend to them the same moral considerations and rights possessed by their human mental equivalents (i.e., the severely neurologically and cognitively impaired). This includes such things as freedom from unnecessary injury and pain and, fundamentally and perhaps most controversially, the right not to be killed and eaten.

Even though I would argue that we have certain fundamental ethical responsibilities to our own species that we do not have to others, I will leave aside the debate over whether membership in a particular species is ethically relevant. I will argue that while animal rights may seek to bridge the boundary between humanity and the rest of the non-human animal world by demonstrating that we too are part of the natural world and are animals, it does so in a way that betrays a certain unease with, even profound distaste for, this connection. Indeed, a large part of the problem that anti-hunting theorists have with hunting is not that it disconnects or alienates us from the natural world, but precisely that *it connects us too closely to it.*

For hunting not only immerses us in the natural world, requiring a considerable degree of knowledge concerning wildlife, it also brings us face to face with the fundamental dynamic of the natural world, the cycle of life, death, and consumption: a cycle from which not even we humans as biological beings (composed of flesh and blood) are immune. This is why much of Western thought has been "consumed" with denying the flesh and our link to the natural world. To recognize our carnal nature and our animality is to recognize our mortality.

Hunting as the Pursuit of Wild "Life"

Hunting is often seen by many of its critics as the paramount example of human domination and control of the natural world. Yet as Garry Marvin points out, hunting differs from other forms of animal killing precisely because of the absence of human control.[2] Relying on Matt Cartmill's definition of hunting, Marvin notes that most sport hunting involves the killing of wild animals (which have not been genetically tamed or otherwise put under our control), and which also must be able to escape or defeat the intentions of the hunter. Indeed, rather than reinforcing a sense of human superiority, hunting can impart in the mind of the hunter a much needed sense of human inferiority.

Living in the modern world, where evidence of human dominance and control abounds, it is easy to forget that in many ways wild animals are far superior to humans. For instance, though deer are often assumed to be helpless and defenseless creatures, in many respects they have physical and sensory endowments that put humans to shame. Not only are they far stronger and faster than any human, but in terms of their sense of hearing, sight, and smell there is no contest. Their panoramic peripheral vision allows them to detect the slightest movement from virtually all directions. Similarly, their large, swivel-mounted ears are sensitive enough to hear the inadvertent snap of a twig, a muffled cough, or the slightest sound of movement and to send these skittish creatures bolting. Yet this pales in comparison to a deer's sense of smell. Generally, if one is anywhere downwind of a deer's location, the game is up.

Of course, it may be countered that modern technological advances completely remove and minimize any advantage the prey may have over the hunter. Yet, it should be remembered that part of the ethos of modern sport hunting is that the hunter deliberately forgoes techniques and technologies that would make the relationship between the hunter and the prey too unequal, or make the hunter's success too easy, let alone a foregone conclusion. Moreover, despite the general public's overestimation of a gun's efficacy, it should be remembered that the accurate range of most hunters and their rifles is about 100 yards, well within range of being detected by the formidable sensory defenses of the deer.[3] In fact, even today, most hunts end without even visually spotting a deer: "Merely seeing the prey marks a good day of hunting."[4] Thus, if hunting were simply about the need to dominate and kill something, then employment in a slaughterhouse would offer a far better outlet for this.

It is the opportunity to spend time in and get close to nature, rather than the need to give vent to some frenzied bloodlust, that hunters routinely invoke when asked why they hunt. Few contemporary activities can rival hunting in terms of familiarizing and enmeshing oneself in the natural world, as hunting requires considerable knowledge of bush craft, the surrounding environment and the habits, behaviors, and spoor of the prey.[5] Furthermore, unlike hiking (and here I speak as an avid hiker), where one is aware of one's natural environment in an almost browsing manner, hunting calls for a much more active and keen attentiveness to one's environment. According to José Ortega y Gasset, this focused alertness towards one's environment is fundamental to the hunting experience and a central aspect of its appeal. Yet not only does hunting stimulate a hyperawareness in the hunter of her surroundings, it also inspires an intense sense of intimacy between the hunter and the prey.

It is often claimed by anti-hunting theorists that the hunter objectifies the prey or treats it as simply an object without any thoughts, feelings, or intentions. Yet the very activity of tracking and stalking the prey requires precisely the opposite: the hunter must assume that the prey has thoughts and intentions, and is in some sense conscious. Throughout the hunt, the hunter needs to continually get inside the mind of the animal, to see the world and the current situation from its perspective. Did the prey hear the rustle of grass as the hunter crept forward? Does the change in direction and speed of its tracks or the tilt of its head indicate that it has caught the hunter's scent? Thus the hunter must constantly imagine the *subjective* state of her quarry, attempting to quite literally perceive the situation though its senses.

T. R. KOVER

Carnal Bonds and the Way of All Flesh

To many anti-hunters, this aspect of hunting is perhaps the most incomprehensible: how can one identify so intimately and viscerally with the mind of another animal and then take its life? Many hunters confess to often feeling profound discomfort at the moment before taking the life of the prey: "Every good hunter feels uneasy in the depth of his conscience when faced with the death he is about to inflict on the enchanting animal."[6] Why, then, does the hunter not heed this pang of conscience? For Ortega, it is a matter of authenticity. If a virtue of hunting is that it enmeshes us in the natural world and confronts us with the fundamental truth of our essential connection to nature, then by taking the shot we face and acknowledge the basic condition of natural existence. As Holmes Rolston, III notes: "In ways that mere watchers of nature can never know, the hunter knows his ecology. Though the hunter succeeds, this is not conquest, but submission to his ecology. It is the acceptance of the way the world is made."[7]

Quite simply, as the old ecological adage goes, "Life feeds on life." Herbivores feed on plants, carnivores feed on herbivores, and when carnivores die, scavengers, worms, and microorganisms eat them, turning them into mulch, which in turn feeds the plants. Each day, our lives are sustained by the deaths of hundreds if not thousands of other organisms, whether one is a strident vegan or supermarket carnivore.[8] For most of us living in largely urban environments, this fact is largely hidden. The hunter, however, is confronted with and must acknowledge this essential fact of her dependency on and debt to the world and other organisms that sustain her. In this light, hunting can be understood as ultimately an act of respect for life, in that it forces us to take responsibility for the true cost of what it takes to feed ourselves and to bear witness to the suffering that sustains our life.

This recognition that "life feeds on life" has often been accused by animal liberationists as a form of "ecological fascism,"[9] which legitimates the perpetuation of human injustice, hierarchy, and dominance. Certainly, many on the political right have seen a justification for human forms of inequality and economic exploitation in the food cycle. But the wolf is not the overlord of the caribou! Indeed, there is no contest between an adult caribou and a wolf pack, as an adult caribou can generally outrun and outfight most wolves. Nor should it be forgotten that not even the wolf escapes death and consumption. In nature, it's not eat *or* be eaten, it's eat *and* be eaten. Nature is the consummate "recycler": everything gets consumed. There is a certain fundamental bio-egalitarianism to this recognition. Death is the great equalizer. Nothing is too high or mighty, too fast or strong to ultimately avoid either death or consumption, including a highly intelligent, bipedal, savanna ape with a very high opinion of itself. While *Homo sapiens* may feel that their intelligence and incredible degree of conscious awareness should grant them special consideration and remove them from this cycle of death and consumption, we are just as much "food for worms" as any elk or rodent. And it is this uncomfortable truth that ultimately confronts the hunter at the end of the hunt.

Just as the successful hunter must attempt to imaginatively inhabit the mind of the prey, such identification does not simply vanish with the quarry's death but continues as the hunter gazes upon its body and begins to gut and butcher it. While in certain respects different than that of humans, the corpse of the prey is uncannily close to ours. Its eyes, "the seat of the soul," stare out at us and, stripped of the fur and skin, the animal's flesh, inner organs, and viscera appear disquietingly similar to our own. Michael Pollan notes that while disemboweling a boar he had just shot, he was overcome with a wave of disgust and revulsion upon realizing how similar its organs were to his own.[10] Jim Harrison recalls of his own decision to no longer hunt deer that "gutting and skinning a deer reminds me too much of the human carcass and a deer heart too closely resembles my own."[11] The corpse of the prey is composed of flesh and blood, and eerily reminds us that we too are little more than a thin visage of skin encasing a body of flesh, blood, and inner viscera and susceptible to death and mortality, just as any other animal. Indeed, in his cross-cultural survey of disgust, the psychologist Paul Rozin notes that much of what disgusts us is that which reminds us of our animal nature.[12] Biological functions that we share with other animals, such as eating, excreting, and sex, tend to cause revulsion. Rozin argues that the root of this disgust with and rejection of our animality is the fearful recognition that we too are mortal and will eventually die.

In *The Denial of Death*, Ernest Becker sees this fear of our own mortality as the ultimate motivation behind the Western tradition's rejection of our animality and the natural world.[13] The fact that we reproduce, eat, and defecate like animals proves that we are incarnate beings who must eat to live and will eventually cease to do so. Humans thus attempt to find protection from this uncomfortable realization of our own mortality by rejecting or suppressing all that reminds us of our animality, such as our carnal embodiment. We seek solace in that which distinguishes us from all other animals – our reason and consciousness – in the vain hope that these might negate the fact of our mortality and that we, unlike all other animals, and by virtue of our reason and awareness, might escape death. Nowhere is this logic more obvious and apparent than in the history of traditional vegetarianism.

Saintly Chewing and the Corruption of the Flesh

Historically, the practice of vegetarianism in both Eastern and Western cultures has been strongly linked to asceticism, the renunciation of the body and the natural world. In his Golden Verses, Pythagoras, one of the first advocates of vegetarianism in the West, advises his followers: "Abstain thou from the meats which we have forbidden in the purifications and deliverance of the soul." The fundamental aim of Pythagoras' teachings was to teach his adherents how to "divest thyself from thy mortal body" so that one arrives at a state of pure immaterial "aether" and becomes "a god, immortal and incorruptible, and death will have no dominion over thee."[14] Eating the flesh of animals was proscribed by Pythagorean doctrine, therefore, because meat eating was seen as reinforcing humanity's animal and incarnate nature and preventing humans from achieving a state of spiritual immortality. Similarly, though abstinence from animal flesh was never central to Christian orthodoxy, it was practiced by some Christian ascetics such as St. Jerome, as well as by certain Gnostic sects, where the renunciation of both sex and "flesh" foods was seen as a spiritual practice by which one attempted to free oneself from the bondage of the material world and demonstrate one's contempt for it.

But given that plants also belong to the living material world, why are they not considered equally polluting? Rozin suggests that this is largely because, unlike animals, there is really little about plants for humans to identify with. Break open a carrot or a pumpkin and it becomes redolently apparent that its interior is nothing like our own. A shaft of wheat does not resemble our own flesh. Similarly, a slab of tofu, a Platonic form of nutrition if ever there was one, does not remind us of our own incarnateness. Hence its saintly status: the benefits of a fleshless diet prevent us from considering the awkward issues of our carnal embodiment. Little wonder then that Paul Shepard refers to vegetarianism as "beatific mastication,"[15] or saintly chewing.

Of course, modern adherents of vegetarianism distinguish themselves from their traditional antecedents by emphasizing that their concerns are more ethical than ascetic. Yet it is difficult not to discern the same symbolic connotations between the flesh, the death of animal life, and human mortality underscoring their own ethical concerns. In his autobiographical paper "The Bird in the Cage," Tom Regan reflects that his own decision to give up meat eating was motivated by the death of his canine companion. He writes:

> My head had begun to grasp a moral truth that required a change in my behavior. Reason demanded that I become a vegetarian. But it was the death of our dog that awakened my heart. It was that sense of irrecoverable loss that added the power of feeling to the requirements of logic.[16]

Unless Regan was planning to sauté and eat his dog, the death of his carnivorous pet from a car accident makes sense in terms of a motivation for vegetarianism only if Regan conceived of it as a wider rebellion against natural mortality. Similarly, the frequent references by vegetarians to meat eaters as "flesh eaters" or consumers of "rotting corpses" reveals a fundamental disquiet among vegetarians concerning the basic connection between life, flesh, and mortality. Yet perhaps the most obvious example of this connection is the frequent rhetorical question asked by vegetarians: "How would you like to be killed and eaten?" This capitalizes on one of the central reasons behind our unease in being connected to the natural world – *our edibility*.

According to ecofeminist Val Plumwood, in many ways vegetarianism can be seen as enforcing the position of human dominance and apartness from nature. Central to the human's conception of being separate from nature, Plumwood argues, is the notion that humans are outside the food chain – a notion, she notes, that is prevalent throughout our culture:

> This denial that we ourselves are food for others is reflected in many aspects of our death and burial practices – the strong coffin, conventionally buried well below the level of soil fauna activity, a slab over the grave, to prevent anything digging us up, keeping the human body (at least sufficiently affluent ones) from becoming food for other species. Sanctity is interpreted as guarding ourselves zealously and keeping ourselves apart, refusing to conceptualize ourselves as edible, and resisting giving something back, even to the worms and the land that nurtured us. Horror movies and stories reflect this deep-seated dread of becoming food for other forms of life: horror is the wormy corpse, vampires sucking blood, and sci-fi monsters trying to eat humans.[17]

Thus, ironically, vegetarianism urges us to relate to the rest of the animal world by extending to animals the human status of being beyond ecology and the food cycle, the very conceit that is at the heart of our radical separation from nature. It is to be wondered whether this fundamental discomfort with the food cycle does not translate into a more basic condemnation of nature itself.

In his paper "Bambi Lovers vs. Tree Huggers," Ned Hettinger asks whether animal rights theorists can condemn all forms of hunting and not, by the same token, condemn the natural world in general and predators in particular. The question Hettinger puts to anti-hunters is, if it is morally condemnable for humans to take the life of animals, then why isn't all animal predation equally as bad?[18]

Critics of hunting have offered a number of counters to this. The first and most obvious move is simply to own up and condemn animal predation as well. The anti-hunting activist Cleveland Amory declared that he would be in favor of a form of ecological apartheid whereby predator and prey would be kept separate.[19] Similarly, the economist Tyler Cowen argues that we should, when economically feasible, take steps to protect herbivores from carnivores up to and including exterminating predatory species.[20] Likewise Marcel Wissenburg has argued that we have an ethical duty "to recreate nature in such a way that no animal shall ever again unnecessarily kill or harm another animal."[21]

Of course, most anti-hunting and animal rights theorists see the incredible contradiction in trying to preserve the natural world from human domination by radically altering it. Consequently, many animal rights theorists attempt to argue that while animal predation and meat eating may be the workings of nature, they should not be the workings of humanity. Peter Singer writes:

> It is odd how humans, who consider themselves so far above animals, will ... use an argument that implies we ought to look to other animals for moral inspiration and guidance! The point is that other animals are not capable of considering other alternatives, or of reflecting morally on the rights or wrongs of killing for food; they just do it. We may regret the way the world is, but it makes no sense to hold nonhuman animals morally responsible or culpable for what they do.[22]

Leaving aside whether the question of whether the fact that predators cannot be considered morally blameworthy is really a robust enough rebuttal to the argument that we should take steps to remove predation,[23] the supreme irony is that Singer, having emphasized our essential continuity with animals in order to advocate for vegetarianism, now supposes a radical discontinuity with them in order to make his case. His case is essentially *yes, natural predation is evil but humans know better and are morally superior to all other animals and the natural world*, or as the vegetarian food columnist Stephany Anne Goldberg succinctly put it, "Nature is an asshole. We know this and other animals don't."[24] In other words, nature is essentially evil and we shouldn't lower ourselves to the level of brutes. Thus, Singer relies on an argument concerning the fallen and radically evil state of nature (which has had a long history in Western thought) to emphasize humanity's essential apartness from nature and other animals.

This same emphasis on the radical discontinuity between humans and animals in order to condemn hunting is also made by Paul Veatch Moriarty and Mark Woods in their paper "Hunting ≠ Predation." For according to them, "meat-eating and hunting are cultural activities not natural activities, [as] ... our distinctly human evolutionary achievement – culture – has strongly separated us from non-human nature. We have found freedom from ecosystems ... and are no longer a part of ecosystems." Thus, because meat eating and hunting are strongly influenced by culture, they can no longer be considered to "involve ... participation in the logic and biology of natural ecosystems."[25] Yet surely most of the basic biological functions we share with other animals, such as eating and sex, also have a heavily cultural component. Defecation, for instance, perhaps an act that is seen as most clearly tying us to the realm of nature, is also in some sense cultural. Not only is it circumscribed by cultural taboos and symbolic meanings, which differ from culture to culture and from historical epoch to historical epoch, but these prescriptions and meanings (as any parent of young children knows) must be acculturated. Does the fact that defecation is also a cultural act mean that it is not natural or that there are no relevant parallels between human and animal defecation? In fact, as both Rozin and Becker note, it is precisely by culturally circumscribing such basic biological acts that humans attempt to convince themselves that they are not animals and hence immune from the fate that awaits all other animals, namely, death and consumption. The tendency to explain away any unpleasant or disquieting aspects of the natural world as simply cultural constructions reaches its zenith with Roger J. H. King, who suggests that Ortega and Shepard's argument that the hunt confronts us with the fundamental and unpleasant reality of our mortality is a manifestation of patriarchal necrophilia.[26]

The Vital Paradox: The Acceptance of Death as Affirmation of Life

The question haunting the hunting debate – indeed, also the meat-eating and ultimately the environmental debate – is the question of death. To recognize our carnal embodiment and kinship to the natural world is to recognize our own mortality – hence the reason why so much of human history and culture have been preoccupied with strenuously denying our connection to nature. However, if we are to save and preserve wild nature – if we are to grant that its existence has value – we must recuperate the very grounds upon which we sought to escape it in the first place: the issue of our mortality. We must come to terms with this disturbing fact and hunting may offer a possible solution. If hunting, by its very nature, requires that we at least visit the wilderness, be familiar with the behavior of wild species, and become aware that in many respects other animals are superior to us, vegetarianism doesn't. If hunting poses the question of how our lives are dependent on taking the lives of other animals, vegetarianism virtually requires that we don't know. If hunting requires that we confront and affirm the fundamental dilemma of all incarnate beings that we die and feed life, then vegetarianism capitalizes on our unease with this carnal fact. As David Petersen writes,

> We are alive the elk and I, precisely because we both must die. Our mortality is the lantern globe that contains shapes and illuminates the brief, flickering flames of our lives, rendering us numinous ... It's the fragility and moment to moment ephemerality of our lives that render them sacred: even as the certainty of our deaths – yours, mine, the elk's – makes us ultimate equals.[27]

Or, to paraphrase the late Paul Shepard, it is by hunting animals that we learn "to love life on its own terms."[28]

NOTES

1 Annie Dillard, *Pilgrim at Tinker's Creek*, in *Three by Annie Dillard* (New York: Harper Perennial, 1990), p. 176.
2 Garry Marvin, "Wild Killing: Contesting the Animal in Hunting," in *Killing Animals* (Urbana: University of Illinois Press, 2006), pp. 10–29.

3 Lawrence Cahoone, "Hunting as a Moral Good," *Environmental Values* 18 (2009): 74.

4 Ibid., p. 78.

5 This would explain why, in demographic surveys, hunters routinely rank above other sections of the population in terms of their general knowledge of wilderness and wild species. See Stephen Kellert, "Attitudes and Characteristics of Hunters and Antihunters," *Transactions of the Fourty-Third North American Wildlife and Natural Resources Conference* (Washington, DC: Wildlife Management Institute, 1978), pp. 412–23.

6 José Ortega y Gasset, *Meditations on Hunting*, trans. Howard B. Wescott (New York: Charles Scribner's Sons, 1972), p. 88.

7 Holmes Rolston, III, *Conserving Natural Value* (New York: Columbia University Press, 1994), p. 125.

8 Many vegetarian theorists claim that the vegetarian diet is cruelty free, for example Brian Luke, *Brutal: Manhood and the Exploitation of Animals* (Urbana: University of Illinois Press, 2007). This overlooks the fact that crop agriculture, particularly in its modern industrialized form, involves a tremendous amount of suffering and death to wild animals. Not only are rodents, birds, and even baby fawns routinely cut to shreds in between the blades of a harvester, but a substantial amount of deer are shot by farmers protecting their crops. As Richard Nelson puts it, "Whenever any of us sit down to breakfast, lunch, dinner or a snack, it's likely that a deer was killed to protect some of the food we eat and the beverages we drink. This is true for everyone: city dwellers and suburbanites; men, women and children; omnivores and vegetarians; hunters, non-hunters and antihunters." Richard K. Nelson, *Heart and Blood: Living With the Deer in America* (New York: Vintage Books, 1997), p. 310.

9 Tom Regan, *The Case for Animal Rights* (Berkeley: University of California Press, 2004), p. 362.

10 Michael Pollan, *The Omnivores Dilemma: A Natural History of Four Meals* (Detroit: Large Print Press, 2006), p. 571.

11 Jim Harrison, "The Violators," in David Petersen (ed.) *A Hunter's Heart: Honest Essays on Blood Sport* (New York: Henry Holt, 1996), p. 212.

12 Paul Rozin, "Food is Fundamental, Fun, Frightening, and Far-Reaching," *Social Research* 66 (1999): 9–30; Jonathan Haidt, Paul Rozin, Clark McCauley, and Sumio Imada, "Body, Psyche, and Culture: The Relationship between Disgust and Morality," *Psychology and Developing Societies* 9, no. 1 (1997): 107–31.

13 Ernest Becker, *The Denial of Death* (New York: Free Press Paperbacks, 1973).

14 Cited in Rod Preece, *Sins of the Flesh: A History of Ethical Vegetarian Thought* (Vancouver: University of British Columbia Press, 2008), p. 82.

15 Paul Shepard, *The Others: How the Animals Made Us Human* (Athens, GA: University of Georgia Press, 1997), p. 315.

T. R. KOVER

16 Tom Regan, "The Bird in the Cage: A Glimpse of My Life," *Between the Species* 2–3 (1986): 42–9, 90–9, quote at p. 93.

17 Val Plumwood, "Animals and Ecology: Towards a Better Integration," in Steve F. Sapontzis (ed.) *Food for Thought: The Debate over Eating Meat* (Amherst, MA: Prometheus, 2004), p. 348. Indeed, this horror and disgust at being eaten are manifest in contemporary artistic works such as Werner Herzog's film *Grizzly Man* (2005), where one cannot but wonder if part of the tragedy concerning Treadwell's end is intimately tied to the fact that he is eaten by an animal.

18 Ned Hettinger, "Bambi-Lovers vs. Tree-Huggers," in *Food for Thought*, pp. 294–301.

19 Amory writes: "All animals will not only not be shot, they will be protected – not only from people but as much as possible from each other. Prey will be separated from predator, and there will be no overpopulation because all will be controlled by sterilization or implant." Cleveland Amory, "Response to a Question: Now, If I Ruled the World ..." *Sierra* (May–June 1992). Available at http://findarticles.com/p/articles/mi_m1525/is_n3_v77/ai_12095996/pg_12/?tag=content;col1 (accessed December 15, 2009).

20 Tyler Cowen, "Policing Nature," *Environmental Ethics* 25, no. 2 (Summer 2003): 169–83.

21 Marcel Wissenburg, "The Lion and the Lamb: Wider Implications of Martha Nussbaum's Animal Ethics," p. 11. Available at www.wissenburg.com/pdf/Nussbaum//.pdf (accessed December 4, 2009).

22 Peter Singer, *Animal Liberation*, 3rd ed. (New York: HarperCollins, 2002), pp. 224–5.

23 Cowen points out the essential arbitrariness of focusing on the moral agency of the killer involved while overlooking the harm done to the victim. He notes that "stopping a human killer does not rest on whether we consider the killer to be a 'moral agent,' mentally retarded, totally insane, or a vampire" (Cowen, "Policing Nature," p. 176).

24 Stephany Anne Goldberg, "Happy, Fat, and Meatless: A Proposal for a 21st-Century Vegetarianism." Available at www.tablematters.com/index.php/plate/vm/vm1 (accessed November 21, 2009).

25 Paul Veatch Moriarty and Mark Woods, "Hunting ≠ Predation," *Environmental Ethics* 19, no. 4 (Winter 1997): 391–405.

26 Roger J. H. King, "Environmental Ethics and the Case for Hunting," *Environmental Ethics* 13, no. 1 (Spring 1991): 80.

27 David Petersen, *Heartsblood: Hunting, Spirituality and Wildness in America* (Boulder, CO: Johnson Books, 2000), p. 105.

28 Shepard, *The Others*, p. 92.

PART IV

THE ANTLER CHANDELIER
Hunting in Culture, Politics, and Tradition

CHAPTER 15

THE SACRED PURSUIT

Reflections on the Literature of Hunting

Those human societies that still live by hunting – in the Arctic, the equatorial forests, and the African grasslands – were, until recently, illiterate. They had the greatest use for words, memory, and song, but no use for literature. The written word belongs to that later stage of human development in which agriculture eats up the land, in which hunter-gatherers become exiles in their territory and in which the city looms on the near horizon, sending messages on paper to all who buy and sell. With the land parceled up and "taken into possession," hunting ceases to be a livelihood and becomes, instead, a recreation. Nevertheless, through hunting we experience something of an earlier, more intimate, and more respectful relation to the landscape, and it is this distant drum-beat in the soul that is awakened by the best of hunting art and literature.

Great writers and artists treat hunting as an activity that takes place outside ordinary life, in which ancient needs and instincts find expression. From the boar hunt that begins at line 428 of Homer's *Odyssey* to the foxhunt that forms the climax of Trollope's *The Eustace Diamonds*, hunting has been used to lift characters from their daily circumstances and to place them in another predicament, which rouses their animal spirits and puts them to a very special kind of test. The wall of domesticity has been broken down, and we cross it to "the other side of Eden," as Hugh Brody describes the world of the hunter-gatherer.[1] In that world animals are not the tamed and subservient creatures of the farmyard or the family house; they are our equals, with whom we are locked in a contest that may prove as dangerous to the hunter as it is to his quarry. In the paintings that adorn the caves of Lascaux we see the beasts of the wilderness portrayed by people who lived in awe of them, and who conjured them into their own human dwelling place. The aura that emanates from these images emanates in a certain measure from our hunting literature, reminding us that we too are animals, and that we live, in our domesticated circumstances, with an unpaid debt towards the creatures from whom we have stolen the Earth.

In a sense we know much about the experience of the hunter-gatherer, since it is the experience that shaped us, and which forms an archaeological stratum beneath the translucent consciousness of civilized man. At its greatest the art and literature of hunting aims to retrieve that experience, to reacquaint us with mysterious and sacred things which are the true balm to our suburban anxieties, but which can be recuperated now only by returning, in imagination, to a world that we have lost. This explains why the art and literature of hunting are so deeply loved, even by those who have no first-hand knowledge of hunting and even among those who campaign on behalf of animals against the humans who abuse them.

Famous among such campaigners was Richard Wagner. Yet no modern artist has evoked the world of the hunter-gatherer so vividly, or used the imagery of hunting so effectively, in order to explore the deeply buried layers of the human psyche. *Parsifal* begins when a community devoted to the Holy Grail – a symbol of our redemption – is disturbed by a hunter. In the community of the Grail all animals are holy, and the redeemer's self-sacrifice on the Cross is understood to have removed the need for further victims. By learning guilt over his quarry's death Parsifal takes the first step towards understanding the place of guilt in the human condition, and exchanges the life of the hunter for that of the knight errant in search of God. In renouncing hunting, and joining the Knights of the Grail, Parsifal is exchanging one sacred pursuit for another.

It is the connection of hunting with old ideas of the sacred and the forbidden that Wagner brings into dramatic focus in his dramas. This we see clearly in *Tristan und Isolde*, the second act of which opens with the most beautiful evocation of a distant hunt in all music (closely rivaled, however, by the royal hunt and storm in Berlioz's *Trojans*), and ends with Tristan himself as quarry to begin the journey into darkness that will shape him as a sacrificial offering, and show his death as the redemption of a love which can have no other fulfillment.[2] Why, you may ask, is

Tristan a sacrificial offering? And the answer, briefly, is that this is a mystery that can be *shown*, but not explained.

Significant in this respect is the role of hunting in *The Ring*, in which hunting is portrayed from the outset as the background condition of the human order, with Siegmund driven as quarry into Hunding's house, there to meet the sister who had been orphaned by hunters, and to flee with her into the forest to be hunted as a pair. (The closing of Act II of *Die Walküre*, with Sieglinde's nightmare of being hunted set against the approach of Hunding's hounds, is surely without compare as a vision of hunting from the quarry's perspective.) The Valkyries are hunter-gatherers of human flesh, and the great turning point of the drama occurs in Act II of *Die Walküre*, when Brünnhilde and Siegmund – hunter and hunted – confront each other, and the work of pity begins. This passage has the grandeur of Greek tragedy: it is the moment of recognition, when the vain charms of immortality lose their luster. Mortals are hunted by the gods; but it is the gods who are the losers. Brünnhilde sees that this is so, and the world changes.

The great culmination of the tetralogy occurs when Siegfried, hunting with his new companions, recounts the story of his life, and so becomes the quarry. This miraculous scene shows the recovery of the victim's innocence at the very moment when he offers himself for sacrifice – so that he offers himself, so to speak, *through* his innocence, thereby under-mining the aggression. The orchestra in this passage becomes the supremely sympathetic observer of its own sacrificial victim, following his narrative in a kind of subdued awe, leading him on with gentle ges-tures as the sacred bull was led to the altar, encouraging him to give the sign of acceptance that will summon the sacrificial blow.

The connection between Siegfried's death and the stories of victims sacrificed and sanctified so that the world might be renewed was noticed by Thomas Mann, in a passage that deserves quotation:

> The overpowering accents of the music that accompanies Siegfried's funeral cortège no longer tell of the woodland boy who set out to learn the meaning of fear; they speak to our emotions of what is *really* passing away behind the lowering veils of mist: it is the sun-hero himself who lies upon the bier, slain by the pallid forces of darkness – and there are hints in the text to support what we *feel* in the music: "A wild boar's fury," it says, and: "Behold the cursed boar," says Gunther, pointing to Hagen, "who slew this noble flesh." The words take us back at a stroke to the very earliest picture-dreams of mankind. Tammuz and Adonis, slain by the boar, Osiris and Dionysus, torn asunder to come again as the Crucified One, whose flank

must be ripped open by a Roman spear in order that the world might know Him – all things that ever were and ever shall be, the whole world of beauty sacrificed and murdered by wintry wrath, all is contained within this single glimpse of myth.[3]

The connections made somewhat breathlessly by Mann need more philosophical and anthropological exegesis than I can give them here, but it is surely right to connect Wagner's many invocations of the hunt with a primeval experience of the sacred. The world of the hunter-gatherer is an enchanted world, in which gods and spirits still roam, brimful of interest in the activities of people. In that world death is not a natural but a supernatural event – either a propitiation of some deity, or a stroke of fate, administered from outside the natural order. The death of the quarry too is seen in that way. The antelope dies so that the species may live, to be worshipped as a totem by the tribe that feeds on its flesh.

Wagner's invocation of a society in which farming and hunting exist side by side, on the edge, so to speak, of the god-haunted forest, is part of an ambitious allegory, whose purpose is to illustrate the godless world into which we human beings emerge when science and industry take over. The prophetic force of *The Ring* is undeniable. But we should remember that it is a work about the modern world which treats hunting as a symbol rather than a subject in itself. By contrast there are works of literature that are explicitly about hunting – both hunting as a way of life and hunting as a ritual intrusion into the world of civilized man. Some of the greatest examples are American. Two stand out for their qualities as writing: James Fenimore Cooper's *The Last of the Mohicans* and Hermann Melville's *Moby Dick*. The first is romantic, thinly characterized, with more than a whiff of schoolboy adventure. The Native Americans described by Cooper are no longer hunter-gatherers. But the book contains incomparable descriptions of the other side of Eden – how it looked, sounded, and smelled, before man the farmer exterminated his hunting brothers.

This extermination of the hunter by the farmer is foretold in the biblical story of the first murder. Cain's offering of fruit from his orchard is disdained by the Lord, who prefers the savory odor that rises from the roasted flesh offered up by Abel who, although a herder rather than a hunter, has retained that intimate relation with the animal kingdom from which Cain has moved on. So Cain kills Abel, in a fit of jealousy for which he is only imperfectly punished. Cain is condemned to wander the Earth, and is thereby deprived for his lifetime of the only thing – settling down – which makes farming profitable. In this story we see a more intuitive and untheoretical glimpse into the psychic residues that were deposited by our hunting fathers. In Fenimore Cooper the story is told more fully by someone who witnessed the extinction of the Native American way of life, and who listened in the American forests for the still lingering voices of vanished gods.

Like *The Last of the Mohicans*, *Moby Dick* is a descriptive masterpiece. But here the characterization is realistic, grim, and strong. Moreover, Melville has a deep insight into the feature of hunting which distinguishes it from other ways of harvesting animals – namely, that hunting is the pursuit of an individual. The hunted quarry is singled out and then hounded to death. (The verb "to hound" is borrowed from the only sport that is called "hunting" in the English spoken in England.) And the singling out also ennobles, transfigures the quarry from general to particular, and from food to foe. The White Whale was an individual enemy for Captain Ahab, respected as such, but also hated. The hatred is abnormal and perverse, a pollution that is brought to the chase by the tensions and resentments of civilized man. But although the relation between Ahab and Moby Dick is bitter and perverse, it recalls another and deeper relationship in which hatred has no part, and that is the sacred bond between totem and clan.

Although Melville's masterpiece offers general invocations of whaling, therefore, it also contains something else: an exploration of a primeval state of mind, which has nothing to do with commercial whaling, but everything to do with the relation between the hunter-gatherer and his prey. In comparison with Melville's example, much that is commonly called hunting literature is really nothing of the sort. Beautiful though it is, Ivan Turgenev's *A Sportsman's Notebook* (1852) touches not at all on the mystery of hunting. It is the diary of a country wanderer, of a pilgrim among peasants, who sees the soil as they do. This kind of wandering, gun in hand, through deeply settled territory, is a recreation, whose goal is to make contact with the simpler forms of human life.

True hunting literature summons up another relation with the earth than that which we know from city life and farming. In this other relation we are at one with the animals, and bound to them by religious ties. And that is why hunting with hounds is so significant to those who take part in it. For the relation between man and dog when joined in common dangers is a healing relation. It closes the wound that was opened by our detachment from the animal kingdom, overcomes the guilt of consciousness and provides a companionship rooted in the earth itself. Homer knew this, and used it in one of his most beautifully understated strokes of drama – the moment of Odysseus' return in disguise to Ithaca, when he is recognized by his favorite hound Argos who lies, neglected and dying, on the muck heap, and who flattens his ears and wags his tail, too weak for any other greeting. The hero wipes away a furtive tear, and, "as for Argos, the fate of black death seized him straightway in his twentieth year."[4]

The same instinctive companionship between man and dog in the hunting field is invoked in the ancient story of Actaeon who, hunting with his hounds, catches sight of the naked goddess Diana. The story, told by Ovid,[5] and beautifully retold by Ted Hughes, provides another vista over that now silent landscape we carry within. Diana is the goddess of hunting, but also the divine keeper of chastity, the goddess who stands aloof from domestic relations, who controls the animal kingdom because she has done away with the animal in herself. She punishes Actaeon by turning him into a stag, removing his humanity and making him fair game to his hounds. It is one of the most poignant moments in the story, as Ovid tells it, that Actaeon pleads with each hound by name as it plants its teeth in his body. The intimate relation that was mediated by naming – the act which distinguishes us above all the other animals – is replaced by another and yet more intimate relation, between the mouth of a dog and the flesh of its quarry.

The ancient world was well aware that hunting with hounds involves a subversion of farming. The hunter is led by his hounds, who are led by the quarry. The quarry is indifferent to legal boundaries: it pays no attention to husbandry and settlement, and the huntsman will be led equally into common land and private property, into wilderness and the sacred groves and temples of the gods. This too is figured in the legend of Actaeon and Diana, and great was the outrage in ancient times when sacred precincts were invaded by the wild horde in hot pursuit of a boar or a stag. Hence Plato's elaborate defense of hunting with hounds in *The Laws*, in which he argues that hunting, properly pursued, is a form of piety with its own place in the landscape.

For Plato the pious hunter should not only respect the sacred places; he should also respect the quarry. Not any way of killing an animal is permissible in the ideal State, as Plato describes it in *The Laws*. Savage butchery is to be avoided, and the quarry itself should be properly singled out. Plato therefore condemned unworthy forms of hunting, like angling, which use hooks and other tricks and contrivances. He compared these devices to piracy, since they make us into "cruel and lawless hunters," seizing advantage by tricks. He distinguished such lawless hunting from "sacred hunting," which is the only sort that should be permitted, since it alone is compatible with human virtue. He defines it thus:

> only the best kind of hunting is allowed at all [i.e., in the ideal State described in *The Laws*] – that of quadrupeds, which is carried on with horses and dogs and men's own persons, and they get the victory over the animals by running them down.[6]

The distinction between virtuous and vicious hunting has been remade and reinforced down the ages. It is often made in Plato's terms, as a distinction between hunting that gives the quarry no chance and uses superior technology in order to place it at a disadvantage, and the attempt to confront the quarry on equal and equalizing terms and to share, to whatever small extent, in its danger. The use of machinery and stratagems is alien to the hunting way of life, which requires us to reenter that earlier condition, if only in imagination, in which man and animal confront each other on equal terms. Plato's point is consciously recalled by José Ortega y Gasset, in his invocation of the aristocratic virtues of a fast vanishing Spain. Ortega's defense of hunting – *La Caza* (1960) – is one half of a book, the other half, *Los Toros*, being devoted to the native Spanish art of bullfighting, the last surviving offshoot of the Roman games, and an after-image of the vanished cult of Mithras. For Ortega hunting with hounds, as opposed to shooting (also called "hunting" in American usage), involves

> the man imposing limitations in the face of the animal, so as to give fair play, not creating an excessive imbalance between quarry and hunter, since to surpass certain limits in their relation disturbs the essentially equal nature of the hunt, transforming it into mere butchery and destruction.[7]

Ortega's contempt for *pura matanza y destrucción* is shared by all hunt followers, who – paradoxical though it seems to those who do not share their passion – are bound to the animal kingdom by a comprehensive web of benevolence. The hunted species stands at the end of strong filaments of kindness that run through man, horse, and dog and which attach the quarry to the rim of their mutual sympathy. Of course, there is no way that the hunted animal can be aware of this, and the books of hunt jollification that pretend that the fox, stag, or hare "enjoy" being hunted are just so much sentimental nonsense. Yet anyone who has shared in the mystery of hunting side by side with horse and hound will be familiar with a deep and atavistic sympathy with the animal kingdom, of a kind that touches on primordial religious needs, and which in my view shows far more respect for animals than the sentimental fantasies of the Bambi-lover.

From Plato to Ortega those who have written in praise of hunting with hounds have written from the vantage-point of civilized people. Only the deeply buried traces have remained in them of the religious awe and totemic veneration that we see recorded on the walls of the Lascaux caves. Hunting, for most artists and writers who have treated the topic, has been a recreation and a sport, in which contact with the animal kingdom comes largely through the horses and hounds, which are its necessary instruments. The religious element survives largely in the ritualization – in the uniforms, the archaic and "liturgical" language, and in ceremonies such as the blessing of the hounds and the "blooding" of newcomers. It is also recalled in the devotional art and literature which hunting has inspired. From the *Books of Saints and Martyrs* to the votive images at popular shrines, devotional art is polluted by kitsch and sacred saccharine, and hunting art is no exception. In many a respectable English country house the walls are encrusted with hunting prints in execrable taste, and the library is given over to books of sentimental sporting lore, fox-hunting ballads, and doggerel verse in the style of "D'ye ken John Peel?"

From this mass of second-rate art and literature, however, there has emerged, from time to time, inspired and lasting classics, in which the ancient meaning of the hunt gives urgency to the narrative and life and soul to the characters. The first example in English is *Sir Gawain and the Green Knight*, which describes a foxhunt in terms that initiate a long tradition in English fox-hunting literature by representing the fox as an object of sympathy. In 1735 there appeared a highly influential poem in blank verse called *The Chase* by William Somerville. This poem is as much a manual as an invocation, and describes hunting as a *domesticated* pursuit, one in which the triumph of the farmer over the hunter-gatherer is entirely taken for granted, yet briefly set aside for the purpose of sport. This new attitude is celebrated in the paintings of George Stubbs (1724–1806) and the novels of Henry Fielding, such as *Tom Jones* (1749). By the time of the sporting tales and novels of R. S. Surtees (1805–64), however – notably *Handley Cross* (1843) and *Mr. Sponge's Sporting Tour* (1853) – a new relation to the landscape has emerged. Stubbs' horses and hounds were the property of aristocrats, who were sovereign in their mansions over all that they surveyed. The novels of Surtees describe a society of incomers, refugees from the industrials cities, finding solace in country pursuits and enjoying the landscape without the first claim to owning it.

Under the guidance of Surtees' cockney hero – the shopkeeper John Jorrocks, MFH, who sells tea to the gentry while jumping beside them over hedges – we see an emerging egalitarian community, united by common danger, charging across a countryside in which the boundaries have been erased and ownership extinguished by the chase. We also find a relation to the quarry which is not utilitarian or pleasure-seeking but again religious. The fox has been redeemed from his vermin status and remade as the sacred totem – the animal who is honored as a divine species, and pursued to the death in his earthly and incarnate form.

In Surtees, therefore, we hear again the distant echo of hunter-gatherer attitudes. Jorrocks and his lunatic companions have slipped out of the orderly world of tilling and sowing, buying and selling, owning and toiling, and have reasserted the old right to the landscape as a common home, a place that we share with the animals, and a field of action with only natural boundaries. Foxhunting provides the perfect literary foil for this shift in attitude, for boundaries are all-important to the sport. They are the obstacles which prove your mettle and which unite you spiritually with your horse, even in the moment when they divide you from him bodily. At the same time these boundaries cease to be marks of ownership and exclusion, and become natural phenomena, parts of our shared habitat, the old meaning of which is rediscovered in the chase.

As a result, the landscape, brilliantly evoked by Surtees and his followers – by the Scottish-born G. J. Whyte-Melville, whose fox-hunting novel *Market Harborough* appeared in 1861, and by the two Irish ladies, writing as Edith Somerville and Martin Ross, to whom we owe *The Experiences of an Irish R.M.* (1899) – is recalled as it was, before the cruel extermination of "our hunting fathers." The egalitarian society celebrated by Surtees, Whyte-Melville, and Trollope is one in which all attempts at status are shown, in the arduous work of hunting, to be no better than a pretense. Anybody who has felt the power of English hunting literature has glimpsed, also, a world of pre-agricultural innocence, to which we can return in imagination, but never in fact, since it has been domesticated, framed by the peaceful occupations of the farmer, and made safe. The dangers of the sportsman are optional, those of the hunter-gatherer are required.

It was to foxhunting that English writers turned in the wake of the Great War, in order to repossess their country and to imbue it once again with the spirit of peaceful settlement. Siegfried Sassoon's *Memoirs of a Foxhunting Man* of 1928 is well known, combining realism, humor, and nostalgia in an intoxicating and very English synthesis. It was preceded by John Masefield's epic poem *Reynard the Fox* or *The Ghost-Heath Run*, published in October 1919. The poem is neither a masterpiece nor a piece of hunting doggerel, but a professional poet's attempt to invoke the loyalty and cohesion of the old village communities. For those country people who had survived the trenches it went some way towards justifying their sufferings. As for the hunts themselves it was a call to resume their former place in the rural order, to replace some of the two million horses that had been killed in the carnage, and to restore a lost icon of peace. The poem went through three reprints in as many months following its first appearance, and went on being reprinted well beyond World War II.

The epic chase, in which all the trials of the hunt are presented through the fox's single-minded determination to survive them, is preceded by a portrait of hunt society that is remarkable for its truthfulness and its easy-going charm. Here, Masefield tells us, is the moral heart of the English countryside. Here all strata of society come together, and all quarrels and passions are brought to order by the oneness established at the meet and rehearsed again in the field. The conflicts and tensions that are the inevitable price of settling side by side are here transcended and purged, by remaking the landscape as a shared possession of the people who dwell in it.

There are few hunting parsons now, squires like Masefield's Sir Peter Bynd are hard to come by, and those old imperial characters typified by Masefield's "Minton-Price of the Afghan border" have gone with the wind. But the rest of the cast – the junior whip who dreams of hunting hounds, the dairy farmer with his "russet-apple mind / That betters as the weathers worsen," the equestrian woman "with white horse-teeth and stooks of hair / Like polished brass," and the rat-catching, pigeon-fancying, terrier-loving chorus – are all evoked by Masefield as they remain today, and to read his cantering rhymes is to enter a world whose contours are intimately familiar, even though it is a world without motorways or mobile phones or plastic wrappings in the hedgerows.

Most striking of all – and it is what caused the astonishing success of this poem when it first appeared – is the representation of the hunt as a symbol of peace. The ritual of the foxhunt both preserves the religious awe of the hunter-gatherer and at the same time domesticates it, incorporates it into the settled ways of the farmer. The transformation of hunting into a community sport repairs the ancient quarrel between Cain and

Abel. The wild chase through the landscape is also an affirmation of our settled ownership, and of the right of a community to be where it is. At every point the reader senses the tranquility of neighborliness, in which tensions and quarrels are submerged by the common interest in a cooperative sport and in the landscape that sustains it. As Masefield evokes it, the peace that reigns in the human community is the other side of the fear and enmity faced by the fox. The poem therefore foregrounds the aspect of hunting that has occupied the attention of anthropologists: the aspect of ritual sacrifice. Death is seen from outside, as the shared condition of the animal kingdom; and the death of the quarry comes as a stroke of fate, and only when the rules and the rituals have been properly obeyed. Death has regained its "supernatural" quality, as an intervention from forces that we can never fathom, but only propitiate.

NOTES

1 Hugh Brody, *The Other Side of Eden: Hunters, Farmers and the Shaping of the World* (New York: North Point, 2000).
2 See my account in *Death-Devoted Heart: Sex and the Sacred in Wagner's Tristan und Isolde* (New York: Oxford University Press, 2004).
3 Thomas Mann, *Pro and Contra Wagner*, trans. Allan Blunden (London: Faber and Faber, 1985), p. 100.
4 *Odyssey* 17: 326–7.
5 *Metamorphoses* 3: 205–27.
6 *Laws*, VII, 824A.
7 José Ortega y Gasset, *La Caza y los toros* (Madrid: Revista de Occidente, 1960), p. 32; my translation.

CHAPTER 16

BIG GAME AND LITTLE STICKS
Bowmaking and Bowhunting

Picture a man in the wild carrying a simple wood bow he crafted with his own hands, a quiver of arrows tipped with stone points slung over his shoulder, following the blood trail of a large animal, hoping to find it before dark, hoping that today he'll bring some meat home for his family. What is the date and location? The Iberian Peninsula, 10,000 BCE? An Algonquin settlement, 1491? Sub-Saharan Africa, late nineteenth century? Or a cornfield on the outskirts of Chicago, Illinois, 2010?

Apart from the scene in the twenty-first century, each of these examples would likely accord with the image of a traditional bowhunter. But the possibility of a contemporary hunter using a stick bow he made himself is as real as any of the others, even when he got to that cornfield in a pickup equipped with a GPS navigating system, cell phone in his pocket, out for a few glorious hours in the open air with a self-made bow. It is a tradition alive and well right now in America.

"I started when there was no such thing as traditional"

The practice of hunting with a self-made bow would seem to be very ancient. It is, and yet it is not. Men (as well as women, but mostly men) have been hunting with bows and arrows for a long time, but what is identified today as traditional bowhunting – as a movement, a sport, a practice, a way of life – is a recent phenomenon. The label "traditional" was not used even a few decades ago, as a 2009 posting on Leatherwall, a popular online discussion site for traditional archers, recently observed. The archer was recalling that he first took up archery in the 1940s using a homemade lemonwood bow, back "when there was no such thing as traditional."[1]

Back then wooden bows were pretty much the only kind of bow around, and if and when men went hunting with them, they simply called themselves hunters or bowhunters, nothing more, nothing less. Today, however, thousands of men and women describe themselves as *traditional* bowhunters, meaning they distinguish themselves from other hunters, even other bowhunters. To explain this phenomenon, we first need some understanding of what traditional means today.

Used today to define an approach to hunting as well as the type of equipment, "traditional" covers all manner of bows, everything from longbows and recurves whose wooden limbs are backed with fiberglass, to bows made from a single stave of wood (known as self-bows), even wooden composite or bamboo-wood composite bows, sinew-backed wood bows, and the more complex composite bows made with horn, sinew, and wood. Longbows, flatbows, bows with recurved limbs, bows of complex deflex-reflex design, bows with snakeskin backings or none at all – what draws these bows of very different designs and materials together under the umbrella of traditional is what they are not: high-tech. As a category, traditional bows represent something other than high-tech equipment.

"Primitive" goes one step further to designate bows made from all natural materials, such as all wood bows, sinew-backed bows, and various composite bows. All "primitive" bows can default to the category of "traditional," but not all traditional bows can be classified as "primitive." The main exception are bows that have fiberglass backings on their limbs. Even though fiberglass is a modern material, having been developed during World War II, a recurved bow that depends upon fiberglass on its limbs for spring and resilience is still considered "traditional" because it predates another type of bow known as the *compound* bow.

To explain, one can turn to various archery publications of the 1970s and 1980s. The first edition of the *Archer's Digest*, a compendium of articles from the popular *Bow and Arrow* magazine, was full of information featuring the recurve in use in hunting, bowfishing, flight shooting, field archery, and so on.[2] Between the first and second editions of the *Archer's*

Digest, however, a significant development occurred. This was the mass marketing of the compound bow, the type of bow recognizable in Sylvester Stallone's series of *Rambo* movies. Made from modern materials and fitted with cables, cams, and pulley wheels, these high-tech bows were developed in the late 1960s and put on the market in the mid-1970s.

Energy efficient and the stuff of engineer's dreams, compound bows could be mass produced at a relatively inexpensive cost. With their surging popularity in the 1970s, it seemed that all forms of archery, with the exception of Olympic archery, were destined to go high tech. The simple longbows of the past, and even the fiberglass composite recurves, were to be relegated to memory. Factory-produced compound bows would be the end of the story.

Or so it would seem. Instead, in the mid-1980s the tide began changing with a revival of interest in "traditional" archery, matched by a desire to return to the use of natural materials and more rudimentary techniques, both in the practice of archery and in the crafting of bows. The appearance of magazines such as *Traditional Bowhunter* and *Primitive Archer* illustrate this phenomenon. *Traditional Bowhunter* entered the market with the lamentation of the degree to which modern technology was overtaking all aspects of life. Quoting Fred Asbell, a bowhunter of some renown, T. J. Conrads' editorial in the first issue promoted the magazine as part of the "phenomenal growth of traditional bowhunting in North America," a movement that reflected the need to "escape a modern technological world that has not only invaded the work place and the home, but also the mountains and the woodlots."[3]

The first issue made little mention of bowmaking, but that soon changed. Issue 2 took up wooden arrow making, and by the summer articles on bowmaking were making a regular appearance in *Traditional Bowhunter*. In comparison with the high-tech compound bows that dominated the field of archery in the 1980s, the wood and fiberglass recurved bows, unencumbered by sights, scopes, pulleys, and so on, represented a return to a simple, natural way of doing things, hence the label "traditional."

Describing itself as taking its readers into the "ultimate challenge in bowhunting," *Primitive Archer* launched its premier issue with how-to articles on techniques of crafting bows and other archery tackle from the most natural materials possible: wood, stone, and bone. With a cover photo showing a hand gripping a snakeskin-backed stick bow fitted with a flint arrow from point-blank perspective, *Primitive Archer*'s first issue took up flint-knapping, how to make selfbows from yew and osage orange, how to join two billets of wood together, and the making of wooden arrows (part of a piece on "How to Make a Tree Fly").[4] This was the popular mechanics of bowmaking. Subsequent issues have continued the tradition of how-to articles, along with hunting tales, articles on the history of archery worldwide, and accounts of traditional archery as found everywhere in the globe.

In the same years that these magazines were launched, the archery ranges and rod and gun clubs that dot much of rural North America began to host traditional shoots, or reserve one day of a shoot for archers using traditional equipment. By the late 1980s and early 1990s, some of these annual events, such as the Great Lakes Longbow Invitational held near Marshall, Michigan, were attracting men and women from all over the continent to talk bowmaking and to swap hunting stories. The energy at some of these early gatherings was frenetic, the air charged with the sounds of draw knives scraping wood as more skilled individuals coached fledgling bowmakers in the arcane – and newly rediscovered – art of transforming wood into a functional bow.

"Follow the growth ring," "limb twist," "out of tiller" – phrases incomprehensible to the uninitiated – circulated freely. Those speaking this language came from all walks of life: medical doctors, insurance brokers, pipe-fitters, office workers, factory workers, CEOs in the telecommunication industry, law enforcement personnel, university professors, electricians, cabinet makers, and writers. If you attended a few of these gatherings, it might have seemed that there were men everywhere bent on making their own bows. There was a movement afoot, with its own language, its literature, its adherents, and its traditions.[5]

Just as these new publications were launched, older works long out of print began to reappear. The new generation of bowmakers and bowhunters reverently turned to the writings of Maurice Thompson, Saxton Pope, and others for inspiration. Thompson's essays on bowhunting in his 1878 *Witchery of Archery*[6] spurred the development of recreational archery in the latter part of the nineteenth century. Contemporary bowhunters turned to his essays to recapture the poetry of being out on the land, alone with little more than a self-made bow.

Pope's 1923 *Hunting with the Bow and Arrow*[7] chronicles the knowledge of bowmaking and bowhunting he gained from Ishi, the last surviving member of the Yahi peoples of northern California. Considered instrumental in creating the sport of bowhunting in the twentieth century, Pope's writings advocated the idea of "fair chase," that in the proper spirit of hunting, the bowhunter should exercise no unfair advantage over the animal. In turning to these older works, the new generation of archers fortified their sense of solidarity with earlier North American expressions of traditional bowmaking and bowhunting.

As easy as it is to document the contemporary surge of interest in traditional bowmaking and bowhunting, pinpointing exactly what prompted this phenomenon is more challenging. One might argue that the making of a bow and using it to hunt is simply a guy thing involving the use of projectiles and concern with performance, that its associations with warrior traditions play into male fantasies, or that it fulfills men's need to tinker in a workshop, a kind of popular mechanics phenomenon involving the manufacture of primitive weaponry.[8] It involves all that, but to suggest that the contemporary phenomenon of bowmaking and bow-hunting is simply an expression of male sexuality misses its deeper ramifications. Like hunting, bowmaking has historically been a male-gendered activity. Recognition of that fact, however, does little to shed light on why in basements and workshops throughout North America today one can find men working to turn a stave of wood into a bow they will use for target practice and for hunting.

In their writings, online postings, and in conversations, bowmakers and bowhunters offer various explanations for the lure of the craft.[9] Multi-faceted and as diverse as the men speaking, these explanations touch on many aspects of life. Enjoyment, appreciation of the outdoors, a love of woodworking, a satisfaction of using something you made yourself, the thrill of hunting with nothing more than a simple bow, and the challenge of doing it well, as well as the affordability of the pastime all figure in these conversations. At first glance, their musings about the appeal of traditional and primitive archery would seem to indicate no core values, and instead offer as many explanations as individuals involved. However, I suggest that a more attentive consideration of their various pronouncements reveals certain shared affirmations that speak to larger questions of meaning, personal gratification, and fulfillment.

This sense of gratification and fulfillment is tied to the meanings associated with "traditional" and "primitive" and how these understandings are expressed through the physical acts of making, using, and hunting with a hand-crafted bow. Recurrent in traditional and primitive archers' reflections are statements about a realness that is both perceived and experienced when working with a bow. For them, the terms "traditional" and "primitive" encode layers of meaning that speak to a capacity – indeed, a human need – to create and use tools, and to do so in a way that acknowledges interlocking relations with the past, with oneself, and with the animals hunted. The understanding of "traditional" and "primitive" speaks to a range of desires for something real, from an unencumbered experience to a quest for authenticity. Involved is a celebration of human ingenuity in its diverse expressions, as well as a return to the basics of life. In the paragraphs that follow I will trace out the interrelated discursive threads that express these attitudes.

"Simple is Good":[10] An Affirmation of Authenticity

Shortly after *Traditional Bowhunter* and *Primitive Archer* appeared on the market, several men who had begun to establish national reputations as traditional bowmakers produced the first volume of a series of works on bowmaking. The title they chose is telling: *The Traditional Bowyer's Bible*.[11] Routinely cited by aspiring bowmakers, the multi-authored series quickly acquired canonical status because of its comprehensive coverage of all facets of the rediscovered craft of traditional bowmaking. Equally important, the series also articulates a worldview expressed in Jay Massey's "Why Traditional?" and "Tradition Begins with the Past," the lead chapters of volumes 1 and 2.[12] According to him, the hunger for traditional ways stems from disquiet with the "more impersonal, more inanimate" quality of mass-produced archery equipment.

To regain what Massey describes as the "romance of archery and the spiritualism of the natural world,"[13] he and other advocates of traditional archery turned to the complete experience of crafting a bow out of natural materials. The making of a bow – a tool – demonstrated a means of regaining control over one's capacity to produce. It is an act of creation that also effects a means of sustaining oneself, in a literal as well as symbolic way. Used successfully in hunting, the self-made bow can bring sustenance to the bowmaker and his family. A self-made bow symbolizes that ability. Moreover, a well-crafted and skillfully used bow is not just an object created by the bowmaker; it is an embodiment of the bowmaker's knowledge. This knowledge is not simple, mindless reproduction as found, for example, in a factory-produced object. "Each bow you make is different," it has its "own identity," is how one man put it. "It is a skill you can develop for years."[14]

The bow of choice in the *Bowyer's Bible* series is the wooden "stick-bow," also described in bowmaking circles as a "selfbow," because such a bow is made from a single stave of wood – in effect, made from itself.

In making a selfbow, the bowmaker is engaged in a self-reflexive act, not only for the bow, but also for the bowmaker. His or her skill and ability to bring a bow to life out of raw materials reflect back onto his own substance. The bow he makes is made out of himself, crafted through the actions of his or her own hands. At the same time, the bowmaker and bowhunter knows he or her has neither invented the bow nor the techniques of hunting with it. Creation comes from partaking in the knowledge shared by so many of other places, times, and cultures.

The word "primitive" is used to describe selfbows, in part because a bow made from a raw stave of wood is associated with earlier eras of human history, with Native and other traditional peoples, but also because "primitive" is associated with a rawness. It is an authenticity that can only be tapped into through a process of doing, as in working with wood to make a bow.[15] Instead of a denigrating term referring to a way of life or a time that people grew out of as civilization advanced, "primitive" as used in bowmaking circles implied a hyperreal state, one that enabled the use of all senses without the intrusion of other mediating forces. This sense was expressed in the initial branding of *Primitive Archer*: "The Ultimate Challenge in Bowhunting," a magazine for those who refuse the entrapments of overloaded technology.

"Primitive" thus becomes a means of celebrating an unencumbered life. It serves as a trigger term to express desire for that life, while simultaneously offering a means of fulfilling that desire. Articles on bowmaking that regularly appear in *Primitive Archer* illustrate this relationship.[16] Often referring to examples of historic bow designs, ancient European and Asiatic as well as Native American, these articles take a hands-on approach, walking readers through the techniques involved as co-participants in the making of these bows. Reader surveys done by the magazine indicate high reader satisfaction with articles of this sort. Providing detailed technical and mechanical information, such how-to articles link the contemporary knowledge of bowmaking with understandings held by earlier peoples, showing how one can participate in that understanding through crafting a bow.

The celebration of tradition expressed by many primitive and traditional bowhunters plays out against a very particular approach to the past. With emphasis placed on the active mode (the *doing*), the past (the *doings* of other times as well as the *doings* of other places) is perceived as a resource. The past is not a time to be understood, explained, or accounted for; instead it functions as a production house with innumerable sources of ideas of things to be produced and reproduced. The past is conflated with tradition, and tradition is associated with an imagined sharing of expression. Making a bow and then using it affirms that understanding, allowing one to celebrate the human ingenuity vested in the tools, the craft, and the exercise of human imagination that brings these possibilities to life. As Arjun Appadurai describes it, the "past is now not a land to return to in a simple politics of memory. It has become a synchronic warehouse of cultural scenarios."[17]

The fulfillment sought in the idea of tradition is not a nostalgic view of the past, or a yearning to escape the present. Rather, it is a sense of the present being fulfilled by the past through participatory engagement. What is expressed is not an attempt to reproduce the past; among the traditional bowmaking and bowhunting movement, there is little interest in reenactment of the sort found among living history proponents. Instead, the past (or the idea of tradition) is accessed for its attainable and reproducible goods, with the fulfillment it intimates demonstrated in the workability of the goods produced (in this case a functional bow). The result is not an imitation of the past or a mimicry of it, but a sense of its diffusion through co-participation. Past times and other places now become the stuff of imagined one-to-one relationships brought to life through shared material production.

Appearing in advertisements selling bowmaking supplies, in how-to articles, and in online discussion sites about hunting, the words "traditional" and "primitive" encode a multitude of meanings that express an existence seen to be both primal and real. Importantly, for individuals drawn to this craft, it is a state of being that is not simply contemplated. The making of a functional hunting bow has a tactile, tangible outcome. The bow is real, and so is the act of hunting; a life is at stake when it is used. "The deer is right there, right in front of you. It's not like a gun when you are 200 yards away," one bowhunter explained, "if you can get your heart to stop pounding, you'll have a chance with that arrow."[18]

Here is the heart of the challenge: not just to dabble in a craft, but also to ensure that what you are doing sustains its purpose. A bow used for hunting has to work and work well, just as the hunter has to trust himself when using it. The bow has to be properly tillered and able to propel an arrow with enough force to bring an animal to its death, and the hunter has to have the skill to do that. Out there in the woods, what you are doing shows. You can't hide from yourself. As the author of an article on primitive hunting puts it, "in my opinion primitive archery is truth and has been for many years."[19] When this writer speaks of truth, he is referring to a state of being that is really real. No gadgets, no technology, no external apparatus mediate; it is a pure experience at the heart of the cycle of existence.

The act is ceremonial as much as anything else. Primitive archers and traditional bowhunters are well aware that there are other, far more efficient and cost-effective ways to obtain animal protein. In the words of one bowhunter, "even a simple .22 caliber rifle is more accurate at a greater distance."[20] Here, the ethic of "fair chase" figures prominently. Armed only with a simple bow, the hunter is positioned in a much closer relationship with the animal.

For many, spiritual and religious feelings figure in this act. In some instances, the feeling is diffuse, described as a sense of participating in a deeply profound act. As one man put it, "It is hard to explain, but when I am out hunting with my bow, I sense something very spiritual about what I am doing."[21] He was referring to a feeling of resonance, explaining that out hunting with a bow he made himself, he felt connected to the earth, to past generations of hunters, to other creatures, even to the animal whose life he might take. He used the term "spiritual" rather than religious to identify the experiential state he was describing, suggesting a distinction between spiritual (a state of being) and religious (an attitude, outlook, or adherence to a set of beliefs).

Other hunters speak of reverence and see their capacity to hunt with a bow they made themselves as an extension of their religious orientation, often Christianity. They see celebration of the bounty of the land, self-sufficiency, a simple life, respect for the law, and activities like hunting – which depict the capacity to provide for the family – as expressive of their religious views. Some go even further and allude to a messianic belief that a change in the world order may well be coming. If and when that happens, people need to be prepared with knowledge of the most basic survival skills – such as the ability to make a functional hunting bow out of a stave of wood. Even bowmakers who don't share these messianic beliefs joke that their craft gives them "a leg up on the population for survival when it all goes kaput."[22]

Not all primitive and traditional archers turn to religious or spiritual language to express their love of the activity. Often, it is simply thought of as creating a special place. It can be a place of renewal, revitalization, or just a personal place. Steeped with meaningful associations that find expression in its doing, primitive archery affirms what matters. A member of the armed forces explains it this way:

Because, after numbing my mind onboard a nuclear powered submarine, surrounded by steel and machinery that controls even the air that I breathe, it's nice to put my hands on something organic, and shape it into something useful. Working with wood takes me miles away from arguments over conflicting policies on what constitutes a radiation area, and measurements that are fractions of decimal places of the radiation we receive when we are exposed to sunlight.... Shooting something made by hand ... puts me in touch with a time before we worried about splitting atoms and doing all the paperwork that goes along with it.[23]

For him and for other bowmakers and bowhunters, these activities matter because they are real.

NOTES

1   Jim Stutesman, posting to "How Old Are You?" Stickbow.com, *The Leatherwall*, October 31, 2009. Available at http://leatherwall.bowsite.com/TF/lw/thread2. cfm?forum=23&threadid=200280&messages=289&CATEGORY=9 (accessed November 25, 2009).
2   Jack Lewis (ed.) *Archer's Digest* (Chicago: Follett Publishing, 1972).
3   T. J. Conrads, "The Way It Is," *Traditional Bowhunter* 1, no. 1 (Fall 1989): 5.
4   Paul Comstock, "Bows from the White Woods"; Bill Akers, "Joining Billets"; Ken Wee, "Arrow Making Secrets Divulged," "How to Make a Tree Fly," "Basic Arrow Making, 101," "Arrow Woods"; and "Tips for the Bowyer," *Primitive Archer* 1, no. 1 (1992): 10–13, 32–3, 42–9, 50–2.
5   Traditional archery events have continued to grow, as seen in the size of gatherings such as the Eastern Traditional Archery Rendez-vous (ETAR), held in central Pennsylvania, and MoJam, a bowmaking jamboree held in Missouri. Now in its twenty-first year, ETAR attracts upwards of 7,000 people over four days with its dozen target courses, two large circus-size tents of vendors, nightly swap meet, schedule of talks and demonstrations, and camping space where conversations continue late every night. As noted above, one encounters a cross-section of North American occupations at such events. At the same time, there is less ethnic diversity. Many people in Native communities continue to hunt, and among certain Native American nations, bowmaking traditions have continued or have been revived. See, for example, Jay Red Hawk and David Gray, "Lakota Sioux Capture Another Lost Art," *Primitive Archer* 14, no. 3 (Fall 2006): 8–13. One finds bowmakers in the Cherokee, Dine, Lakota, Mohawk, and other communities, but the aficionados of traditional archery today are for the most part of European ancestry, a legacy of the history of sports archery in North America.

6   Maurice Thompson, *The Witchery of Archery: A Complete Manual of Archery* (Walla Walla, WA: Martin Archery and Sylvan Toxophilite, 1878; repr., 1981). See also Clifford H. Huntington, "Maurice Thompson: The Man and Legend, Part 1," *Primitive Archer* 9, no. 2 (Summer 2001): 48–51 and "Maurice Thompson: The Man and Legend, Part 2," *Primitive Archer* 9, no. 3 (Fall 2001): 40–3.

7   Saxton Pope, *Hunting with the Bow and Arrow* (n.p.: Sylvan Toxophilite, 2000).

8   It is not that women are not interested in traditional archery, as women both hunt and do target archery. Likewise, some women have tried their hands at bowmaking, but by and large, they have not taken to the craft in the same way as men. By all accounts only one woman, Hilary Greenland out of the UK, is a full-time bowmaker; no other women have made bowmaking a profession. See Hilary Greenland, *The Traditional Archer's Handbook: A Practical Guide* (Bristol: Sylvan Archery, 1993). The work is now in its fourth edition.

9   See, for example, "Why I Love Primitive Archery," Primitivearchery.com, *Anything Else*. Available at www.primitivearcher.com/smf/index.php/topic,16145.0.html (accessed November 25, 2009).

10   Kegan McCabe, posting no. 11 to "Why I Love Primitive Archery," Primitivearchery.com, *Anything Else*, November 2, 2009. Available at www.primitivearcher.com/smf/index.php/topic,16145.0.html (accessed November 25, 2009).

11   Jim Hamm, Steve Allely, Tim Baker et al., *Traditional Bowyer's Bible* (Goldthwaite, TX: Bois d'Arc Press, 1992). The series is now up to four volumes. Volume 4 was released in 2008.

12   Jay Massey, "Why Traditional?" *The Traditional Bowyer's Bible*, vol. 1 (1992): 15–18, and "Tradition Begins with the Past," vol. 2 (1993): 14–19.

13   Massey, "Tradition Begins with the Past," p. 15.

14   Chuck Styles, posting no. 14, "Why I Love Primitive Archery," Primitivearchery.com, *Anything Else*, November 22, 2009. Available at www.primitivearcher.com/smf/index.php/topic,16145.0.html (accessed November 25, 2009).

15   See Gary Ellis, "What Primitive Archery is all About," *Primitive Archer* 1, no. 1 (1992): 2.

16   See Judson F. Bailey, "Let's Get Back to Bowsics," *Primitive Archer* 5, no. 4 (October 1997): 8–15.

17   Arjun Appadurai, "Disjunction and Difference," in *Modernity at Large* (St. Paul: University of Minnesota Press, 1996), p. 30.

18   Anonymous, personal communication, November 26, 2009.

19   Tim Murphy, "Primitive Hunting," *Primitive Archer* 4, no. 1 (January 1996): 38.

20   Robert Wayne Atkins, "How to Make a Primitive Homemade Bow and Arrows," 1998. Available at http://grandpappy.info/wbow.htm (accessed November 25, 2009).

21 Herman Levy, personal communication, November 25, 2009.

22 Kegan McCabe, posting no. 11, "Why I Love Primitive Archery," Primitivearchery.com, *Anything Else*, November 22, 2009. Available at www. primitivearcher.com/smf/index.php/topic,16145.0.html (accessed November 25, 2009).

23 Mark Sizemore, HMC(SS)IDC, USN, posting no. 15, "Why I Love Primitive Archery," Primitivearchery.com, *Anything Else*, November 24, 2009. Available at www.primitivearcher.com/smf/index.php/topic,16145.15.html (accessed November 25, 2009).

CHAPTER 17

GOING TO THE DOGS

Savage Longings in Hunting Art

 "In the mountains of Germany I killed an enormous stag, a stag of twelve points," declared French painter Gustave Courbet (1819–77) in 1859. "It is the largest that has been killed in Germany in twenty-five years. He weighed, with an empty stomach, 275 pounds; in summer, alive, he would have weighed 400 pounds. The whole of Germany is jealous of my adventure."[1] Hunters have been known to exaggerate, telling big fish stories about tasty mammals with fur. What's peculiar about this declaration from Courbet, however, is not the size of the stag, but rather the fact that the storyteller was a painter.[2] To rehearse the stereotypes: the artist is a pale and fussy vegetarian who chain smokes and keeps cats, whereas the hunter is ruddy of cheek and hale of limb, whose keening sensibilities willingly abandon the soft pleasures of the city for a bracing jaunt through the forest. Ironically, it is partly to Courbet that we owe the latter set of beliefs, for he consciously set out to create a visual representation of the robust and vigorous hunter as a cultural reference. His vision of the hunter has remained relatively stable into the present, even as philosophies concerning hunting have dramatically shifted, reflecting the changing dynamics of human–animal relations as well as the continued retreat of "nature" to the margins of the urban imagination.

In his unpublished manuscript, "Notes on Hunting," Courbet wrote: "The hunter is a man of independent character, who has a free spirit or at the very least the feeling of being free. He is a wounded soul, a heavy

FIGURE 17.1   Gustave Courbet, *The Quarry.* © Museum of Fine Arts.

heart that longs for the dark and the melancholy of the forest."[3] Arguably, this is how he portrayed the hunter in a painting of 1856, *La chasse au chevreuil dans les forêts du grand Jura: la curée*, known in English as *The Quarry* (Fig. 17.1). The life-size canvas shows a hunting scene set in the forests of the Jura mountain range running through the Franche-Comté region in France. In the foreground, a freshly killed roe deer dangles by one leg from a pine tree. Two hounds approach it with raised tails and lowered heads. In the background, a young man is sitting on a stump. His bright red vest identifies him as a *piqueur*, whose role is to follow the deer on horseback and to encourage the dogs by sounding the horn. The chief hunter, who is responsible for the kill, leans laconically against a mature tree in the center of the canvas.

The hunter is Courbet, though it would be missing the point to consider this work simply as a self-portrait. With a closely cropped beard, waxed moustache, black felt hat, faded blue hunting tunic, and weathered leggings mottled with mud, he looks like an illustration out of a Grimm Brothers' fairy tale. He is a figure suspended in time, surrounded by trees that are both geographically specific yet extracted from history. In brief, the hunter represented the crisis of urban man precisely because he refused to relinquish a particular engagement with nature, an idealized and sheltering nature still untamed by the feminizing forces of civilization. By 1859, however, the wilderness was a Romantic myth, and his hunter was already an endangered species that could only roam freely inside the nostalgic preserves of fiction. Hence, he is "wounded," and the forest is "melancholy." Resigned, the hunter smokes his philosophical pipe and ponders the future that has already arrived.

The Dangerous Sport of Social Climbing

In 1858, the humorous periodical *Le Charivari* published the latest installment of Honoré Daumier's "Croquis de chasse (sketches of the hunt)." The long-running series mocked weekend hunters whose main skill as outdoorsmen consisted of wearing the appropriate clothes. One print from the series showed an outraged hunter tumbling backwards, head over heels, as a young deer bounds by him. Dryly, the caption reads: "Parisians aren't used to encounters with ferocious animals." Other hunters are shown stuck and whining in deep snow, staring incredulously at hares as if encountering aliens, and ducking into a comfortable shelter at the first sign of rain "because the animals are just as afraid of rain as we are." One revealing image shows two weekend hunters standing in a location just outside Paris. They are cold, irritated, and hungry. "Brrrr!" the fat one complains. "I am furious that I came here to hunt in the St. Denis-Plain. It's just too cold!" Shivering, his skinny friend replies, "[It's] one of those days when you would love to catch a bear. His fur would be more than welcome right now!" They are both bandy-legged, soft-skinned weaklings with hands shoved in their pockets and heavy scarves wrapped around scrawny necks. Their best option is to quit. In every example from this series, the city folk are miserable, incompetent, and hilariously unsuccessful at hunting. So why are they bothering to go?

Until the French Revolution forced the country's laws to change, the hunt was the privilege of the aristocracy and the hunting of stags traditionally reserved for the king. Throughout the nineteenth century, the practice remained coded to elite social circles at the highest echelons of power. Social-climbing Parisians used the hunt as a means to elevate their social position, much in the same way that today's junior executives might join a country club in order to golf with captains of industry; it's irrelevant whether they like the game. In this regard, it is important to recognize that Daumier wasn't mocking the deep sociocultural shifts manifested by the emergence of hunting as a leisure activity among the middle classes. He was savaging hobby hunters for their pretentiousness. The specific groups being shot down by Daumier were petty bourgeois or faded aristocrats whose main motivation for hunting was to showcase the money that paid for their excursions. Being both shallow and foolish, they were unaware that their flabby, teetering bodies exposed their crass ambitions, their knobby knees and cirrhotic noses serving as the visible sign of weak moral character. Despite their social prestige, they cannot buy courage, fortitude, or a feel for the forest. The dreadful reality was that these qualities no longer mattered.

Across the span of the nineteenth century, France was undergoing profound transformations marked by the rise of capitalism replacing rural economies, dramatically changing human relationships with nature in general, and with animals in particular. It was no coincidence that this period saw the creation of "pets," i.e., domesticated animals suitable for cramped city apartments, transforming spaniels, dachshunds, and terriers from hunting companions into lapdogs. In their swift segue from working animal to fetish object, one sees the transformation of wild nature into living artworks, as well as the female appropriation of the dog as an urban fashion accessory. Who now associates French poodles with birding? By contrast, it is now taken for granted that the authentic hunter is never a woman and his dogs are, rather, hardy "hounds" that earn their keep by working.[4] The very antithesis of the dandy, i.e., the metrosexual of nineteenth-century London and Paris, the urban hunter insisted on earthy, rustic values that rejected the (feminine) fripperies of fashion. To do so was an act of defiance, specifically revolving around changing ideas of masculinity. Problematically, these same reactionary values were coded to the peasantry, men and women of the soil who worked the land, possessed physical strength out of necessity, were often mired in poverty, and lived hard lives that were far from quaint or charming. It is precisely because the nineteenth-century hunter attempted to mediate painful ruptures between wildness/civilization, country/city, instinct/reason, and so on, that he

FIGURE 17.2   John Byrd, *Tricky Buck*. Reprinted by permission of John Byrd
© 2009. Photograph by John Byrd.

represented the active, masculine principle that was conservative in its values and yet, for that very reason, also a complex sign of social rebellion.

As the son of prosperous farmers in the rural village of Ornans, Courbet was acutely aware of the complex stew of social snobbery, sexualized envy, and the cult of authenticity that his (rural, illicit, savage) skill with hunting represented to Parisians. The wall sculpture *Tricky Buck* (2003) by contemporary artist John Byrd (Fig. 17.2) helps us understand the confrontational aspects of Courbet's hunter in terms of class differences, as both works offer the figure of the hairy male (deer) as a form of calculated aggravation. Byrd exhibits the "taxidermied" head of an eight-point buck, co-opting the bourgeois practice of turning the wild animal into a decorative object. The trophy head is conventional as far as the presentation of the hide, head, neck, and antlers is concerned. However, the anthropomorphized buck is smoking a glowing cigar and the entire head is covered in a clear glaze, turning it into a parody akin to a sofa preserved in Saran wrap. As a work of fine art that edges toward kitsch, the buck's animated swagger is an act of defiance against domestic narratives that increasingly frame hunting as promoting cruelty to animals, narratives that not only express an underlying utopian sentiment for complete social control extending to the "correct" governance of animals (which magically cease to be vermin, pests, predators, competition, or viable food), but correspondingly repudiate the mammalian reality of human existence as something "solitary, poor, nasty, brutish, and short."[5] Much like Courbet's *Quarry*, Byrd's *Tricky Buck* explicitly retains the southern, regional, parochial elements of an aspect of rural culture rejected by urban aesthetes because of its perceived vulgarity, and does so specifically by tweaking masculine stereotypes as well as middle-class hypocrisy regarding its mantle of moral superiority. Deprived of its body and turned to stone, the tricky buck still retains more vitality than passive viewers denatured by cities, reduced to pushing buttons to make the cigar glow red instead of lighting real fires to roast fresh meat.

Whether understood as physical specimens or as role models for a practice of hunting, Daumier's hobby hunters do not correspond to Courbet's vision in *The Quarry*. Strong limbed and clear browed, Courbet's hunter is comfortable in the forest. Relaxed and integrated with his surroundings, he seems not to feel hunger, thirst, or overwhelming fatigue after a successful hunt, the proof of which hangs casually in front of us. As a hunter at home in the forest, Courbet's urban "savage" accepts the death of the deer as a reminder of the mortality of all living things. By contrast, Daumier's hobby hunters lack all feeling for the pathos of earthly existence. The breezes disturb their coifs. The bugs are a source of despair. Their bodies are outdoors but their minds remain bottled in glass. Voyeurs, they derive pleasure from telling themselves: "we are not prey." They stare wistfully at rabbits getting away and think themselves mighty hunters. They go home empty-handed.

Not a Doe but a Roe

For Courbet, hunting was a form of "violent exercise that I do not find displeasing," and he hunted at every opportunity because of its expansive physicality.[6] He confessed to being "an incorrigible poacher," and found himself once in conflict with the police after hiking up and down mountains while hip-deep in snow, chasing after hares and wolves.[7] Given that he was a boastful man, it is noteworthy that the roebuck in *The Quarry* is modest in proportions, very far from the "enormous" twelve-point stag he would get a few years later in Germany. Courbet is known to have painted his own kills in other depictions of the hunt, giving the scene an anecdotal charge. The buck cannot be read as a trophy kill. Instead, the roebuck shown here is small and young, as evidenced by the short length of the antlers (known colloquially as "spikehorns"). Unremarkable as a kill, its presence nonetheless cements this forest as a man's world. Hunter, horn player, and buck are bound together by the exercise of hunting, making it clear that if men do the killing, it is also males that do the dying.

By the mid-nineteenth century, roe deer were the only member of the deer family in the Jura, as both fallow deer and red deer (traditionally the most prestigious of game animals) had been driven away. Bears were an expected presence among the wildlife populations of Switzerland, naturalist Victor Fatio noted in 1869, and "wolves, lynxes, and wild cats are not uncommon in the forests of the Juras."[8] Courbet's single-shot hunting rifle hangs on a tree branch immediately behind him, the leather strap and wooden butt clearly outlined in front of a pine sapling. (In a kind of visual pun, the butt of the rifle is juxtaposed next to the deer's upturned butt, and the animal's upstretched limb exactly repeats the shape and coloring of the instrument used to kill it.) His eyes are downcast but his folded arms and leaning stance indicate a posture of relaxed defense. In other words, the hunter in reverie is not oblivious to his surroundings: he remains alert to the possibility of an attack from an opportunistic carnivore, and keeps his rifle within arm's length and himself ready to move swiftly.

The threat of such an attack was greatest when the smell of blood was intense, as was the case when field dressing has begun. Notably, the original painting had consisted simply of the hunter and the deer inside a compressed frame. As he worked on the painting, Courbet added a strip of canvas above the hunter's head, and then added the large piece on the side which eventually featured the *piqueur* and the two dogs.[9] If understood as a painting consisting of one deer and one man, the inelegant one-legged hoist of the deer may reflect conditions a lone hunter might have faced. He tied a short rope around a hind leg and tossed the other end over a low tree branch. The belly of the roe deer is hidden, making it difficult to determine the exact stage in the field-dressing process. It is assumed that the splayed position of the legs is a result of the pelvic bones having been broken and the anus and intestines having been removed, with the goal of conserving as much viable meat as possible. If this is the case, however, it would confirm that two centuries-old French hunting traditions, the "ritual hunt" and the "subsistence hunt," would not only have been conflated but their cultural meanings reversed by the mid-nineteenth century in France.

The ritual hunt is chiefly a symbolic activity. Highly scripted, it presents itself as a spectacle with banners, songs, and other forms of group celebration. By contrast, the subsistence hunt is driven by the need for food, with no ceremonial value. Formerly, the ritual hunt was the prestige hunt *because* it did not result in food. Arguably, Courbet expressed the inversion of symbolic values by hanging the roebuck prominently in the foreground of the canvas, upside down, and broken. While full-length hunting portraits were not uncommon, the hunters were aristocrats. Their kills would be nearly hidden in a heap immediately behind them; they would not be gutted and hanging prominently from a limb, as such a display would have been considered both pointless and in bad taste. Courbet puts himself literally in the place of the aristocrat, yet he positions the roebuck in such a way that makes it clear that it is being dressed in the field. His hunter is not embarrassed by this frank admittance of need and/or desire. This is new.

By referencing the "period eye," or the cultural, social, political, philosophical, and economic views shaping audience reception, we can better understand the depth of the social changes implied by Courbet's display of the deer and his relationship to it. In this regard, the captions to Daumier's hunting caricatures helpfully give voice to the period eye. In another print from this popular series, we see an urban hunter standing in his living room. He'd promised his wife he'd bag a game bird for dinner and found a creative explanation when he failed to catch anything. "But I did bring you a partridge!" the hunter protests to his perplexed wife. "Only this time, I preferred to buy it as a pâté!" Among other things, the caption reveals that economic power has replaced marksmanship as the surest means to obtain game meats. It also confirms that Parisian hunters were practicing what Claude d'Anthenaise called "la chasse gourmandise," or hunting for gourmets, a phenomenon recently revived by Michael Pollan and the locavore movement in the United States. As a philosophy of hunting, the chasing of wild animals to enhance the table seems highly defensible, even necessary. However, it only seems this way because sensibilities have changed. And much depends on the animal being served: the rationale does not work with armadillos or squirrels.

Contemporary hunters may be startled to learn that the traditional hunt, as practiced by French kings for centuries, rejected framing the killing of deer in terms of provisioning the table, as this lessened the hunt's symbolic value as a surrogate form of war. Though meat was obtained from the kill, it was chiefly consumed by the servants and dogs. First, the deer was skinned and gutted by the dog handlers. The master of the hounds collected the hounds' fees (*menus droits*) owed to the king as his right. The most prized bits were "the muzzle, tongue, ears, testicles, *franc-boyau*, heart artery, and the little strings attached to the kidneys." These parts were bundled together, hung from a hook, and taken away to be presented in a dish served to the royals near the conclusion of the hunt.

That the choicest bits destined for "the mouths of the king and queen" strike us today as being perfectly vile makes sense if one understands that their highly ritualized preparation was driven neither by culinary interests nor by hunger. Instead, the custom of *menu droit* symbolized royal authority over all that lived on the land, in accordance with God's law (the testicles) and obedient to the king's will (the muzzle). The ritual hunt was exceptionally elaborate, involving several hundred people, dozens of horses, and up to a hundred dogs per outing. As part of their training, the dogs would receive what was known as the *curée* at the conclusion of each successful hunt. The usual mixture consisted of a mash of blood and bread, sometimes heated together with milk, to which was added the deer's intestines, the whole mixture spread out on the hide like a picnic blanket. The *curée* concluded with the serving of "dessert." This dessert was the *menu droit*, i.e., the sack of delicacies presented to the royals at the beginning of the ceremony. Renamed *le forhu*, the sack was held up high in the air by a dog handler, who then dispensed the contents among the dogs as if handing out treats.

For socioeconomic and political reasons, the practice of *la curée* has become unthinkable. Yet the French title of Courbet's painting tells us that this is its subject: *La chasse au chevreuil dans les forêts du grand Jura: la curée*; the last word was mistranslated as "the quarry," probably because the word has no English equivalent and nothing in American hunting practice approximates it. Indeed, very little of the original information carried in the title would have made sense to an American audience. This painting is not about the prey, and the carcass is not being cured. Instead, the title suggests, as does the forced inclusion of the *piqueur*, it is about feeding the deer to the dogs. Except it is not.

There is no sign of the tell-tale mash of entrails, milk, and blood served on the deer's hide. If the dogs have already eaten the intestines, they did so delicately, as if using utensils, instead of partaking of the throat-ripping attacks that were also allowed as part of their training. In short, the title's reference to *"la curée"* here functions as the French version of a doggy bag. The dogs aren't going to be eating those leftovers from the restaurant. *You are* – as a function of extracting maximum value ("that meal was expensive!") as well as the perceived immorality of wastefulness. Among Courbet's peers, the indignities suffered by the roebuck passed without remark, probably because it was less the manner of the animal's death that registered than its middle-class desirability as red meat. Given that France is a country where butchers had elevated the dressing of animal carcasses displayed in their shop windows to an art form, it is safe to say that the French have never been squeamish about the animal sources of their protein. Indeed, the painting's reception was remarkably free of contention, almost certainly because it flattered bourgeois aspirations with enough subtlety to avoid becoming parody. Newly invested with a social charge, the roebuck revises the role of the kill as a sign of prosperity, of mastery over the land that is the natural right of the enlightened man. Not the king but the hunter now claims the *menu droit* as his due. But it is no longer a symbol of monarchical authority over nature, of wilderness tamed by the forces of civilization. Tellingly, by the nineteenth century, the word *curée* had entered the vernacular in reference to humans begging for scraps of food, or an act of charity to the most desperate of the poor. From *menu droit* to *le forhu*: the doggy bag is human food.

The Belly of the Beast

At this juncture, we can understand Courbet's hunter as standing inside a cultural forest that is literally not cut from the same cloth. Whereas the hunter and deer represent a certain kind of nostalgic ideal, the world around him has changed. One could almost propose the forest setting as a staged reverie the hunter is incapable of fully inhabiting. The oddly sunny, spatially compressed right half of the canvas is a collection of visual quotations from hunting's aristocratic past, nominating ceremonial traditions that by 1857 would have been laughably pretentious for a man of his station to emulate. But he did so in much the same way that t-shirts labeled "Chanel" or "Dior" are flaunted by individuals who could never afford haute couture clothing. Consumers take such appropriations for granted, and hardly perceive the irony of these displays. Indeed, the *piqueur* can best be understood as the pictorial equivalent of a lawn

FIGURE 17.3   Christopher Carroll, *Doubt(ing)*. Reprinted by permission of
Christopher Carroll © 2009. Photograph by Gregory Vershbow.

jockey popped on suburban American lawns. Red-vested riders of expensive mounts, they function as vestigial signs of the aristocratic tradition
of the ritual hunt (deer hunt, steeplechase, fox hunt) and they are coveted precisely because they invoke the immense socioeconomic power
that horses, riders, and hunts formerly required.

When the artist added the two dogs and the *piqueur* to his painting,
and then designated the whole as "*la curée*," his painting took on the
contours of Daumier's mocking series by poking fun at his viewership.
His audience saw the young man in the red vest. It did not see the rest of
the aristocratic hunting party being called by the horn (because there

FIGURE 17.4   Image 3 from the *Trophy* series. Reprinted by permission of
Christopher Carroll © 2009. Photograph by Gregory Vershbow.

was only the artist hunting, alone). It saw two shaggy hounds, sniffing
vaguely at the ground. It did not see the ritual of the *curée*. It saw the deer
carcass, prominently hung from the tree. It did not see the eviscerated
belly. The artist suppressed the realistic details that were too close to raw
violence and death, and displayed a set of ideas regarding hunting instead.
The humor and pathos of this work reside in the fact that the public
didn't see what it missed.

Recent work by contemporary artist Christopher Carroll helps us to
better understand this point. Carroll's *Doubt(ing)* (2009) gives us a carved
and "gutted" tree dangling from a portable game hanger (Fig. 17.3). We

are able to see the tree as a dressed buck because he invokes the same conventions of display, encouraging the zoomorphic projection. The rough branch functions as a privileged sign of wildness, a role that the roebuck in Courbet's painting also fulfills. The branch continues to represent the animal in the series *Trophy*, where Carroll explores the relationship between hunter and quarry as one of active and passive roles, casting the hunter as a kind of soldier-scientist who observes nature in order to master it. Wearing army surplus instead of camouflage, the hunter surrounds himself with signs of the untamed outdoors: tall grass, open sky, and gnarled trees (Fig. 17.4). The hunter is Carroll, though here, too, it would be an oversimplification to consider the work a self-portrait. Most importantly, his hunter's trophies are more specimens of dead trees, which he displays as if they were large and prestigious kills. By showing the hunter as a collector of relics instead of a killer of animals, Carroll's work illuminates the surprising point that the hunter's role is not primarily defined by his hunting of game but by his intermediary position between wilderness and civilization. As those boundaries shift, so too do his opportunities and permissions, resulting in a fluctuating level of cultural value assigned to his role.

Carroll's urban hunter represents man's inability to return to a state of nature, a state which he nonetheless seeks to possess. Doomed to fail, he takes what he finds and preserves what he can – usually the head, that part of wild nature that is most like him. It is also the most inedible, thanks to taboo and toughness. This is the lesson of the *menu droit/le forhu*: the same parts that are most coveted in the beginning are the most despised at the end. However, in times of rapid social change and weakened political authority, the cultural boundaries are unclear. Thus the struggle over the trophy head of Courbet's twelve-point buck yields comedy, because no one is exactly sure what it means when a French painter takes a prize stag from forest lands in Germany. As Courbet relates with glee, "The Grand Duke of Darmstadt said he would have given a thousand florins for it not to have happened."[10] The trophy head was taken away from Courbet by this titled aristocrat, and then it was restored to him, thanks to the intervention of the Society of Sportsmen. In this story, there is nationalism (the French vs. the Germans), class conflict (a Grand Duke bested by a farmer's son), crude theft, and old systems of authority running up against new ones (a titled aristocrat forced to cede the head by a bourgeois association of sportsmen).

Perhaps unsurprisingly, it is the hunter's intuitive relationship to nature – defiantly represented by Courbet as something proudly lower class, vitally masculine, swaggering and vulgar – that has tended to disappear from hunting as a philosophy, though it remains in hunting as a practice. The idea of the hunter as primordial man fails to flatter the social aspirations promised by education. Depicted as a hunter of deer, Courbet's hunter represented the new social freedoms that allowed ordinary citizens to partake in an activity once reserved for the king. As a self-sufficient man standing on his own two feet, meditatively smoking a pipe instead of gnawing mindlessly on bread, he distinguishes himself from the sniffing dogs answering only to their hunger, for humans dine rather than feed. As a contemplative male at home in the forest, his melancholic hunter is also a defiant anachronism: a self-styled "savage" who feels at one with nature because of his naïve emotions and sentiments. As a social practice with symbolic value, the hunt cannot be understood apart from works such as Courbet's, which provides a powerful statement regarding the conflicted streams of thought that idealistically imagines a human nature free of violence, even as it celebrates the hunter who walks without fear in the forest.

NOTES

1 Letter from Gustave Courbet to his sister Juliette, recounted in Léonce Bénédite, *Gustave Courbet* (Philadelphia: J. B. Lippincott; London: William Heineman, 1913), p. 63.
2 Bénédite, *Gustave Courbet*, p. ix. Courbet's ego and self-promotional tendencies were well documented by his contemporaries.
3 Gustave Courbet, "Notes sur la chasse," manuscript, quoted in Kerstin Thomas, "La mise en scène du sauvage: Gustave Courbet et la chasse," *Romantisme* 35, no. 129 (2005): 85.
4 Until the Revolution ended the privileges of the aristocracy, the huntress Diana/ Artemis was a popular artistic and literary motif. In Molière's play of 1664, for example, *La Princesse d'Élide* (the princess of Elid), the eponymous heroine is mad for hunting, rising early and going out every day, much to the vexation of her male suitors. Her image was prominently featured in the châteaux at Fontainebleau and Versailles, both of which were country residences for hunting.
5 Thomas Hobbes, *Leviathan* (1651).
6 Bénédite, *Gustave Courbet*, p. 63.
7 Ibid.
8 E. Ray Lankester, review of Victor Fatio, *The Mammalia of Switzerland/Faune des vertébrés de la Suisse* (Geneva and Basle: H. Georg, 1869), in Norman Lockyer (ed.) *Nature: International Journal of Science* (London: H. Macmillan and Co., 1870), p. 282.

9 Physical details provided in "Hunting the Roebuck in the High Jura: *The Quarry,*" *Bulletin of the Museum of Fine Arts, Boston* 16, no. 98 (December 1913): 84–5. In the original version, the hunter's hat touched the top of the frame. See Bruce K. MacDonald, "*The Quarry* by Gustave Courbet," *Bulletin of the Museum of Fine Arts, Boston* 67, no. 348 (1969): 60–9. Though routinely recognized as one of his more important works, *The Quarry* has received very little scholarly attention. Thomas' article (see note 3) is the first to focus on the importance of hunting in Courbet's oeuvre.

10 Bénédite, *Gustave Courbet*, p. 64.

CHAPTER 18

THE NEW ARTEMIS?

Women Who Hunt

When I was nine or ten years old, my father taught me how to shoot. Rifle and pistol alike were loaded, cocked, aimed, and fired at paper targets. He wanted me to learn the power weapons have and what it means to fire one. I was born and raised in the upper part of Michigan's lower peninsula in an agricultural and hunting area where guns were common accouterments. Every fall and winter dozens of deer and other animals were killed. Some by car, some by carbine. I clearly remember dead deer suspended head first from trees being "bled out," and their dead, gutted-out bodies slung across the hoods of pickup trucks parked outside the local bar. To be squeamish about killing animals wasn't unusual for a girl; in fact, it was almost expected. Hunting was a man's activity. It was men who got up before dawn to bond with their buddies deep in the forests, leaving sleepy wives and daughters warmly at home. Women, in fact, weren't welcome.

In modern cultures, hunting typically falls under the purview of other traditionally male-dominated activities such as sport and waging war (two not unrelated activities). Nearly 88 million Americans hunt, fish, or watch wildlife. Of that figure, 13 million Americans hunt, the majority of whom are male.[1] However, in the last few years the number of men who hunt has declined, while the number of women and girls has grown.[2]

What attracts women to hunting? How do they see this activity and themselves in relation to it? How did they start? Online conversations with women who hunt revealed similarities in motivations to those of men. Using a Yahoo Group (*Women Hunters*), I posed questions to members about why they hunt, how they started hunting, whether or not they hunted as children, if they found hunting-related magazines helpful or relevant, and whether or not they experienced any challenges based on gender. Using Kheel's categories of men who hunt (happy, holistic, and holy),[3] I asked of the findings: do they fit women?

In this chapter I take an ecological feminist view of hunting, recognizing "important connections – historical, experiential, symbolic, and theoretical," psychological and ecological – "between the domination of women and the domination of nature."[4] In the following sections I describe the historical underpinnings for the gendered nature of hunting, explore women's roles as they relate to hunting culture, and present illustrative examples of online responses of women who hunt in relationship to Kheel's categories. Finally, I discuss the importance and implications of participation for the socialization of girls and women.

Humans and Hunting

In the book *The Hunting Hypotheses*, Robert Ardrey describes the widespread, popular belief that humans are the singular primate hunter.[5] Truth is, based on the research of ethologists and behaviorists, we now know that baboons sometimes capture and consume infant antelope and that chimpanzees hunt and eat monkeys. Some hunt individually, others in groups. Similar to other primates, humans traditionally live in groups, watch out for one another, work together in order to remain safe, and were, and in some places of the world still are, vulnerable to being prey. In our sanitized, mass-mediated worlds, our being hunted by animals is rare compared with our killing of them. Yet the fear still motivates a posturing of humans, particularly males, as "the macho, meat-eating, kill-'em-dead Top Predator."[6]

In many anthropological studies, men are presumed to be and to always have been the primary tool users and hunters. Yet, what men do (hunt) and what women do (gather) often are, when interrogated, similar activities: "Women's hunting is often overlooked by researchers either because they do not see it while emphasizing men's activities to the exclusion of women's or because they deem it unimportant or irrelevant to studies of subsistence."[7] Yet, human fossil and primate evolutionary history show that the majority of tools were used by women for domestic tasks and

60–90 percent of food used and collected in the tropics today is by women.[8] In "The Paleolithic Glass Ceiling," Zihlman challenges the male dominance theory of sexual attraction and gathering of sustenance: "anthropologists reach a wide audience through textbooks, television specials, and museum exhibits [but] women in evolution are rendered either invisible non participants or as the handmaidens to men in prehistory."[9] Why?

Drawing on Freud, hunting is often justified as fulfillment of a primal "instinctive urge" which, "like the sexual drive, cannot and should not be repressed."[10] A boy's first hunting experience is often considered a form of initiation and one of the few remaining rites of passage. Hunting can be viewed as an act that requires boys and men to make the ultimate break with women/mothers and "forsake the 'longings for the prelapsarian idyll of childhood'" by participating in the ultimate public act of separation from the source of life – killing.[11] Hence hunting operates as a substitute for the risks of battle, which, at other times and in other places, is used to symbolize who is a "real" man evidenced by blood: "men nurture their society by shedding their blood, their sweat, and their semen, by bringing home food for both child and mother, by producing children, and by dying if necessary in faraway places."[12]

In patriarchal societies, maintenance of sex and gender roles is also about power. Similar to war and sports cultures, access to and participation in men's hunting practices have been tightly controlled by men. The socially constructed view that men are more rational, capable, and effective than women creates borders between the private and public lives women and men occupy. Thus gender ideologies about one's "proper place" come to be seen as normal, natural, and eternal in the form of the sexual division of labor, which is "concretized through material objects" such as access to and participation in the hunting domain.[13]

Kheel takes the analysis further by identifying and critiquing "the mental and moral framework that underlies the ties between hunting and the environmental movement."[14] Focusing on Western industrialized cultures, Kheel distinguishes three kinds of hunters who participate in this "predominantly male activity": the happy hunter, the holistic hunter, and the holy hunter.[15] All three hunt not for need but to fulfill a desire, consist mainly of white men, believe that "hunting has some redeeming benefit beyond individual satisfaction,"[16] and find pleasure and release in a combination of self-restraint and actualizing what is seen as "man's inherent aggressive drive."[17] Differences exist in motivation and justifications for hunting. The happy hunter is the only one of the three to admit to hunting as a sport and for the sheer pleasure of it. The holistic hunter claims to be doing so for the sake of the environment, or "biotic whole."[18] The holy hunter hunts because of the "spiritual communion" he finds with nature, which serves as a linguistic cover for a "spiritualization of violence."[19]

There is a complex relationship between an erotics of hunting, objectification, (dis)regard of women, and cultivation of codes that actively contribute to a "harsh environment" of masculinity.[20] Whether it is the kind of weapons used (bows, arrows, i.e., penetration), sexual names for weapons, or the language of conquest, hunting is a dramatic expression for the performance of stereotypical male roles, defined by violence, aggression, and power. The paraphernalia of hunting is coded with sexual innuendo coupled with violence: bullets are called balls, a weapon is discharged, when the weapon accidentally fires it is called "premature discharge,"[21] and when a bullet hits the target it is said to have penetrated it. Thus, hunting discourse includes a "logic of domination"[22] in which animals and human women are tracked/chased, killed, and consumed: "Bow hunting is manly, exciting, intimate, and – above all, *sexual*."[23] Hence, "resilient popular culture images that celebrate and glorify weapons, killing, and violence, [lay] the ground work for the perpetuation of attitudes of domination, power, and control over others."[24] In hunting publications, women are represented as synonymous both with hunting and with animals as acceptable targets of male predation.[25] For example, Kalof, Fitzgerald, and Baralt examined the content of *Traditional Bowhunter* magazine (1992–2003) and found a "juxtaposition of hunting, sex, women, and animals."[26] In another study, Kalof and Fitzgerald examined photographs of trophy animals and found extensive similarities between the portrayal of dead animals and dead female bodies as shown in sci-fi and other film genres.[27] Given the gendered culture in which women are viewed at the least as an annoyance and at times as sexual prey, why would they want to enter such an uneven playing field?

Women Who Hunt

In a study of "women's place" in post-World War II American outdoors magazines, Andrea Smalley found ample evidence of women's participation in hunting.[28] However, with the rise of advertising-supported mass circulation magazines, women's place being in the home and out of the forest was normalized. By the 1970s, women were seen as a threat to

DEBRA MERSKIN

masculine identity and to hunting, threatening male dominance and control. In the 1980s and 1990s, women began venturing into the forest, not just as companions or cooks for male hunters. The hunting industry has been actively recruiting women and girls since the 1980s when the numbers of American hunters plateaued and among men declined.[29] Women's participation was 1.5 percent in 1980, but grew to 2.7 percent in 1990.[30] Studies show that not only is more than 95 percent of the hunting population male, it is also white (91 percent), of lower education and social status than non-hunters, and most live in small towns.[31]

If a woman who hunted was one of the most venerated goddesses in Greek and Roman mythology, what happened to this regard for her prowess and position? How and when did hunting become the bastion of men? While answers to these questions go beyond the scope of this chapter, to begin unraveling the thorny knot of women's attraction to hunting I asked questions to an online group of women hunters about why they hunt, how they started hunting, and if they find the same forms of pleasure, release, and communion as men do. In the following section I present illustrative dialogue organized by responses to the following questions:

- Why do you hunt?
- How did you learn to do so? With whom?
- Did you have any childhood experiences hunting?
- Do you find any hunting-related magazines useful?
- Have you faced any challenges as a *woman* who hunts?

Not every woman answered every question, but most answered some of them. The explanations and justifications were remarkably the same as Kheel's three hunter types: happy, holistic, and holy. The responses are quoted here unedited. Online identities are protected using aliases.

Why Do You Hunt? The Thrill of the Kill

Respondents' answers typically began with descriptions of the beauty of nature, of peacefulness, and a holy hunt. Some hunted animals for food, some to learn, others to test skills, sometimes to feel powerful. Helen said:

I'm sure most women will agree that we hunt to get in touch with nature. Some get in touch by photographing animals, whereas I like to take it one step further. I love the challenge of bow hunting. You have to get within a certain range to get a clean, ethical shot at the animal. It's more of an up close and personal interaction. My family loves to eat wild game and I enjoy the thrill of the chase and the feeling of satisfaction after a successful hunt.

This posting suggests not only Kheel's "holy hunter," but also the idea of there being an ethic of "good sportsmanship." Helen said she takes an "ethical shot at [an] animal," but then describes another reason – the "thrill of the chase" inherent in Kheel's first type, the "happy hunter," someone who states unequivocally that he/she hunts for pure pleasure. Another respondent, Melanie, said, "i can make the choice to let an animal go, and have the responsibility to do it right the FIRST time."

One of the list members suggested an article titled "What to Say to a Person Who Has Never Hunted,"[32] in which 2,500 hunters, average age 55, were asked about events that opened their hearts and engendered compassion. Most women responded about becoming a parent, while the men said, "taking the life of an animal." Giving and taking life. Words recreational hunters used to describe the animals they killed were "respect," "admiration," and "reverence." The article advocates for hunting as a rite of passage for boys and argues that it teaches compassion and recognition of something or someone greater than ourselves.

One list member sent an essay by hunting advocate Wanda Garner titled "Why Women Hunt," in which she claims the reasons are similar to men's:

> The magic of the forest and the creatures which inhabit it, or the awe you feel while sitting in your stand as that first morning light emerges and the world comes alive one critter at a time. The emotions are deep. How do you explain the world standing still for a time? I am alone, at peace with the world around me, yet fully alert, and ready for anything. At the same time, I never feel closer to God than when sitting in that deer stand, bundled in layers of clothing trying to stay warm, feeling the cold morning air on my face. Often I am reminded of the verse in Psalms that says, "Be still and know that I am God."[33]

The essay further describes the motivations of all three in the hunter typology:

> I hunt for the adrenaline rush I feel when I see a swollen necked buck chasing a doe in hopes of that once a year opportunity to mate. I hunt for the

challenge of taking a wild animal on his own turf, using my brain and wits to outsmart the hunted and to successfully stalk my prey, ghosting from tree to tree undetected. I hunt to put meat on my table and feed my children. I hunt because I can.

Another respondent, Melanie, viewed hunting as a kind of test:

My will and spirit and reflexes against those that are far superior to my own (wild animals). there is a huge amount of satisfaction in working and planning really hard and have it pay off with 100 pounds of deer in the freezer, or that turkey that can be deep fried for the next 4 dinners ...

Besides the practicality of Melanie's reply, both the "holistic" and the "holy hunter" perspectives are revealed. She acknowledges strategizing, but also that "something more," a communion through spirit and will. In another response, she describes the feeling of power hunting brings to her: "Its a passion. Would rather be sitting in the woods than inside a building. Cant get enough of the thrill of the kill."

How Did You Learn to Hunt? With Whom?

Since far fewer women hunt (1–5 percent of the total hunting population), I wondered what the circumstances and context were in which they were introduced to the activity. In every case, men and boys had influence and were present at a girl's or woman's first kill, whether it was a brother, cousin, boyfriend, father, or husband. According to Sarah,

I was not introduced to hunting until I was an adult and thankfully have a husband who was patient enough to teach me what I needed to know to get started. At the time, I had teenage sons in the home and they had a field day taunting me when I announced my decision to hunt. They figured Mom would last about thirty minutes in the woods before whining and begging to go home. Instead, I remained in the woods that first day from early dawn until nearly sundown in awe of the wildlife which kept me entertained throughout the day and the sheer enjoyment of being outdoors, away from the hustle and bustle of the world. I might also add that

I brought home a whitetail buck that evening in the back of my truck as an added bonus to an already splendid day outdoors.

Karen said:

> my grandpa and i used to track wolves with these strange "old guys" that hunted timber wolves and trapped all kinds of things north of montreal in the laurentians. the first time i ever saw a timber wolf i was about 5 and the "old guys" had shot it and hung it in the tree and my dad didn't want me to see it, so of course i raced over to see what it was … and have been fascinated by wolves ever since.

Leslie said, "My husband has been hunting since he was 16 (now 43). He was with me at the time." Sheila learned about it this way:

> As a child and into my teen years hunting was a sport my brothers and cousins enjoyed. However it was not something the women in the family did so I never really thought twice about it. Later on, into my twenties I started working in the hunting industry by luck. It was there that I decided this was something I could do.

Jennifer said, "I didn't start hunting until I was about 18 years old when I met my present husband. I had known his family for years and they were born hunting just about." Julie said:

> In 2002, I married my best friend and hunting partner. He's taught me a lot of what I know and love about hunting and deer management. In 2004, my husband bought me a bow. This has turned out to be one of the best gifts I have ever received. I harvested my first buck with my bow that first season. I've harvested a buck or doe with it every season since.

Some of the women describe hunting in the same way the National Rifle Association's *Women on Target* program[34] and other hunting and gun-supporting organizations do – as a bonding opportunity, rite of passage, and an opportunity to educate girls and boys about the environment.[35] Jennifer said,

> I developed a LOVE for hunting many years later when I realized the sport taught so many life lessons and built so much character and discipline that I wanted my girls to develop in these areas also. Hunting took care of all these character issues.

DEBRA MERSKIN

Women Hunting

Do women face any gender-related challenges as hunters? As described earlier, hunting is traditionally constructed as a male activity. As a "cultural act" hunting appears to reflect not only gendered roles but also the times within which roles shift.[36] According to Karen:

> i think (at least here) there is still an awful lot of "hunting is a MAN's sport. women shouldn't be doing it." i get it all the time at the hunting stores (we only have bass pro here, and they are the WORST for it!), and the gun shop it's always "wow, you hunt and you're a girl?!." i must admit ... the most embarrassing moment for me was the instructor in the firearms course announcing that i was the only 100% on the firearms course and getting hit on by this guy in class who just walked up to me and said "wow. you got 100% on the firearms. i've owned and shot guns all my life. would you like to go out for dinner and a date?" while i'm wearing my wedding band ...

Even finding hunting clothes to fit women's bodies is a challenge, but one quickly being addressed by American consumer culture. As Linda described:

> Being a woman hunter isn't the easiest thing in the world. It's getting better, but some men look down on women hunters. Sure we have our limitations. I think every hunter does. I'd have a heck of a time putting up a ladder stand on my own and I'm kind of afraid of the dark. I can field dress a deer better than a few men I've watched, but hate taking a fish off of the hook without some gloves on. (My hubby laughs at me for that.) The hunting industry is starting to recognize that the sport of hunting isn't just for men. It's still pretty hard for girls to find hunting apparel that fits, but until we have it available, most of us gals will cinch up our belts to keep our pants from falling off and put on an extra pair of socks to make our boots fit because we know it's worth it.

What Does It Feel Like?

After the first set of questions, I returned to the chat group and asked the women to describe the experience of the moment they fire and shoot an animal or bird. While only a couple of them replied, their answers were interesting:

Kim:

The feeling you get when you have spotted, targeted, and killed the animal is un-describable. Your heart is racing in the beginning then you slow your breathing down to stay focused. Keeping your eye on the target without making noise or sudden movements, and then once he is down it feels like your heart will pound out of your chest, and the excitement is racing through your veins.

Marybeth added,

Afterwards, WHAT A FEELING OF ACCOMPLISHMENT! The bear dropped right there. I don't know who was more excited, me or my husband. Now that I know what to expect, I have to admit I am nervous/excited, but know that when I am about to pull the trigger, focusing is very important. The thrill is still there after the kill.

The New Artemis?

I sing about Artemis of the gold arrows, chaste virgin of the noisy hunt, who delights in her shafts and strikes down the stag … She ranges over shady hills and windy heights rejoicing in the chase as she draws her bow, made all of silver, and shoots her shafts of woe.[37]

Homer describes Artemis' personality, her relationship to and with nature, and the pleasure she takes in the chase and the hunt.[38] Artemis, sister of Apollo and daughter of Titan Leto and God Zeus, is known as Diana in Roman mythology. While the hunter extraordinaire, she is simultaneously the protector of young animals. She is goddess of the wilderness and originally a goddess of fertility.[39] In later tellings of her myth, Artemis chose not to be in relationship with men. For example, when the mortal Actaeon spied on her while she was bathing, she had him killed by his own dogs for his voyeuristic violation. Women who hunt resist confinement to socially constructed categories of appropriate conduct by threatening men's roles as *the* provider. Self-sufficiency, confidence, and autonomy are viewed as defeminizing traits.

A cinematic example is the 1947 Scottish-themed film *I Know Where I'm Going*.[40] In the fifth scene, "Can you skin a rabbit," one of the characters, Catriona, is first seen in silhouette, standing in fog-soaked scenery on a hillside, accompanied by several Irish wolfhounds, all pulling on their leads. The handsome naval officer, Torquil, and feminine visitor Joan Webster chat in Catriona's living room. Suddenly the hounds bay, and Catriona, with soaking wet hair, bursts into the room, holding a dead rabbit, before throwing it aside to greet Torquil, a childhood friend. She is bold and enthusiastic in cloak and hunting attire while Miss Webster is tidily dressed in a smart suit with sparkling lapel pin. Joan is described as a "queer girl." Throughout the film Catriona is regarded as eccentric for her independence, ability, and interest in bagging and preparing game, and enthusiasm for outdoor life. Her heterosexuality is affirmed in the mention of having had a husband at one time. Accompanied by her hounds and rifle, Catriona is pure Artemis.

My asking about women's hunting experiences revealed how little I knew and how much I am influenced by Western industrialized culture, which says men hunt and women gather. Something about (women's) being socialized to be the more emotional, nurturing, and sensitive members of the species suggested to me that women would have a more difficult time than men pulling the trigger. This is true for some, but not all. For example, a 1948 *Outdoor Life* magazine featured an article titled "I Just Like to *Kill* Things" by Kristin Sergel, who was featured in a photo wearing gingham and pigtails.[41] The story Sergel wrote wasn't so much about gender as it was about defending hunting as recreation and sport. A more current example is Republican vice-presidential candidate Sarah Palin. An advocate of trophy and "recreational" hunting and a lifelong NRA member, Palin was born into a family of "outdoor enthusiasts," which included hunters. Her mother, Sally Heath, said Palin was "raised to hunt, shoot, fish and play sports. She and her daddy would wake up at 3am on schooldays to hunt moose."[42] She can dress them out and loves to eat them. As Alaska's first female governor, Palin represents what several special interest groups wanted to see: a beautiful (hockey mom/pit bull) woman who hunts and is proud of it and yet retains her femininity and (re)productivity as the mother of five.

Are women who hunt the new Artemis? Noddings reminds us, "Bloody jaws belong to the same creature who licks her young with such affection."[43] A goal of feminist theory is to break away from narrow either-or, this-or-that dichotomous gender roles. I argue, as does Mary Zeiss Stange, that an ecofeminist consideration of women and hunting must consider women as multi-dimensional.[44] Unlike stereotypes of women that say we are only and always the emotional, passive, nurturing sex, Artemis was capable of both caring and killing. The discourse of women who hunt reminds us that aggression is a *human* characteristic. Whether women who hunt do so to challenge a male-dominated field, to take back an activity they once participated in, or to challenge stereotypes is less relevant than the topic's omission from feminist analysis. Whether hunting is the right or wrong moral outcome is grist for another mill. What matters is that participation be based on individual directive rather than cultural constructions of appropriate gender roles.

NOTES

1   Doug Nadvornick, "More Women Hunt, Seeking Food and Togetherness," National Public Radio, September 29, 2009. Available at www.npr.org/tem plates/story/story.php?storyId=113279429 (accessed December 2, 2009).

2   US Fish and Wildlife Service, "National Survey." Available at http://wsfrpro grams.fws.gov/Subpages/NationalSurvey/National_Survey.htm (accessed December 2, 2009).

3   Marti Kheel, "License to Kill: An Ecofeminist Critique of Hunters' Discourse," in Carol J. Adams and Josephine Donovan (eds.) *Animals and Women: Feminist Theoretical Explorations*, 2nd ed. (Raleigh, NC: Duke University Press, 1999), pp. 85–125.

4   Karen J. Warren, "The Power and Promise of Ecological Feminism," *Environmental Ethics* 12, no. 3 (1990): 126.

5   Robert Ardrey, *The Hunting Hypothesis* (New York: Macmillan, 1976).

6   Donna Hart and Robert Wald Sussman, *Man the Hunted: Primates, Predators and Human Evolution* (Boulder, CO: Westview, 2009).

7   Susan Kent, "Egalitarianism, Equality and Equitable Power," in Tracy L. Sweely (ed.) *Manifesting Power: Gender and the Interpretation of Power in Archaeology* (New York: Routledge, 1999), p. 36.

8   Hart and Sussman, *Man the Hunted*, p. 215.

9   Adrienne Zihlman, "The Paleolithic Glass Ceiling: Women in Human Evolution," in Lori D. Hager (ed.) *Women in Human Evolution* (New York: Routledge, 1997), p. 91.

10 Marjorie Spiegel, *The Dreaded Comparison: Race and Animal Slavery* (New York: Mirror Books, 1997), pp. 89, 105.

11 David D. Gilmore, *Manhood in the Making: Cultural Concepts of Masculinity* (New Haven, CT: Yale University Press, 1990), p. 29.

12 Ibid., p. 230.

13 Henrietta L. Moore, *A Passion for Difference: Essays in Anthropology and Gender* (Bloomington: University of Indiana Press, 1994), p. 72.

14 Kheel, "License to Kill," p. 86.
15 There are three additional categories of hunter: the hired (for commercial profit), the hungry (for food), and the hostile (to "eradicate 'villainous' animals"); ibid., p. 87.
16 Ibid., p. 89.
17 Ibid., p. 95.
18 Ibid., p. 87.
19 Ibid., p. 88.
20 Gilmore, *Manhood in the Making*, pp. 220–1.
21 Kheel, "License to Kill," p. 92.
22 Warren, "The Power and Promise," p. 48.
23 Linda Kalof, Amy Fitzgerald, and Lori Baralt, "Animals, Women, and Weapons: Blurred Sexual Boundaries in the Discourse of Sport Hunting," *Society and Animals* 12, no. 3 (2004): 240.
24 Ibid., p. 247.
25 Brian Luke, "Violent Love: Hunting, Heterosexuality, and the Erotics of Men's Predation," *Feminist Studies* 24, no. 3 (1998): 627–55.
26 Kalof, Fitzgerald, and Baralt, "Animals, Women, and Weapons," pp. 237–51.
27 Linda Kalof and Amy Fitzgerald, "Reading the Trophy: Exploring the Display of Dead Animals in Hunting Magazines," *Visual Studies* 18, no. 2 (2003): 112–22.
28 Andrea L. Smalley, "'I Just Like to Kill Things': Women, Men, and the Gender of Sport Hunting in the United States, 1940–1973," *Gender and History* 17, no. 1 (2005): 183–209.
29 Jan E. Dizard, *Mortal Stakes: Hunters and Hunting in Contemporary America* (Amherst: University of Massachusetts Press, 2003); Thomas A. Heberlein and Elizabeth Thomson, "Changes in US Hunting Participation, 1980–1990," *Human Dimensions of Wildlife* 1, no. 1 (1996): 85–6; US Fish and Wildlife Services, "Factors Related to Hunting and Fishing Participation in the United States, Phase IV," Mark Damian Duda et al., 1996-404-991/4406 (Washington, DC: Government Printing Office, 1998).
30 Heberlein and Thomson, "Changes in US Hunting Participation."
31 Dizard, *Mortal Stakes*, p. 43.
32 Randall L. Eaton, "What to Say to a Person Who Has Never Hunted," Hunting the Great Kalahari. Available at www.kalahari-trophy-hunting.com/reasons-for-hunting.html (accessed December 2, 2009).
33 Wanda Garner, "Why Women Hunt," Women Anglers and Hunters Too! Available at www.womenanglers.us/wanda_whyhunt.html (accessed December 2, 2009).
34 The Women of the NRA, "NRA's *Women on Target*," National Rifle Association Headquarters. Available at www.nrahq.org/women/wot.asp (accessed December 2, 2009).

35 The NRA and other organizations literally want to "sell" hunting. As the numbers of individuals who hunt declines, so do retail revenues for hunting-related paraphernalia. For example, according to the US Fish and Wildlife Department, hunting expenditures in 2006 totaled nearly $23 billion.

36 Smalley, " 'I Just Like to Kill Things,' " p. 204.

37 Homer, "Homeric Hymn to Artemis 9," in Mark P. O. Morford and Robert J. Lenardon (eds.) *Classical Mythology* (New York: Oxford University Press, 2003), p. 200.

38 Ibid., p. 27.

39 James George Frazer, *The Golden Bough* (New York: Penguin, 1922).

40 *I Know Where I'm Going*, dir. Michael Powell and Emeric Pressburger (The Archers, 1947).

41 Smalley, " 'I Just Like to Kill Things,' " p. 183.

42 Ken Herman, "Palin's Speechwriter Not a Fan of Hunting," *Austin American Statesman*, September 3, 2008. Available at www.statesman.com/blogs/content/shared-blogs/washington/washington/entries/2008/09/03/palins_speechwr.html (accessed December 3, 2009).

43 Nel Noddings, *Women and Evil* (Berkeley: University of California Press, 1989), p. 124.

44 Mary Zeiss Stange, *Woman the Hunter* (Boston: Beacon Press, 1997).

CHAPTER 19

OFF THE GRID

Rights, Religion, and the Rise of the Eco-Gentry

Hunting: A Rite of American Secular Religion

... I live back in the woods, you see
A woman and the kids, and the dogs and me
I got a shotgun, rifle and a 4-wheel drive
And a country boy can survive
Country folks can survive

... We came from the West Virginia coal mines
And the Rocky Mountains and the western skies
And we can skin a buck; we can run a trot-line
And a country boy can survive
Country folks can survive[1]

Early American game laws were not about to let landed urban gentry insinuate their way into our anti-aristocratic rural nation. We were American citizens, meaning free people.[2] Consequently, hunting became an intrinsic aspect of our inalienable rights – divinely inspired – in and for the common man. From the very start, hunting was a crucial touchstone of our national identity. The right to hunt became no less than a sacred rite of the revolutionary secular religion of America.

Americans knew the pain of the English commoners who had been excluded from possessing the fruits of nature given to them from the

Old Testament God and vowed that nobles would never again keep the common people of America's democracy from enjoying the fruits of "Nature's God." But Nature's God was *not* identical with God Almighty. Nature's God was the American Deist divinity named in the Declaration of Independence. The predominance of Nature's God over all other gods was also made explicit in the First Amendment: the freedom to worship as one pleased meant that individual liberty – given to each citizen by Nature's God – was more important in America than any particular divinity a citizen might worship.

Hunting became an icon of the American secular religion of individual natural rights. Unlike the Judeo-Christian God, Nature's God did *not* give us the wild land itself and the game upon it. Nature's God gave us instead the inalienable right – the liberty – to go into that wild land, unenclosed by any privileged class, and transform that land through our labor. Each American bumpkin was told he had direct intuition of the self-evident truth that nature was his to enter,[3] and to own any part of that nature required the individual stamina and skill embodied by hunting. The commons, therefore, had to remain open to hunters. Our democratic government provided legal protection of public hunting and ready access to game land to demonstrate that the brutality of British land enclosures would end in America. Even so, in Jeremy Bentham's words, rights remained "terroristic language."[4] As I will show below, talk of individual human rights terrorized the noble gentry of the eighteenth century, and individual human rights continue to terrorize the eco-gentry of the twenty-first century.

Hunting as the perfect symbol of American secular religion is made even more evident by Walter Burkert in his book, *Homo Necans* (Slaughtering Man). Burkert provides a sustained demonstration of the intimate link that exists between hunting, sacrifice, and religion. In his words, "[B]lood and violence lurk fascinatingly at the very heart of religion. ... For this is the act of piety: bloodshed, slaughter – and eating. Nourishment, order and civilized life are born of antithesis: the encounter with death. Only *Homo necans* can become *Homo sapiens*."[5]

As with most religions, the American secular religion entails blood sacrifice. In America, with so much game available, each American can perform the sacrificial rite of the hunt. When it comes to Nature's God, Americans understand – and have understood from the beginning – that one needs the courage to embrace one's religion, not because it is true, but because it *has to be* true. Despite Bentham's assertion that rights were merely "nonsense on stilts,"[6] human rights have to be true, and public hunting illustrated they were. According to Joseph Ratzinger: "Even the one who does not succeed in finding the path to accepting the existence of God ought nevertheless to try to live and to direct his life *veluti si Deus daretur*, as if God did indeed exist."[7] *Veluti si Deus daretur* could be the motto for Nature's God who gave Americans their inalienable natural rights and the sacrificial rites of hunting. Whether or not Nature's God or rights exist in an absolute sense is irrelevant: they both exist, palpably, concretely, in the cultural reality of America.

Rights and the Burden of Ownership

> As I went walking I saw a sign there
> And on the sign it said "No Trespassing."
> But on the other side it didn't say nothing,
> That side was made for you and me.
>
> In the shadow of the steeple I saw my people,
> By the relief office I seen my people;
> As they stood there hungry, I stood there asking
> Is this land made for you and me?
>
> Nobody living can ever stop me,
> As I go walking that freedom highway;
> Nobody living can ever make me turn back
> This land was made for you and me.[8]

American game laws grew in strident opposition to the tragic conse- quences of the enclosure laws of seventeenth- and eighteenth-century England. These enclosure laws eliminated access by the common people to common land and thereby forced them off of the land upon which their lives depended.[9] When Georgia law explicitly rejected the Black Act, the American state of Georgia made clear that America is not and will not become England. "That landowners possessed status privileges similar to those exemplified by English qualification laws" was simply rejected by early American courts as being un-American.[10] All men are created equal, and the commoner is as free to hunt as the aristocrat or the gentry. Land – *all land* – in America would be open to hunting for Americans: "The American belief in common rights to wildlife was man- ifested in doctrines that rejected landowner claims of special privilege and allowed free taking *even on private lands*."[11] Still today, most American states require landowners to actively post their land to exclude hunting.[12] The presumption is that unenclosed land is open to hunting, and this supersedes trespassing laws.[13]

Americans had taken a different reading of John Locke's natural rights: it was not merely private property that was to be protected in America – it was the individual's liberty to *create* private property through pursuit and ingenuity. It was no accident that Jefferson ultimately chose "pursuit of happiness" to replace the words "estates" and "property" that figure so prominently in Locke's *Second Treatise*. For the American, possession of property did not come through birthright but from effort conjoined with actual capture. This ultimately led to the principle of adverse possession which, in America, meant one could lose one's land through indolence, inattention, or inability. Mere pursuit is irrelevant to property ownership, whereas actual capture of the property is paramount, and that even applies to property inherited or presumed owned.[14] In America, to own property, you must hold it in your hand like a shot partridge.[15]

Off the Grid: Civilization's Joyous Discontent

"Paw," says my little brother, as the old man loads the shotgun, "let me shoot the deer this time."

"You shut up," I say.

Our father smiles. "Quiet," he whispers, "both of you. Maybe next year." He peers down the dim path in the woods into the gathering evening. "Be real still now. They're a-comin'. And Ned ..." He squeezes my shoulder. "You hold that light on 'em good and steady this time."

"Yes, sir," I whisper back. "Sure will, Paw."[16]

Hunting is not conservation. No hunter goes off into the woods to thin the herd. That is a lie hunters tell to mollify those who don't hunt, and perhaps to themselves to qualm their fears about their own bloodlust. If hunting were really for the sake of conservation then early each spring we would simply use our tax dollars to pay a small army of lab technicians to go about the forests and fields with the most advanced satellite-enhanced equipment and, with relative ease, find the most fragile fawns and other animals scientifically deemed unbeneficial to the ecosystem, and euthanize them – efficiently, painlessly, and silently. Thankfully, we do not do this. In fact, the US federal government created two special "excise tax[es] on sporting equipment … and fishing gear"[17] to help states provide hunters with prime game land and sufficient game to assure them successful hunting. Rather than a conservation strategy, hunting is an end in itself and part of the cost of the boots, shells, and camo we buy helps pay for the killing we ultimately intend.

Since the advent of the Neolithic age some ten thousand years ago, hunting has not been necessary for human subsistence. Once humans began to domesticate animals and plant grains, we have virtually always had a better chance of survival by spending our energies herding, farming, and trading than by expending our energy hunting. José Ortega y Gasset illustrates this by explaining one of the essential aspects of hunting as the simple fact that game is scarce, and has *always been* scarce.[18] Hunting has never been a sure bet: if anything, the likelihood of a successful hunt is probably much higher for us than it was for our Paleolithic ancestors. Though many hunters like to pretend they hunt for food, clearly a short trip to the grocery store and a low-paying job are vastly more effective uses of one's time and energy: hunting provides no comparative advantage.

Yet another lie hunters tell is that "hunting is just as good when I don't get anything." Nonsense. If one does not intend to kill the prey, one simply does not hunt. Despite the pleasure of the hike, any hunt that does not end with a kill is a failed hunt. Killing the animal we hunt is by no means an unavoidable evil: we intend to kill the animal, and yes, we like it and yes, we also feel clear ambivalence and a bit of regret: "Every good hunter is uneasy in the depths of his conscience when faced with the death he is about to inflict on the enchanting animal."[19] Ortega also asserts that "hunting is counterposed to all that morphology of death as something without equal, since it is the only normal case in which the killing of one creature constitutes the delight of another."[20] It may be disturbing, but that is the truth of it: we enjoy hunting when we have possessed the game we pursue by killing it.

Despite the secular religiosity of hunting, there can be no honesty discussing hunting by hoping to explain away what it is. Invoking contemporary romanticism, neo-animist mysticism, or any other misguided return to paganism is a degradation of what it is to hunt. Intrinsic to the joy of hunting – and it is thoroughly a joy – is the killing of a wild animal one hopes to eat. The hunter stands still; he sees the prey before he is seen or forces the prey out of its cover. The hunter must then kill the prey with absolute clear intent. Unabashedly killing a wild animal for consumption gives the hunter an atavistic awareness that survival is possible despite the precarious and various concretions of civilization. The hunter's relationship with the rabbit is ultimately more secure than his relationship with the skyscraper. He is off the grid. In the off-the-grid world of the hunt, there is an ancient understanding that wild animals – the squirrel, the whitetail, and the partridge – will assuredly feed him and his family even if the city, the university, and the satellite vanish. Though a low-paying job may have a better comparative advantage, in the American Deist religion an off-the-grid hunter is more secure in the Cathedral of Nature's God than in the cubicle of his man-made job.

To hunt is always to imagine and remember one's self, at least for a moment, as able again to live by one's own wits in the woods and the wildness. Modern humans, *Homo sapiens sapiens*, have been here approximately half a million years, worn woven clothing for only a tenth of that time, and ceased needing to hunt for only *one fiftieth* of that time. In our genetic bones, man evolved as a hunter and remained a hunter for a vastly longer time than he has been a herder or farmer. There is a biological familiarity with hunting, just like there is a biological familiarity with holding a child's hand. In a deep, ineffable way, hunting – stalking, capturing game – feels bodily right.

Civilization is a joyous discontent for the hunter, for at the moment the gun is loaded or the arrow knocked, the hunter is ever so slightly, ever so deliciously free of civil constraints. He is an armed man, and he is mortally dangerous. All his hopes are on killing game for his family. Not only must civil society control our human propensity to join irrational urban mobs, but it must also control our propensity as individuals to separate from civil society and live as unitary hunters. Civilization suffers an uneasy relationship with each individual's capacity to step off the grid, alone, to kill and eat an animal. Fundamentally, social ambivalence toward hunting is not a consequence of antagonism to killing animals, but an expression of civil society's attempt to dampen the hunter's propensity to individuation in the wild. This is particularly visible in stipulations on the hunter's use and ownership of game land.

The game animal, though described as "wild," is actually the "civil animal" par excellence, and is the only animal legally hunted. The legal notion of a "wild animal" is fully an artifice of civil society.[21] We can legally raise or kill our own domesticated livestock at any time. Not so with civil wild animals: to keep a wild rabbit or deer as a pet on one's own land requires a special license issued by a state fish and game department. Wild game animals remain controlled state property regardless of the particular land on which the animals live. Hunting, killing, or otherwise capturing legally designated wild animals requires government permission for the individual's transformation of state property into private property. And yet, that licensed transformation remains troubling to civil society. The bear or the moose, despite the state's attempt to create a civic creature by legally designating it "game," can be transformed in an instant into private meat by the skilled hunter. Hunting, from this perspective, is always a challenge to the public order of things.[22] Game animals are artificial public organisms, protected by the state for individual sacrificial hunting. The hunter, by eating the state's boar, glorifies the power of the individual while threatening the social contract. He who can kill the king's stag may also kill the king.

Big Green: The New Nonsense of the Eco-Gentry

What we see evolving in contemporary environmental law is the return to a new gentry, an *eco-gentry*, whose elite knowledge of urban values has transferred to them ownership of wild animals. The expense of this new gentry's luxury falls upon the common landholder, for whom the takings clause of the Fifth Amendment provides little protection. If one's land is designated "park" or "protected wetland," one loses it, and it often becomes land where hunting is now considered poaching. Under the auspices of the eco-gentry, the deer and the rabbit have again achieved a royal status beyond the common man. To imagine that land or wild animals have achieved rights that supersede the human rights of the owner of the land or the hunter on the land destroys the sanctity of American Deistic human rights.

If it is people who create the legal notion of nature, then neither land nor animals have rights. People – commoners – we alone have rights, and though I love rabbits in my gun sights more than I love some people, those people have rights beyond my beloved rabbits or even all of Yellowstone Park. Should we fight to protect Yellowstone Park from development? Yes, of course, but not because the buffalo, the wolf, the elk, or the grizzly have rights; rather, because those who love the buffalo, the wolf, the elk, and the grizzly have rights. The tragedy of the commons is not that the land is destroyed: it is that people destroy what people love, often unto death. Muir was right: Yellowstone is a Cathedral. But a Cathedral has no rights. The Grand Canyon in all its unfathomable glory is not the divinity of our secular American religion – our individual liberty is.

To forget this is to allow the civil invention of wild animals to slip again into the domain of the gentry – a new gentry, a new royal elite – for whom there is a new urban museum aesthetic, an aesthetic that can only arise in those living far from the actual land where the game lives and competes daily, often dangerously, with the men and women who live in common on that land.

This new aesthetic presumes it is only the scholar who understands why the raw wilderness gives definition and meaning to the human enterprise:

> The land ethic simply enlarges the boundaries of the community to include soils, waters, plants, and animals, or collectively: the land.
>
> ... In short, a land ethic changes the role of *Homo sapiens* from conqueror of the land-community to plain member and citizen of it. It implies respect for the community as such.
>
> ... In the biotic community, a parallel situation exists. Abraham knew exactly what the land was for: it was to drip milk and honey into Abraham's mouth. At the present moment, the assurance with which we regard this assumption is inverse to the degree of our education.[23]

The "land ethic" as envisioned by Aldo Leopold, and later adopted by animal rights advocates like Tom Regan,[24] is born *not* out of respect for wild animals but out of antipathy for the uniqueness of the human being. Their shared, mistaken notion that all animals, as part of the "biota,"[25] have rights equivalent in kind if not degree to human rights is a sacrilege to the American "divinity itself" who wrote "the sacred rights of mankind."[26] Leopold conflates human rights with the pretense of some essential inhuman identity of the soil, the molds, a bacterium, a snowflake. In effect, the land ethic of the eco-gentry is very much the sort of antipathy the elite English gentry held toward the eighteenth-century commoners. The eco-gentry of today have similarly elevated themselves to a position of moral privilege based on their self-confirmed erudition. They alone now grasp the genuine beauty of the hunt – the photo-hunt and the eco-tour. An ecological notion of "humankind" has replaced the commoner, and humankind – a mere resident life-form of the biosphere – has been reduced to the carbonate chemical compounds we share with animals and plants. We are all brethren of the land, the biosphere. Commoners and chemicals are equivalent. This is the fallacy of composition: attributing an aspect of the whole to an individual part. However, before we return to dust, we are so much more than dust. Even so, the fallacy of Leopold and Regan is incomparable to the true absurdity of Garret Hardin's eugenic nightmare described in "The Tragedy of the Commons."[27] In this much reprinted article, we are told the commons must inevitably come to destruction without severe limitation of access by either property owners or the government. Unavoidably, commoners will over-graze their flocks through their reasonable, yet selfish, competition with one another until their shared commons will be despoiled, utterly starving them all. Hardin's solution – elegant in its cruelty – is that only through the forced reduction of the human population (i.e., the commoners) can the commons be well controlled. In essence, we must sterilize the Bushmen for the sake of the bush meat:

> But the air and waters surrounding us cannot readily be fenced [like private property], and so the tragedy of the commons as a cesspool must be prevented by different means, by *coercive laws*. ... Perhaps the simplest summary of this analysis of man's population problems is this: the commons, if justifiable at all is justifiable only under conditions of low population density. Every new enclosure of the commons involves the infringement of somebody's personal liberty. The only way we can preserve and nurture other and more precious freedoms is by *relinquishing the freedom to breed*, and that very soon.[28]

Man, like Descartes' animal, becomes only another "mineral."[29] You and I and our children are only breathing, yearning bits of the Earth's biosphere. The eco-gentry confuse the Cathedral where Nature's God is worshipped with Nature's God itself: they merge the Sacrament with the divinity. This is idolatry of the most dangerous variety. The god of human rights is only clothed in nature. But from the perspective of the eco-gentry, every unnecessary common person has become an accidental poacher leading inexorably to the tragedy of the commons. Every human being must succumb, by the morality of the equivalent rights of the biosphere, to the eugenic enclosure of human thinning. Animals have not at all been elevated; rather, man has been demoted. What an animal is man!

The eco-gentry are not merely royal idealists: they include those with simple commercial interests as well. Not only did commercial hunting virtually eliminate the bison from the American plains, but in recent years, under new cover, these same sorts of commercial exploitations have arisen in unexpected places. The very organizations that promote conservation have themselves been implicated in the exploitation of wild land for simple profit taking. "Big Green" was the title of a series of three major articles published in the *Washington Post* from May 4–6, 2003, detailing the disreputable practices of conservation groups:

> The Arlington-based Nature Conservancy ... [is] the world's richest environmental group, amassing $3 billion in assets by pledging to save precious places. Yet the Conservancy has logged forests, engineered a $64 million deal paving the way for opulent houses on fragile grasslands and drilled for natural gas under the last breeding ground of an endangered bird species.[30]

Over the course of a year, in no fewer than 14 articles, the *Washington Post* demonstrated that, among other strategies, the Nature Conservancy had been using land conservation easements and other dubious accounting techniques to raise money to buy and sell land for profit in order to purchase more land. By creating tax benefits for major corporations, the Nature Conservancy had, in effect, forced American commoners to pay to have land enclosed for the exclusive benefit of the Nature Conservancy and their corporate partners. These same corporations also used the Conservancy logo to promote unrelated products, from beef to toilet cleaner. By July 2004, the IRS finally began "focusing on easements that have questionable public benefit or have been manipulated to generate inflated deductions."[31]

In September 2009, *Economist.com*, quoting recent separate works by eugenics-minded scientists Thomas Wire, Roger Short, and Malcolm Potts, reported why the World Wildlife Fund's historic support of eugenics for the sake of saving the world's wildlife has come back into fashion:

> Sir Julian Huxley, the first director-general of the United Nation's Education, Science and Cultural Organization, remarked that death control made birth control a moral imperative. Sir Julian went on to play a role in establishing what was then the World Wildlife Fund, a nature conservation agency, linking population growth to environmental degradation.[32]

The eco-gentry have arrived. Their distaste of hunting is not rooted in respect for animals, but rather in their justifiable fear of the hunter and hunting itself. Through the narrow edge of game and conservation laws, they have begun to exert more control over human rights and human life than we might have imagined. International commons will be enclosed to preserve the land *ethic*, if not the land. Equal rights for all carbonates:

the coney, the deer, and the human. To hunt is to subvert this growing hegemony of the eco-gentry and their conflation of all life into an inhuman unnatural carbonate biosphere. I accept that the notion of nature is man-made – as too are rights – but the hunter rejects Big Green's notion of nature and rights. To hunt and kill a rabbit is to reserve the dignity of humanity for humans. I am not biosphere, nor are my children.

The sacrificial rite of hunting always opposes the arrogance of any civilization that imagines it can defeat humankind's own slaughtering nature. Humans worship, and to worship we kill: that is a human absolute. Every hunt brings the hunter full face again with the tragic understanding that *Homo sapiens* is indeed *Homo necans*. To retain our humanity we need to be honest about our humanity. Ultimately, we hunt because we worship. That worship means we cannot degrade the rituals of our religion. The American hunter is brought up with a series of rituals all geared to show respect for the game: if you kill it you eat it; know what you are shooting at; don't shoot if you aren't confident you can kill it with the first shot; aim carefully. No hunter respects the beastly killer who leaves a deer carcass to rot just to take the antlers. No hunter respects the fool who kills a doe or a spike and then leaves it to spoil only because he believes he may save his tag for one that is better. These and other acts of obscene killing are not consistent with the hunting rite of the American secular religion of individual rights.[33] Doused with fox urine and dressed in camouflage, the hunter enters the Cathedral of Nature's God to worship respectfully. The rifle is loaded and sighted in; the cartridges are new. The hope is to kill a buck with a single lethal shot. Each of us anticipates the somber thrilling boom and the sight of the deer shot dead with one well-placed round. There is death and there is blood and the dark smell of intestines and there is the significant work of dragging the animal out. But throughout all of it there are the rituals of respect for the Cathedral within which we worship Nature's God in the American sacrificial rite of slaughter, *hunting*.

NOTES

1 Hank Williams, Jr., *Hank Williams, Jr.'s Greatest Hits*, vol. 1 (Curb Records, 1993).

2 Thomas A. Lund, *American Wildlife Law* (Berkeley: University of California Press, 1980), p. 27. This excluded slaves and Indians, for whom there would initially be extremely restrictive game laws.

3 Declaration of Independence, July 4, 1776, para. 2.

4 Jeremy Bentham, "Anarchical Fallacies," in *Works of Jeremy Bentham*, vol. 2, ed. John Bowring (London: Simpkin, Marshall and Co., 1843), p. 4.

5 Walter Burkert, *Homo Necans: The Anthropology of Ancient Greek Sacrificial Ritual and Myth*, trans. Peter Bing (Berkeley: University of California Press, 1986), pp. 2, 212.

6 Bentham, "Anarchical Fallacies," p. 501.

7 Joseph Cardinal Ratzinger (Pope Benedict XVI), *Christianity and the Crisis of Cultures*, trans. Brian McNeil (San Francisco: Ignatius Press, 2006), p. 50.

8 Woody Guthrie, "This Land Is Your Land," in Elizabeth Partridge, *This Land Was Made for You and Me: The Life and Songs of Woody Guthrie* (New York: Viking, 2002), p. 85.

9 E. P. Thompson, *Whigs and Hunters: The Origin of the Black Act* (New York: Pantheon Books, 1975); Douglas Hay, "Poaching and Game Laws on Cannock Chase," in Douglas Hay et al., *Albion's Fatal Tree: Crime and Society in Eighteenth-Century England* (New York: Pantheon Books, 1975), pp. 189–253; see Christopher Hill, *Liberty Against the Law* (London: Penguin, 1997), chs. 2 and 7 for extensive descriptions of the Black Act, poaching, and enclosure laws in eighteenth-century England.

10 Mark R. Sigmond, "Hunting and Posting on Private Land in America," *Duke Law Journal* 54 (2004): 555.

11 Lund, *American Wildlife Law*, pp. 24, 20, 57; emphasis mine.

12 Sigmond, "Hunting and Posting," pp. 558–64.

13 Lund, *American Wildlife Law*, pp. 24–5; Sigmond, "Hunting and Posting," pp. 558–68.

14 Aaron Larson, "Adverse Possession," *ExpertLaw Library: 2004–2007*. Available at www.expertlaw.com/library/real_estate/adverse_possession.html (accessed September 23, 2009).

15 *Pierson v. Post.* [No Number in Original], Supreme Court of Judicature of New York, 3 Cai. R. 175; 1805 N.Y. LEXIS 311, August, 1805, Decided.

16 Edward Abbey, "Blood Sport," in David Petersen (ed.) *A Hunter's Heart* (New York: Henry Holt Owl, 1997), p. 16.

17 Lund, *American Wildlife Law*, p. 89.

18 José Ortega y Gasset, *Meditations on Hunting*, trans. Howard B. Wescott (Belgrade, MT: Wilderness Adventures Press, 2007), pp. 66–81.

19 Ibid., p. 98.

20 Ibid., p. 101.

21 Sigmond, "Hunting and Posting," p. 553.

22 Lund, *American Wildlife Law*, p. 103.

23 Aldo Leopold, *A Sand County Almanac and Sketches Here and There* (London: Oxford University Press, 1968), pp. 202–5.

24 Tom Reagan, *The Case For Animal Rights* (Berkeley: University of California Press, 1983).

25 Leopold, *A Sand County Almanac*, p. 178.
26 Alexander Hamilton, "The Farmer Refuted," in *The Works of Alexander Hamilton*, vol. 2, ed. John C. Hamilton (New York: Charles S. Francis, 1851), p. 80.
27 Garrett Hardin, "The Tragedy of the Commons," *Science* 162, no. 3859 (December 13, 1968): 1243–8.
28 Ibid., pp. 1245, 1248.
29 Ortega, *Meditations on Hunting*, p. 98.
30 David B. Ottaway and Joe Stephens, "Nonprofit Land Bank Amasses Billions: Charity Builds Assets on Corporate Partnerships," *Washington Post*, May 4, 2003, p. A1.
31 David B. Ottaway and Joe Stephens, "IRS Toughens Scrutiny of Land Gifts," *Washington Post*, July 1, 2004, p. A1.
32 *Economist*, "Fewer Feet, Smaller Footprint," September 21, 2009. Available at www.economist.com/world/international/displaystory.cfm?story_id=14488619 (accessed September 23, 2009).
33 Leopold, *A Sand County Almanac*, pp. 178–9.

NOTES ON CONTRIBUTORS

ALISON ACTON, PhD, teaches interdisciplinary social science at the Open University in the East of England. She attended the University of Nottingham and graduated with a BA (Hons) in Sociology. Her doctoral thesis, completed at the University of Essex, explored the interrelationship between foxhunting, landscape, and identity. Her fieldwork was based predominantly on her ethnographic participation in English and Irish mounted foxhound packs. Alison still rides to hounds and uses this as a means by which she can continue to learn about hunting culture and practice.

JAMES CARMINE, PhD, is an Associate Professor of Philosophy, and the token classical liberal, in the Humanities Division of Carlow University. He also teaches philosophy and moral reasoning to third-graders, sixth-graders, and high school students for the Penn Hills Public Schools, developed "Take Your Father to School Day" for the Pittsburgh Public Schools, and was the Republican candidate for Mayor of the City of Pittsburgh in 2001. He received his PhD in philosophy at SUNY, Stony Brook, where he developed a passion for blue fishing and squirrel hunting. He has three sons, one daughter, and a wife who is a crack shot.

A vegan-turned-deer-hunter, TOVAR CERULLI has been wondering about humans and other animals since he was a boy. His undergraduate career spanned Dartmouth College in New Hampshire, Kansai Gaidai University in Japan, and the New School for Social Research in Manhattan. He has worked as a carpenter and as a logger, and has written on hunting, forestry, wildlife, and conservation for Outdoor America,

Bugle, Northern Woodlands, and Massachusetts Wildlife, among others. After 15 years away from academia, he was awarded a Graduate School Fellowship by the University of Massachusetts-Amherst, where he is currently researching diverse perspectives on human relationships with the natural world. He lives in Vermont with his wife Catherine and their affectionate labrador retriever, Kaia.

GREGORY A. CLARK is Professor of Philosophy at North Park University, but his most widely read article was published in *Traditional Bowhunter*. He is a decent archer, a mediocre bowyer, and (after three seasons) still a novice traditional bowhunter. He is also a member of Reba Place Fellowship, a Mennonite intentional Christian community in Evanston, Illinois.

JANINA DUERR graduated with her MA from Ruprecht-Karls-Universität, Heidelberg, Germany, and recently finished her PhD in prehistory and cultural anthropology on hunting history, myths, and rituals at the University of Kiel, Germany, in cooperation with the University of Basel, Switzerland. She is a member of CLIOHRES – a European Network of Excellence working on European history. Her research interests include human–animal relationships and comparative, intercultural studies. She has written articles on the advent of dairying in European prehistory and on rituals concerning hunting, the revitalization of animals, and meat-sharing.

VALERIUS GEIST, PhD, is Professor Emeritus of Environmental Science at the University of Calgary, where he was the first Program Director for Environmental Science and founding member of the Faculty of Environmental Design. A zoologist by training, he branched out into research on how to maximize human health environmentally. This and his interest in the biology of Ice Age mammals, of which humans are a splendid example, led him deeply into interdisciplinary studies. He also published and became professionally involved in policy issues pertaining to wildlife conservation. He is the author or editor of technical and popular award-winning books, as well as several hundred technical papers and book chapters, popular essays, and encyclopedia entries. He is a hunter, fisherman, gardener, hobby farmer, mushroom and berry picker, cook, and avid brewer. He and his wife Renate are now living in retirement, if one can call it such. They have three children and four grandchildren.

JESÚS ILUNDÁIN-AGURRUZA is fascinated by weapons, both edged ones and firearms. He practices regularly with the katanas and longsword he owns, and enjoys shooting his bolt-action rifle at targets. He fancies himself a good shot – until his wife outdoes him, bringing a measure of his own Socratic medicine. An Assistant Professor of Philosophy and Allen & Pat Kelley Faculty Scholar at Linfield College in Oregon, his main areas of research and publication are the philosophy of sport and the philosophy of art. He has edited, with Mike Austin, *Cycling – Philosophy for Everyone* for this series, and published in journals such as *Sports, Ethics, and Philosophy*, as well as in anthologies on sports and risk, the Olympics, soccer, childhood and sports, and more (some in Spanish). He hails from Pamplona in Spain, where more than once he wished for a gun as he got into trouble with the bulls. His dream gun is a lever action – a Winchester 73 or 92 in .45LC, bit of a romantic there. Had he been born in El Paso in the late 1800s he would surely have been a hunter. Times being what they are, the cute squirrels around his house are safe.

ROGER J. H. KING is Associate Professor and Chair of the Philosophy Department at the University of Maine. Having received his PhD from Boston University, he moved to Orono, Maine, in 1986 and has lived in the area ever since. While he has not hunted anything, he does enjoy sharing his bioregion with the plants and animals of northern Maine. Professor King's publications have mostly been in the area of environmental ethics, including articles on hunting, eco-feminism, the ethics of eating, feral animals in ecological restoration projects, and the environmental ethics of built environments.

A nomad at heart, KAY KOPPEDRAYER has done scholarly nosing around in places as diverse as Rosebud, South Dakota; the Kingdom of Bhutan; Pawhuska, Oklahoma; and Tiruvavatuturai, Tamilnadu. Her forays have taken her into the world of expressive culture to study performance, sports, ritual activities, and visual display. Recently retired from the Department of Religion and Culture at Wilfrid Laurier University, Waterloo, Ontario, she is widely published in popular archery magazines as well as academic journals. Since 1999 she has been an associate editor of *Primitive Archer*.

TIHAMER RICHARD KOVER is a PhD candidate in philosophy at the Katholieke Universiteit Leuven in Belgium, and is currently completing his doctoral thesis on Paul Shepard's environmental thought. His main research interests include environmental philosophy, philosophy of technology as well as other areas of social, political, and ethical thought, specifically the interplay between modernity, postmodernism, transhumanism, and neoprimitivism. Aside from serving as the assistant editor of this volume, he has published several papers, one of the most recent of which was "The Beastly Familiarity of Wild Alterity: Debating the 'Nature' of our Fascination with Wildness." When not working, he enjoys nothing better than hiking and camping in the Alberta Rockies.

A hunter before he was a philosopher, **NATHAN KOWALSKY** still manages not to completely gross out his colleagues at St. Joseph's College, University of Alberta, Canada, with the dead deer mounted on his office wall (it's not actually his, it's Grandpa's – Nathan prefers European skull mounts). To add to intra-collegial harmony, he's made a habit of sharing venison with priests, struggling vegans, and other deserving non-hunters who can appreciate it. His research interests primarily concern environmental philosophy, philosophy of religion, and philosophy of culture, but truth be told he'd rather be trying to make a living outside. Probably too much of a Romanticist, Nathan would willingly give up his professorship if he could join a tribe of hunter-gatherers milling about the shortgrass prairies of southeastern Alberta, where his true home always will be – that is, if he could convince his wife and kids to come along!

LISA KRETZ completed both her Bachelor of Arts in Honors Philosophy and Visual Arts and Bachelor of Education at the University of Western Ontario. She received her Master of Arts in Philosophy with a focus on Environmental Aesthetics and Ethics from the University of Alberta. Lisa was awarded her doctorate from Dalhousie University, and her doctoral research was at the intersection of ecological selfhood and ethics. She currently divides her time between teaching and writing philosophy, not-for-profit environmental work, and painting. She has been a vegan for the last five years, and was a vegetarian for seven years before that. She advocates for locally grown, organic, and native produce.

PAULA YOUNG LEE holds a doctorate in art history from the University of Chicago. The editor of two anthologies on slaughterhouses (*Meat, Modernity and the Rise of the Slaughterhouse* and *The Slaughterhouse and the City*), she is also the author of a forthcoming book entitled *The Birdcage of the Muses: Observing Animals at the 17th-Century Menagerie at Versailles*. She is not squeamish. In her spare time, she is working on a cook book on game meats, and builds bird traps based on seventeenth-century hunting manuals.

GARRY MARVIN, PhD, is Reader in Social Anthropology at Roehampton University, London. Garry's main research interest is in the performance of human–animal relations. This interest began with his doctoral research into the culture of Spanish bullfighting and developed through studies of cockfighting, zoos, and human–wolf relations. For the last few years he has been working on a long-term anthropological study of English foxhunting. His work with Spanish hunters who visit England for deer hunting keeps his freezer full of venison.

DEBRA MERSKIN received her PhD from the S. I. Newhouse School of Public Communication at Syracuse University. She teaches Communication Studies courses in the School of Journalism and Communication at the University of Oregon. Her teaching and research focus on the representation of women and other minorities in mass media content. She is completing a second PhD in depth/ecological psychology at Pacifica Graduate Institute exploring the connections between racism, sexism, and speciesism. Her publications appear in journals such as *Human Behavioral Science*, *Howard Journal of Communication*, *Mass Media & Society*, and *Sex Roles*. She is a vegetarian, a yoga devotee, and companion to two dogs and two cats.

JONATHAN PARKER is currently a doctoral student and graduate research assistant in the Department of Philosophy and Religion Studies at the University of North Texas. He holds degrees from Loyola College in Maryland and the Katholieke Universiteit Leuven in Belgium. His essay in this book is a snapshot of his master's thesis, which critiques the extension of animal rights and liberation theories to wild non-human animals and nature. His recent work has examined the role of traditional ecological knowledge in confronting contemporary environmental issues, and the relationship between science and society.

DAVID PETERSEN is a former Marine Corps helicopter pilot turned writer and conservation activist. Before joining Trout Unlimited as their Colorado Field Director for public lands conservation projects, David authored nine books, including *Heartsblood: Hunting, Spirituality and Wildness in America* (www.davidpetersenbooks.com), and edited several more including the journals, poetry, and letters of his friend and mentor

Edward Abbey. Recently named Conservationist of the Year by the Colorado Wildlife Federation, David is a passionate traditional bowhunter and co-chair of the all-volunteer public lands conservation group Colorado Backcountry Hunters and Anglers.

STEPHANIE PYNE is a PhD candidate in geography at Carleton University in Ottawa, Canada, with a professional career related to governance and legislative policy. Stephanie's longstanding commitment to a multi-perspective disciplinary approach is reflected in her academic history, with a BA in Philosophy and Psychology focusing on developing a holistic approach to cognition and emotion, and an MA in Philosophy focusing on applying this holistic approach to development ethics. Stephanie's doctoral work involves integrating theory and practice in a manner that enhances awareness of different perspectives and worldviews through the creation of a cybercartographic (online, interactive, multimedia) atlas. The atlas is being designed and developed to tell the story of the Robinson Huron Treaty along multiple dimensions with multiple storytellers, and explicitly incorporates Anishinabe approaches to gathering knowledge and interpreting events. In this regard, inspired by Anishinabe understandings of hunting, a tracking method is being developed to interpret the worldviews, motivations, and intentions of the various actors in this treaty story, which took place in colonial Canada around the mid-nineteenth century.

ROGER SCRUTON is a writer and philosopher who is currently a resident scholar at the American Enterprise Institute in Washington. He has written on hunting for *Hunting* magazine, *Country Life*, and other prestigious and not so prestigious publications. His short book *On Hunting* was published by Yellow Jersey Press in 1998. Recent publications include *Understanding Music* (Continuum) and *I Drink Therefore I Am: A Philosopher's Guide to Wine* (Continuum). When not drinking or hunting he is usually thinking, writing, or composing. His second opera *Violet* was performed to critical acclaim in London in 2006, and his first opera, *The Minister*, was last performed at St. Andrews in March 2009. He is currently at work on *Going Home*, an opera for a railway station.

BRIAN SEITZ lives in Brooklyn, New York, and is Associate Professor of Philosophy at Babson College in Wellesley, Massachusetts. He is the author of *The Trace of Political Representation* and *The Iroquois and Athenians: A Politology*. He is also co-editor of *Eating Culture, Etiquette,* and *Fashion Statements*, as well as having authored numerous articles in the area of social and political philosophy and continental philosophy. He fishes wherever there is water, and hunts and gathers mostly in New York and Montana.

THEODORE R. VITALI, CP, was ordained a priest in the Roman Catholic Church as a member of the Passionist Religious Community on May 29, 1969, in Union City, NJ. He received his MA (Research) in Philosophy (1974) and his PhD in Philosophy (1976) at Saint Louis University. He taught philosophy at Bellarmine College (University) from 1976 to 1989. He chaired the Philosophy Department at Bellarmine from 1980 to 1989. From 1989 until the present, he has been Chair of Philosophy at Saint Louis University. He has published in the areas of philosophical theology, Whiteheadian philosophy, and applied ethics in the area of hunting and environmental ethics. He is presently a professional member of the Boone and Crockett Club.

JACOB WAWATIE (MOWEGAN) is the founder and director of Kokomville Academy, a knowledge-sharing institute committed to combining theory and practice and to integrating traditional approaches to knowledge with Western approaches. First acknowledged as an elder at the age of 28 for his knowledge of Anishinabe culture and language, Jacob has been a teacher since the age of 16. Through his studies of linguistics at McGill University, Jacob developed a writing system for the Algonquin language, which he later applied in his teaching. With a special interest in curriculum development, he has participated in the design of a number of learning programs geared to integrating the traditional Anishinabe approach to education with the standard Western science approach. In 1984, Jacob took what turned out to be a 12-year sabbatical from his position as director of the Rapid Lake School to begin living on the land and learning the traditional knowledge and education system from his grandmother, Lena Jerome Nottaway. Lena had been raised living on the land with no usage of European resources, and received an honorary doctorate from Carleton University (Ottawa, Canada) for her knowledge of traditional law, language, and culture. Throughout his life of hunting and trapping, Jacob has always thought of hunting simply as part of life, as something that is necessary to participate in existence.